ATOMIC ROBO

VOLUME SIX

THE GHOST OF STATION X

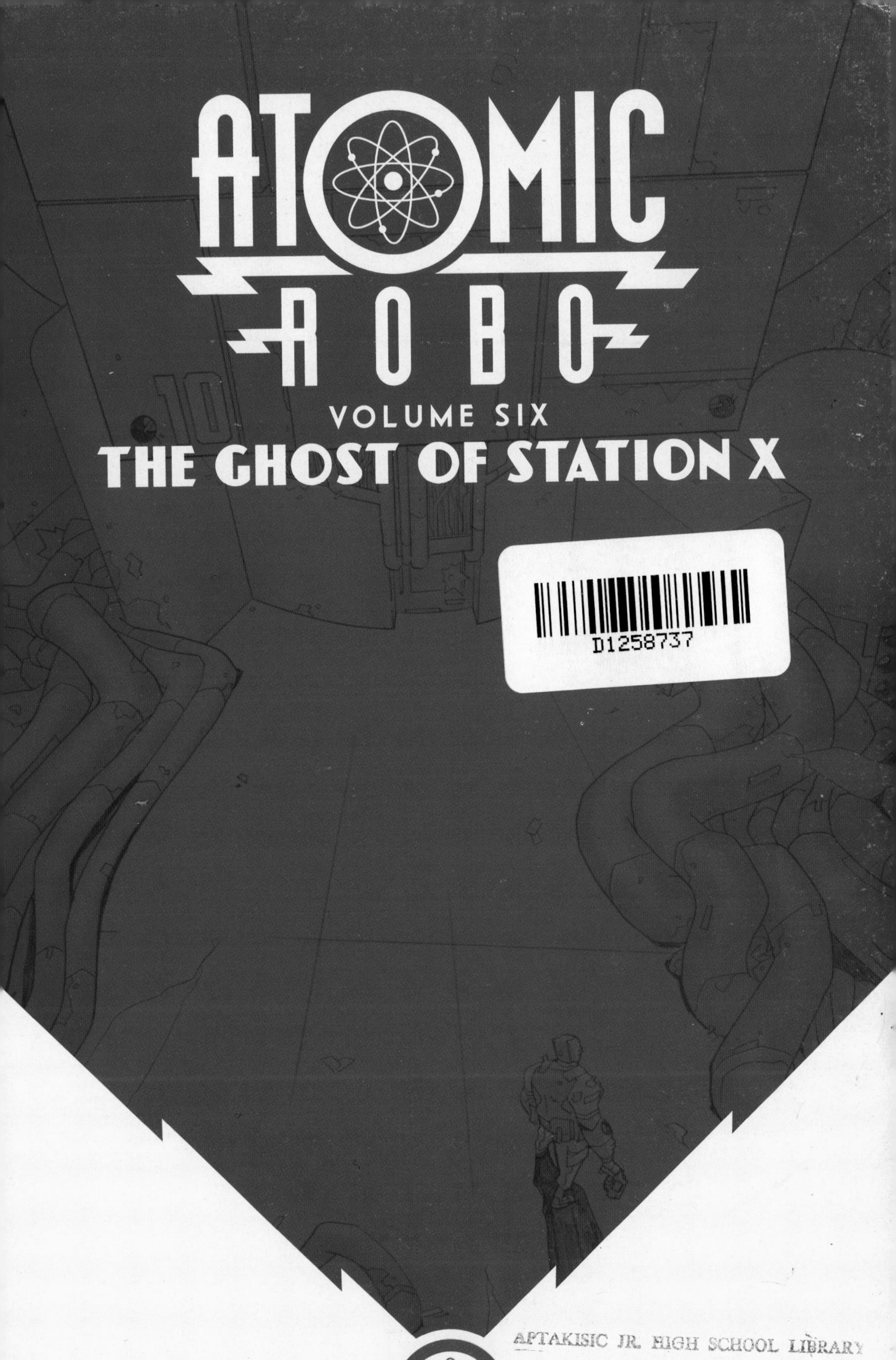

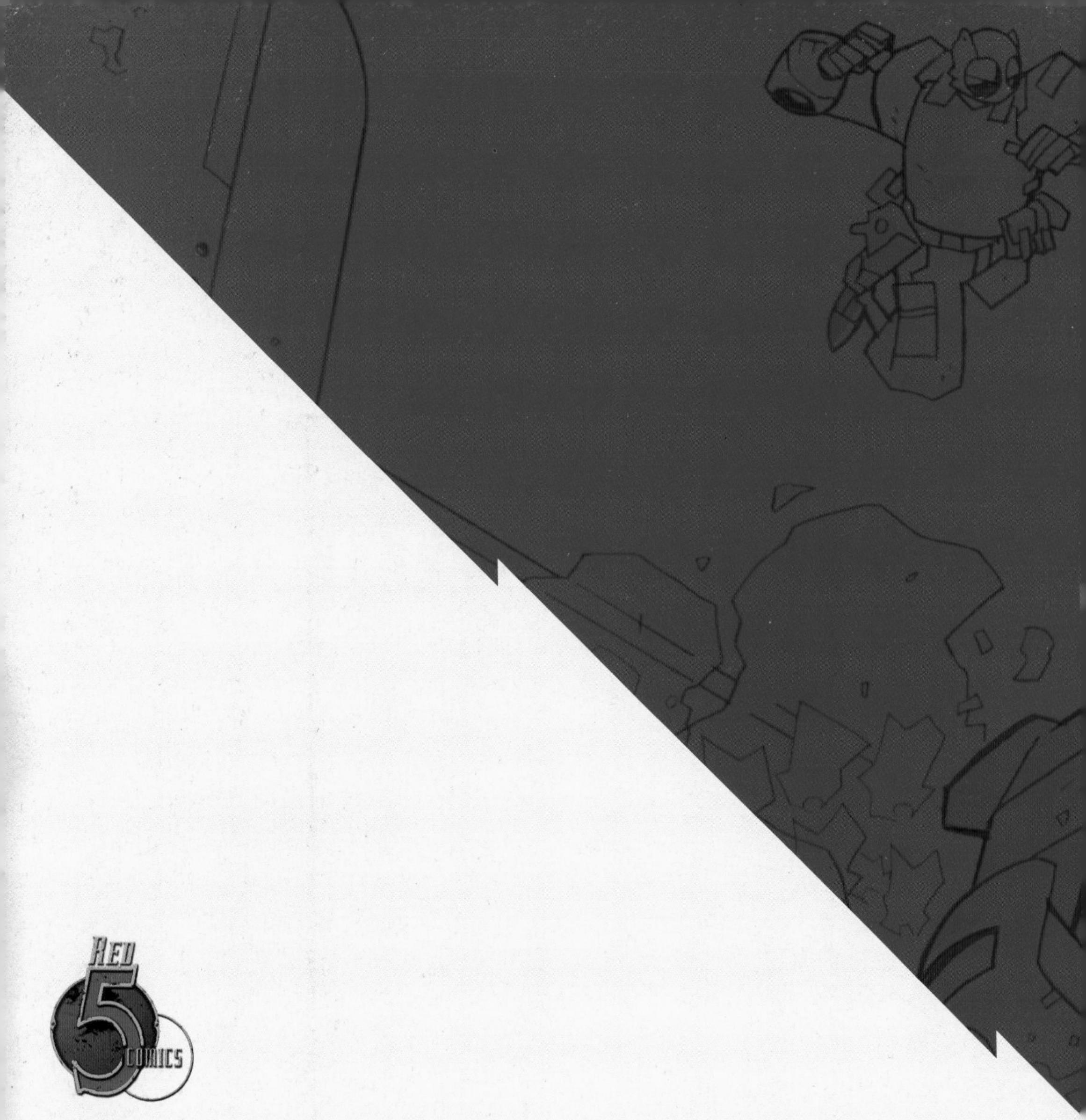

Publishers
PAUL ENS and SCOTT CHITWOOD

Book Design
JEFF POWELL

ATOMIC ROBO VOLUME SIX: ATOMIC ROBO and THE GHOST OF STATION X

This volume collects ATOMIC ROBO: THE GHOST OF STATION X #1 through #5 and ATOMIC ROBO FREE COMIC BOOK DAY 2010 of the comic-book series originally printed by Red 5 Comics.

Published by
RED 5 COMICS
298 Tuscany Vista Rd NW, Calgary, Alberta, Canada, T3L 3B4

www.red5comics.com

To find a comics shop in your area, call the Comic Shop Locator Service toll-free at 1-888-266-4226

First edition:
ISBN: 978-0-9868985-4-5

Printed in Canada.

ATOMIC ROBO

VOLUME SIX
THE GHOST OF STATION X

WORDS
BRIAN CLEVINGER

ART
SCOTT WEGENER

COLORS
RONDA PATTISON

LETTERS
JEFF POWELL

When Brian asked me, several months back, if I might consider writing an introduction "eventually" for one of the *Atomic Robo* future trades, I said yes immediately, and almost as quickly began drafting the piece in my mind. My plan was to write something about the Arthur C. Clarke quote concerning science and magic, and comparing Atomic Robo's "action science" to the "magic" of creation, as executed by Brian and Scott. This introduction was going to aspire to wit, and try to be clever, and genuinely fawn and foam, as such introductions often do.

And, I should add, it would've been quite sincere, because I quite sincerely love *Atomic Robo*.

I would have been happy to write that introduction, and throw in a couple jokes about Doctor Dinosaur and crystals ("Crystals!") and I probably could've left it at that, because, number one, I'm doing this because I *want* to, and number two, I'm not getting paid for it, either. So if Scott and Brian didn't like it, well, they could lump it, as far as I was concerned.

Or so I thought.

This is true:

In early 2009 I had reached a breaking point with comics, particularly in regard to my work in the mainstream. I'd put in over ten years of hard labor at DC, with the occasional dead-of-night border crossing over to Marvel, and in that time I had written quite literally hundreds of comics, and some of them - if I may say so myself - were actually rather good.

At the start, it had been joyous, and fun, and hard work, but the best kind of hard work, where I was eager to put in the hours. But by the time 2009 had rolled around, those years of fun were long gone, and the hard work was just hard, and there was no joy. Prior to March of 2009, I'd spent the better part of the previous three years in near-constant battle with one publisher or another. Most of these fights were bloody, and almost all of them I lost, and more often than not the work suffered as a result, and the instances of books making it to press and market as I and my collaborators had hoped were few and far between. I wasn't sleeping, I wasn't healthy, I wasn't happy. I was actually miserable, the kind of misery where one cannot see it because one has been living within its walls for a very, very long time. There was no sign of things changing. In fact, all the signs were that it was only going to get worse.

I was disgusted with comics in general, and the industry specifically. I was so disgusted, in fact, that it had become almost impossible for me to even read comics without finding something to hate in them. Comics, a form I had loved since I was six years old, had metastasized into something I sincerely loathed.

So I quit.

Which isn't nearly as easy as it sounds. It was, in truth, one of the hardest decisions of my life, and one of the most frightening things I've ever done.

But I did it, I walked away. I washed my hands and I turned my back and stopped going to comic books stores and stopped reading comics. Mostly. But every so often, I'd pick up this book or that book, and read something, and invariably it would just confirm that I'd made the right choice to begin with, and that I was gone, long gone from the medium.

This lasted just over a year, until Free Comic Book Day 2010, whereupon I found myself at Olympic Cards & Comics in Lacey, Washington, with fellow writer and very good friend Eric Trautmann. Eric was half the reason I was even there. The other half was his wife, Gabi, who owns and runs the store.

It was Eric who forced - and he really did have to force them on me, I was that reticent - *Atomic Robo* into my hands. With the same gleam in his eye you normally find amongst the attendees of revival shows, the same foaming, near-crazed passion of a True Believer.

"Read this," he said. "Seriously, trust me, read this. Doctor Dinosaur is the greatest nemesis in the history of comics. Read this. Crystals!"

I left with the first four trades. A two hour drive home, and ten at night, I opened Volume 1, not expecting very much at all. I was tired, I was grumpy, I was suspicious, and I didn't trust comics, even if I did trust Trautmann.

I started reading.

What Brian Clevinger and Scott Wegener do so well, so beautifully, elegantly, forcefully well, is love comics.

They love comics with an abandon that bursts from each page, each panel, again and again, issue after issue. They love comics with a joy and a glee that, sadly, is missing in the majority of works you see on the stands. They love comics the way we all used to love comics when we first discovered them, the books shabby and with torn covers. They love comics like children, entirely and unashamed.

We are an industry that, really, doesn't know if it's going or coming. We've got corporate oversight on one side and self-loathing Creators on the other. We are bombarded with events and promotions and tempests within teacups all designed to make it seem that things matter when they really couldn't matter less. We have writers and artists who seem to hold their audience, their fans, in contempt, as if to say, yes, comics, but me? I'm better than this.

Atomic Robo doesn't just reject this attitude, it forces it to its knees and puts one in the back of the head.

There is not a fraction of self-loathing in Robo; there is no hint of resentment in Robo; there is no whiff of arrogance in Robo. What exists, instead, is reverence and respect. What Wegener and Clevinger deliver, month after month, is the goods, precisely as promised; the old promise, that a comic book will transport you to another world, another time, another place, full of adventure and excitement and dashed with humor and sometimes with romance. A book that delights in the story it tells, and that honors our intelligence; because amidst all of these things, there's also the fact that *Atomic Robo* is a smart comic book, and by being such, its creators pay the (increasingly rare) compliment of thinking us smart, as well.

That's not just refreshing. In this day and age, in this market?

That's practically revolutionary.

I finished all the trades within 24 hours of starting the first, and then I did something that you hear about folks doing all the time, but which I think most people tend to lie about. I promptly read them all again.

They were, astonishingly enough, better the second time around. Subtleties were revealed. Accents of craft become more apparent. The funny was even funnier. The smart was even smarter.

Then I gave them to my wife to read. And then I gave them to my then-11 year-old son to read. Pause and think about that for a moment, or better, ask yourself the following: how many of the comics *you've* read in the last year would you share with a child? Your son or daughter or niece or nephew or whoever? Without hesitation? Without worrying about what they were going to discover within? How many comics out there play successfully to such a wide audience?

Robo can. Robo does. That's by design, not by accident. That's by effort, not by chance. That was a choice that Scott and Brian made at the start, and one they've continued to honor, even when it would be easier to narrow the field.

(As an aside, this volume, *The Ghost of Station X*, veers into some very, very dark places, but does so via insinuation and implication, never overtly. It is, in truth, the most chilling story these two have given us so far. Yet I would not hesitate to put this book into my son's hands. Further credit to the creators.)

All of this would have been enough. Given the state I was in when Trautmann gave me the books, it would have been *more* than enough, certainly far more than I could've hoped for. I had found a comic that genuinely delighted me, that I had read eagerly, without trepidation, and that I wanted more of, and wanted it now. I remembered why I loved comics. More than enough.

But there was an unintended consequence. Because if there was a book like this one, why couldn't there be more of them? And so, with fear in my heart and my pulse pounding at my temples, I went back into my LCS for the first time in almost a year. I dug amongst the shelves and pulled titles I'd never heard of, and tried, again, several that I had forsaken.

A lot of what I brought home was the same miserable mill-product it had been before, to tell the truth. Sound and fury, signifying little by way of entertainment. Yet there were also gems buried within, books that I was glad to have discovered, and sorry I had been missing. There were titles that deserved more than I had initially given them.

I started reading comics again, that's what I'm trying to say. I came back, hesitantly, nervously. With all the apprehension of a beaten puppy. But I came back.

And it was better.

Time, they say, heals all wounds, and maybe that's true, but the right medicine does wonders, as well. It's January of 2012, now, and I'm healthier and happier and doing better work than I was three years ago.

Which is more than I can say for Robo himself.

Yes, that's oblique. You'll see why.

Robo's world is about to change for the worse.

Yours is about to change for the better.

Greg Rucka
Portland, Oregon
January 2012

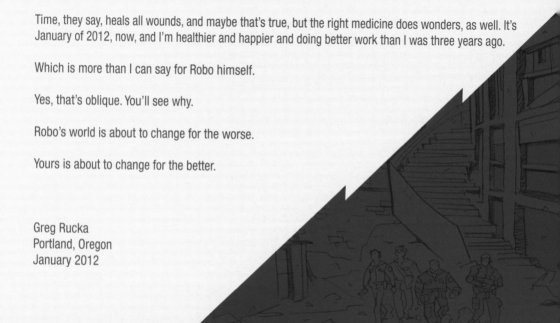

Rather unexpectedly, *Atomic Robo and the Ghost of Station X* ended up being a real watershed event for me. For some time I'd felt that my art had plateaued. It was missing something, but I had no idea what. And then, quite by accident I stumbled upon the thing that would end up turning on the creative lights for me. Again.

Katsuhiro Otomo's AKIRA. One of the most painstakingly illustrated and composed manga ever. Specifically the version published in America by Marvel's EPIC COMICS imprint and colored by Steve Oliff. I feel like I need to be that specific for a reason. While the original black and white art is masterfully illustrated, and speaks with a strong voice, the addition of Steve's colors made it absolutely sing.

Purists who insist that coloring a book intended to be B&W is an abomination can blow it out their ears. Otomo and Oliff worked closely with one another to ensure that the colors enhanced the mood, focused the viewer's eye, and never distracted the reader with garish effects and cheap tricks. As a result, more than twenty years after it was released in America, AKIRA is still one of the best looking books out there.

What blows my mind most about AKIRA is how I was able to forget all about it.

When I was a kid I owned exactly two, non-sequential, issues of the comic. That was all I could find. Manga was just "comics from Japan" back before the Internet, and they were hard as hell to come by. Even the shops that wanted to carry them seemed to have trouble finding stock for their shelves. Despite not knowing what was going on in the story, or how to get more, I devoured these books. I copied panels, I stole poses, I traced the coolest most badass motorcycle I had ever seen and will ever see in my life. Over and over and over again.

And then I lost them. A decade and a half slid by, and I forgot about them. Then I was standing in a used book store and coffee shop near my house, and there on a shelf was a nearly complete collection of the Epic Comics AKIRA graphic novels. A psychedelic wormhole opened up between 2011 and 1989. I think I screamed. And the next thing I new I was lying on the floor with a barista splashing hot coffee on my face, telling me I couldn't sleep there.

Between finishing *Deadly Art of Science* and beginning *Ghost of Station X* I studied the hell out of those books, then dove into the 6th volume of Atomic Robo with all the reckless abandon of an alcoholic in a brewery (thank you James Burke). My first attempts at applying the lessons I'd learned were less than elegant. I spent a lot of time pacing my studio muttering angrily to myself. More than usual, I mean.

And then Robo fell out of space. It was time to make it all work or just give up in frustration. I think it more or less worked. There were still plenty of mistakes on my end of things, most of which were so masterfully intercepted and dealt with by the other creatives working on this book that you will be hard pressed to find them.

I own a huge creative debt to Katsuhiro Otomo and Steve Oliff. This book is for them.

Scott Wegener
January 2012, Staten Island NY

FROM THE CREATORS

This volume started with Scott and I asking, "What if something like Advanced Idea Mechanics existed in Robo's world?"

We already snuck a group called DELPHI into the setting years ago, so that became the hook we'd hang the story on. We were positively giddy about weaving a vast and secret anti-Tesladyne corps into the framework of Robo's life – I went to work filling in the whos, hows, whens, and whys. And, man, this thing was complicated. Easily the most ambitious narrative we'd tackled.

And then I started taking things out of it. Wrinkles here and there that were cool but inelegant. Interesting, but labored.

By the end I'd removed all the AIM-like bits with DELPHI, and put Robo through the wringer of a conspiracy he thought he understood only to find out it was wrapped up in another one he'd never heard of. It was the same kind of story, but faster, sleeker, and with fewer gangly parts poking out at odd angles.

Then I had the unenviable task of convincing Scott it was not merely a good idea but actually in our best interests when I gutted everything we'd been excited about in this volume. He was on the fence until he saw how there'd be more room for explosions. I can get anything past that guy if I provide explosions as recompense. Scott actually makes little exploding sound effects the whole time he draws them. I bet you think that's a joke.

Oh, and don't mourn too much for poor neglected DELPHI. We'll get to see what became of that idea when...well, that'd be telling, wouldn't it!

Brian Clevinger
January 2012, Richmond VA

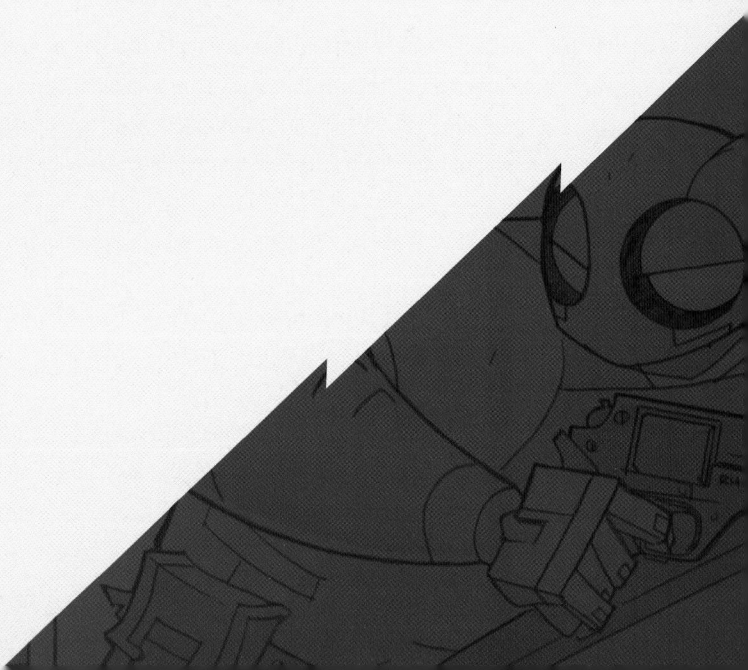

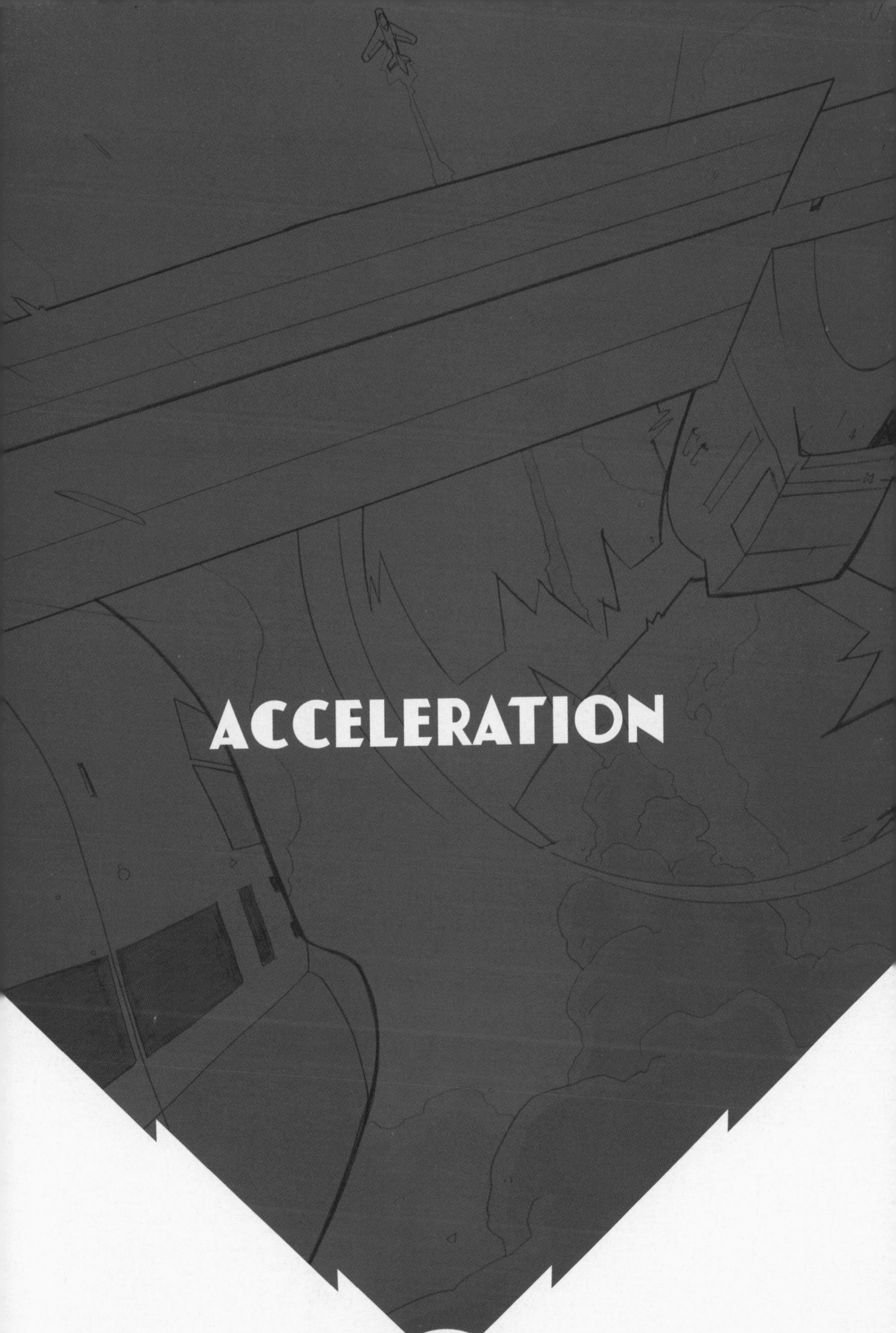

ACCELERATION

1

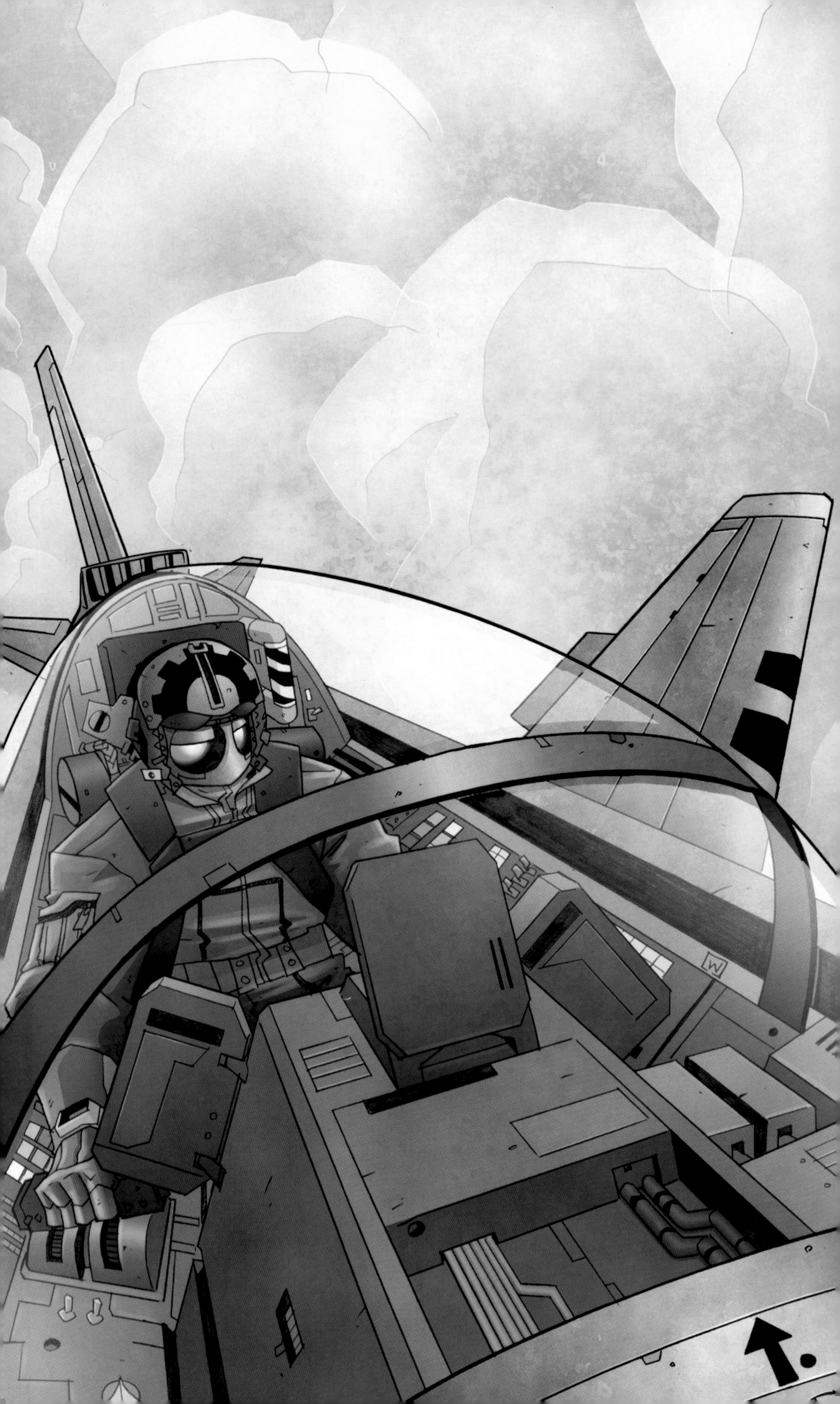

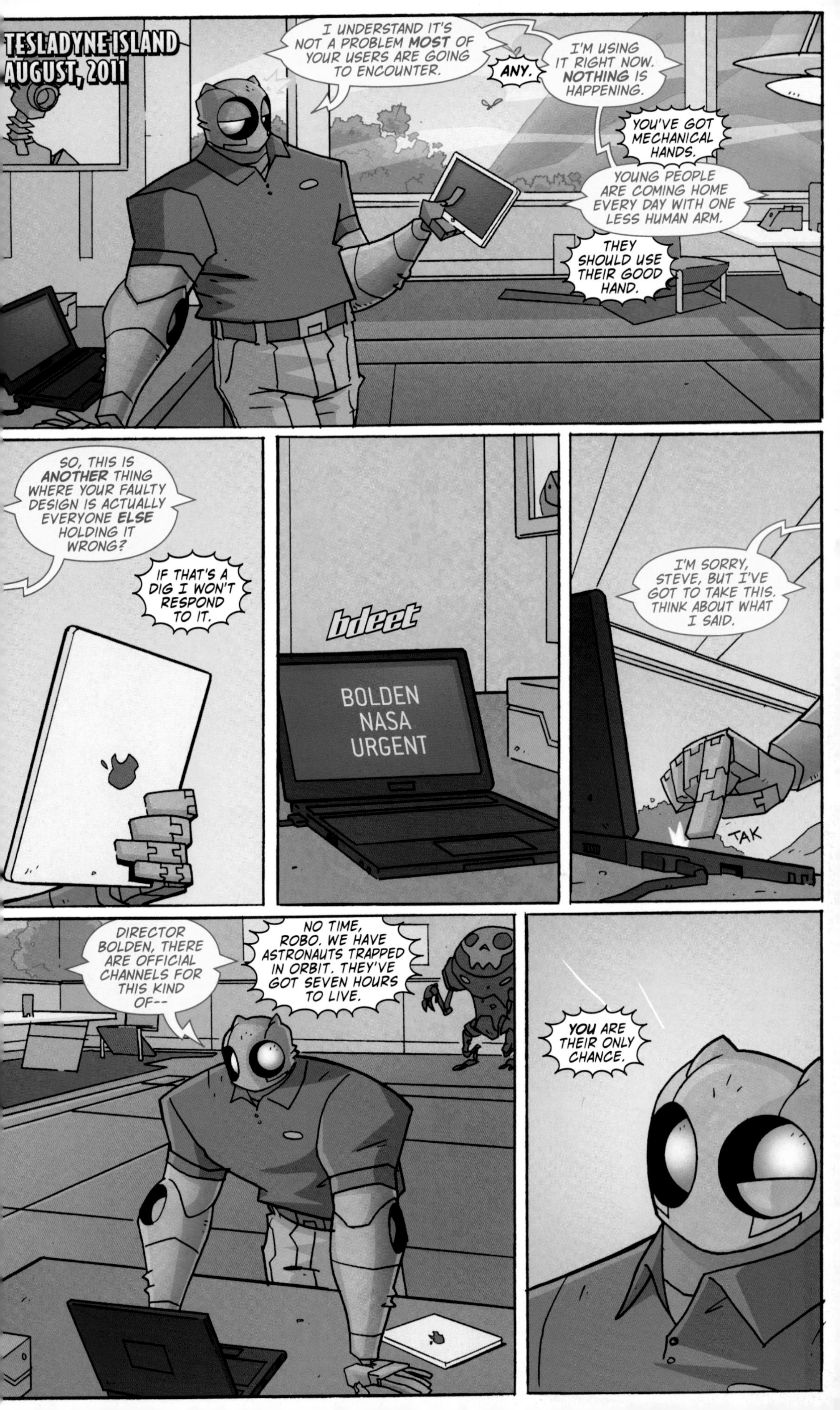
TESLADYNE ISLAND AUGUST, 2011
I UNDERSTAND IT'S NOT A PROBLEM MOST OF YOUR USERS ARE GOING TO ENCOUNTER.
ANY.
I'M USING IT RIGHT NOW. NOTHING IS HAPPENING.
YOU'VE GOT MECHANICAL HANDS.
YOUNG PEOPLE ARE COMING HOME EVERY DAY WITH ONE LESS HUMAN ARM.
THEY SHOULD USE THEIR GOOD HAND.
SO, THIS IS ANOTHER THING WHERE YOUR FAULTY DESIGN IS ACTUALLY EVERYONE ELSE HOLDING IT WRONG?
IF THAT'S A DIG I WON'T RESPOND TO IT.
bdeet
BOLDEN NASA URGENT
I'M SORRY, STEVE, BUT I'VE GOT TO TAKE THIS. THINK ABOUT WHAT I SAID.
TAK
DIRECTOR BOLDEN, THERE ARE OFFICIAL CHANNELS FOR THIS KIND OF--
NO TIME, ROBO. WE HAVE ASTRONAUTS TRAPPED IN ORBIT. THEY'VE GOT SEVEN HOURS TO LIVE.
YOU ARE THEIR ONLY CHANCE.

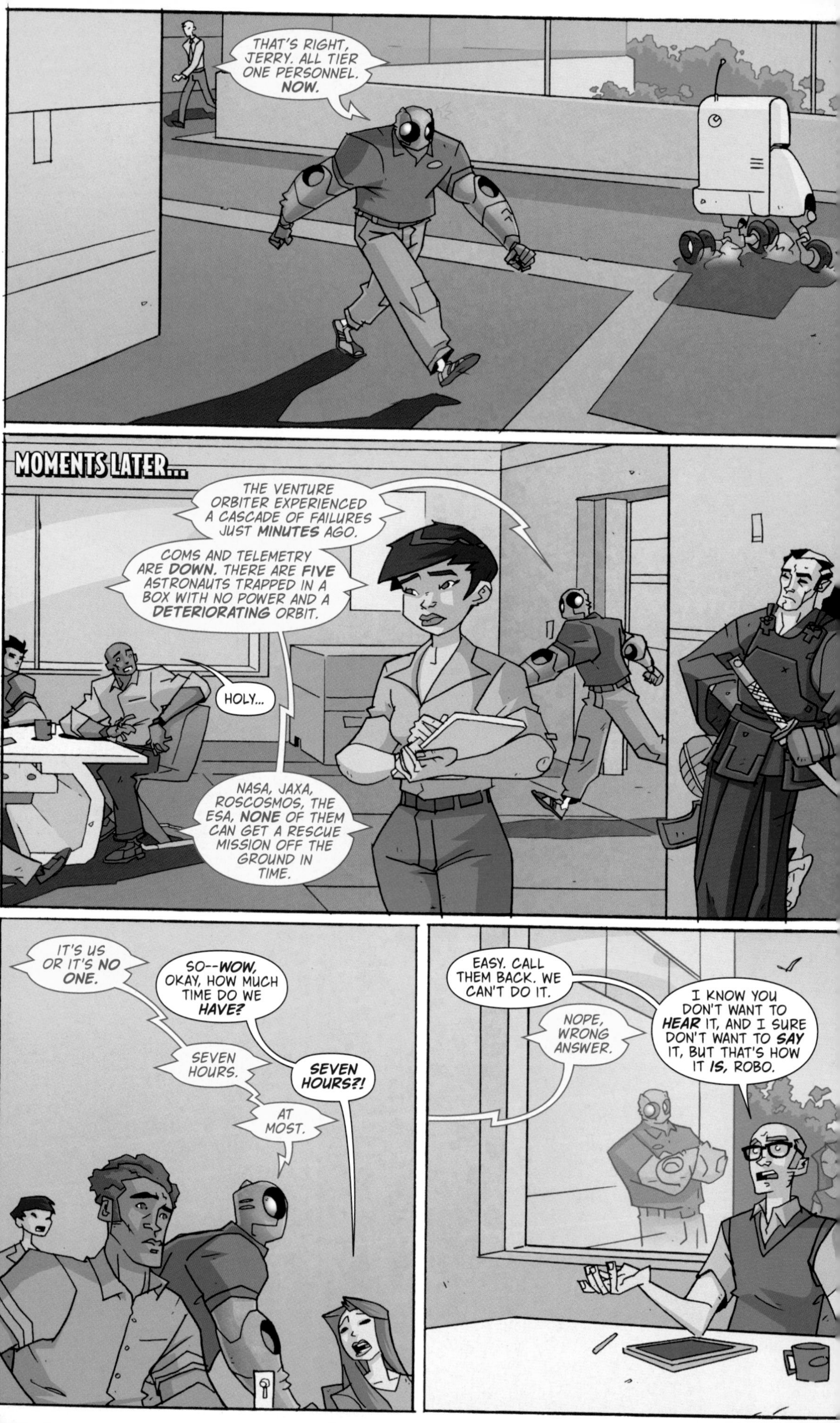
THAT'S RIGHT, JERRY. ALL TIER ONE PERSONNEL. **NOW.**
MOMENTS LATER...
THE VENTURE ORBITER EXPERIENCED A CASCADE OF FAILURES JUST **MINUTES** AGO.
COMS AND TELEMETRY ARE **DOWN.** THERE ARE **FIVE** ASTRONAUTS TRAPPED IN A BOX WITH NO POWER AND A **DETERIORATING** ORBIT.
HOLY...
NASA, JAXA, ROSCOSMOS, THE ESA, **NONE** OF THEM CAN GET A RESCUE MISSION OFF THE GROUND IN TIME.
IT'S US OR IT'S **NO ONE.**
SO--**WOW,** OKAY, HOW MUCH TIME DO WE **HAVE?**
SEVEN HOURS.
SEVEN HOURS?!
AT MOST.
EASY. CALL THEM BACK. WE CAN'T DO IT.
NOPE, WRONG ANSWER.
I KNOW YOU DON'T WANT TO **HEAR** IT, AND I SURE DON'T WANT TO **SAY** IT, BUT THAT'S HOW IT **IS,** ROBO.

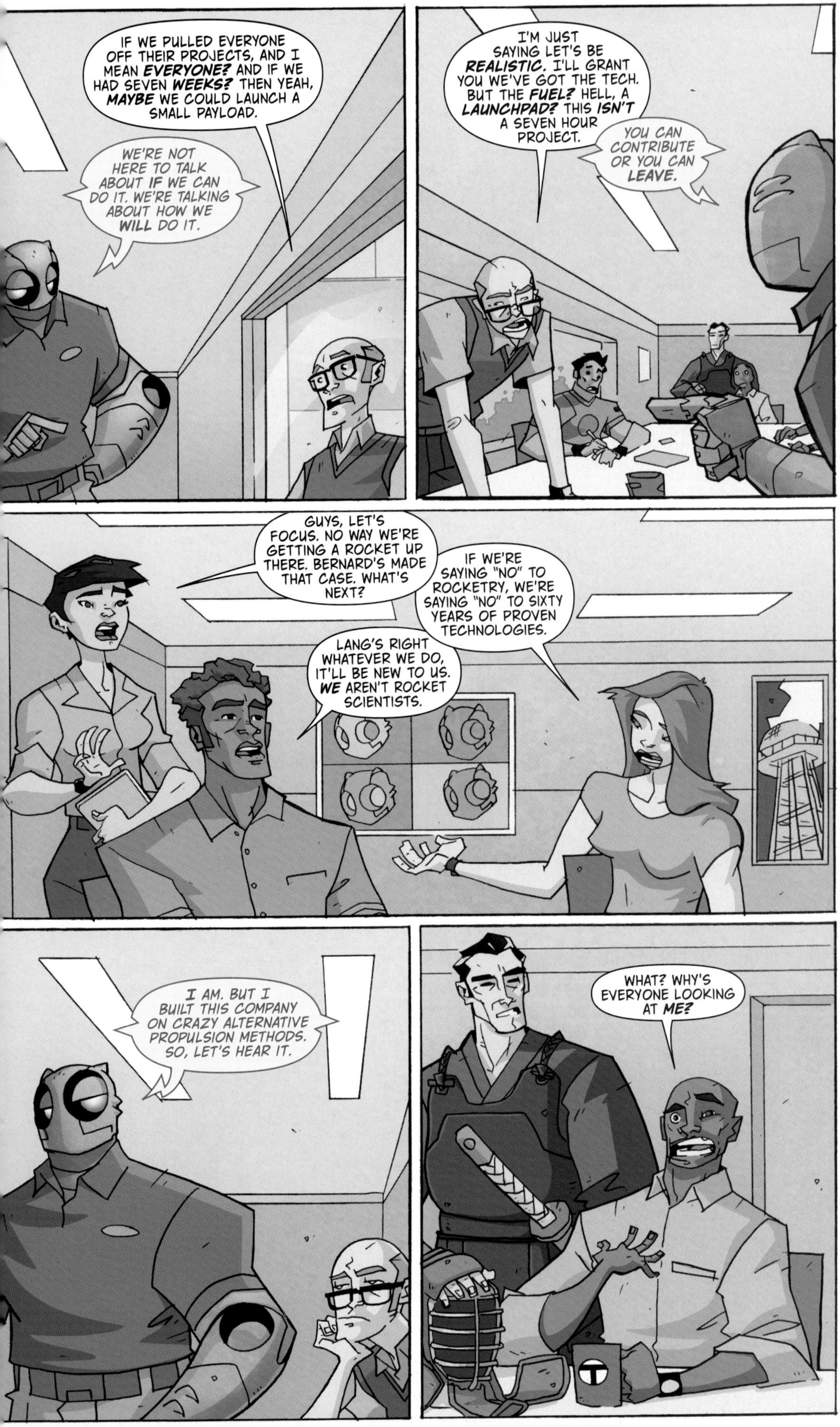
IF WE PULLED EVERYONE OFF THEIR PROJECTS, AND I MEAN **EVERYONE?** AND IF WE HAD SEVEN **WEEKS?** THEN YEAH, **MAYBE** WE COULD LAUNCH A SMALL PAYLOAD.
WE'RE NOT HERE TO TALK ABOUT **IF** WE CAN DO IT. WE'RE TALKING ABOUT HOW WE **WILL** DO IT.
I'M JUST SAYING LET'S BE **REALISTIC.** I'LL GRANT YOU WE'VE GOT THE TECH. BUT THE **FUEL?** HELL, A **LAUNCHPAD?** THIS **ISN'T** A SEVEN HOUR PROJECT.
YOU CAN CONTRIBUTE OR YOU CAN **LEAVE.**
GUYS, LET'S FOCUS. NO WAY WE'RE GETTING A ROCKET UP THERE. BERNARD'S MADE THAT CASE. WHAT'S NEXT?
IF WE'RE SAYING "NO" TO ROCKETRY, WE'RE SAYING "NO" TO SIXTY YEARS OF PROVEN TECHNOLOGIES.
LANG'S RIGHT WHATEVER WE DO, IT'LL BE NEW TO US. **WE** AREN'T ROCKET SCIENTISTS.
I AM. BUT I BUILT THIS COMPANY ON CRAZY ALTERNATIVE PROPULSION METHODS. SO, LET'S HEAR IT.
WHAT? WHY'S EVERYONE LOOKING AT **ME?**

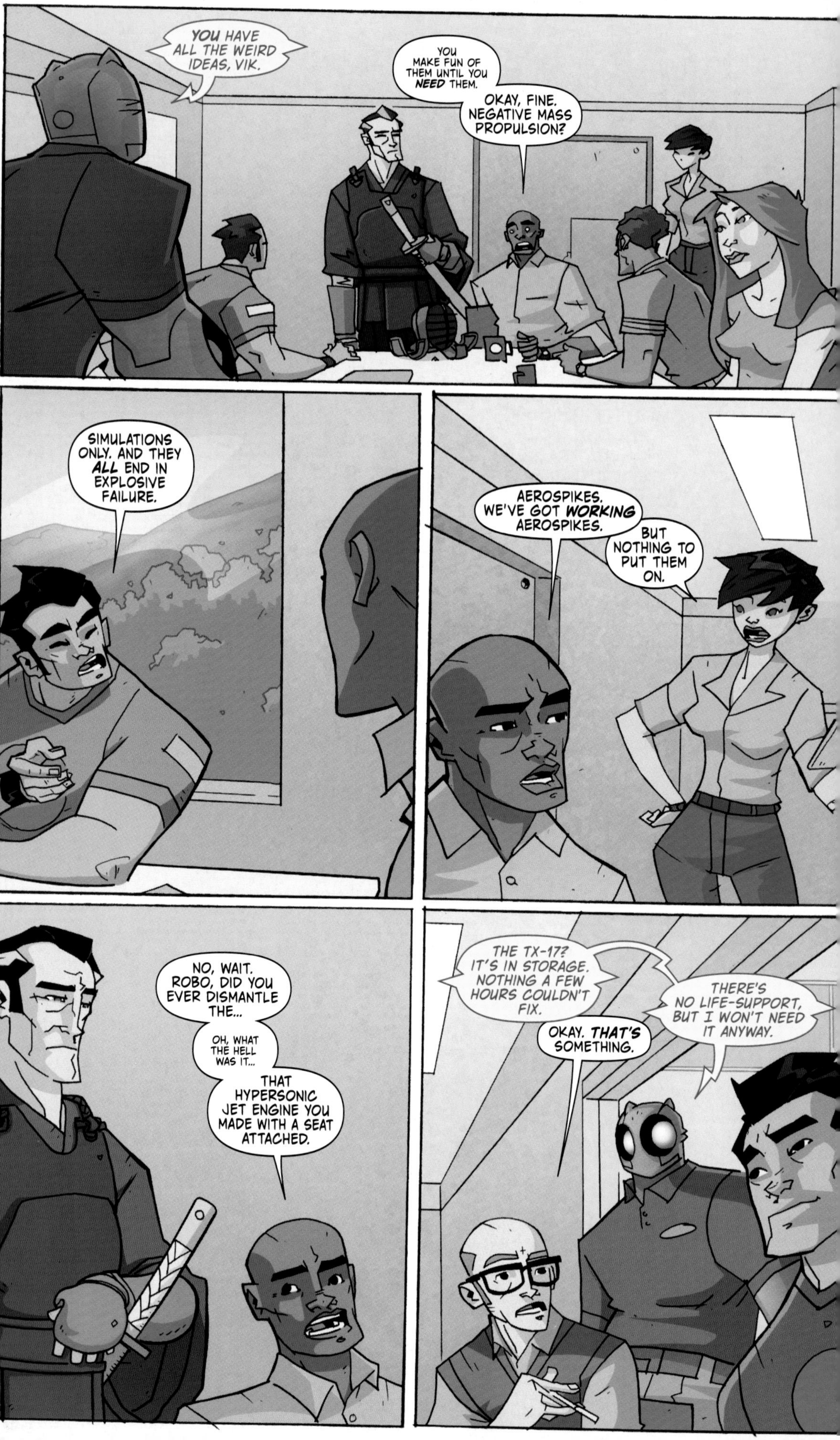
YOU HAVE ALL THE WEIRD IDEAS, VIK.
YOU MAKE FUN OF THEM UNTIL YOU NEED THEM.
OKAY, FINE. NEGATIVE MASS PROPULSION?
SIMULATIONS ONLY. AND THEY ALL END IN EXPLOSIVE FAILURE.
AEROSPIKES. WE'VE GOT WORKING AEROSPIKES.
BUT NOTHING TO PUT THEM ON.
NO, WAIT. ROBO, DID YOU EVER DISMANTLE THE...
OH, WHAT THE HELL WAS IT...
THAT HYPERSONIC JET ENGINE YOU MADE WITH A SEAT ATTACHED.
THE TX-17? IT'S IN STORAGE. NOTHING A FEW HOURS COULDN'T FIX.
OKAY. THAT'S SOMETHING.
THERE'S NO LIFE-SUPPORT, BUT I WON'T NEED IT ANYWAY.

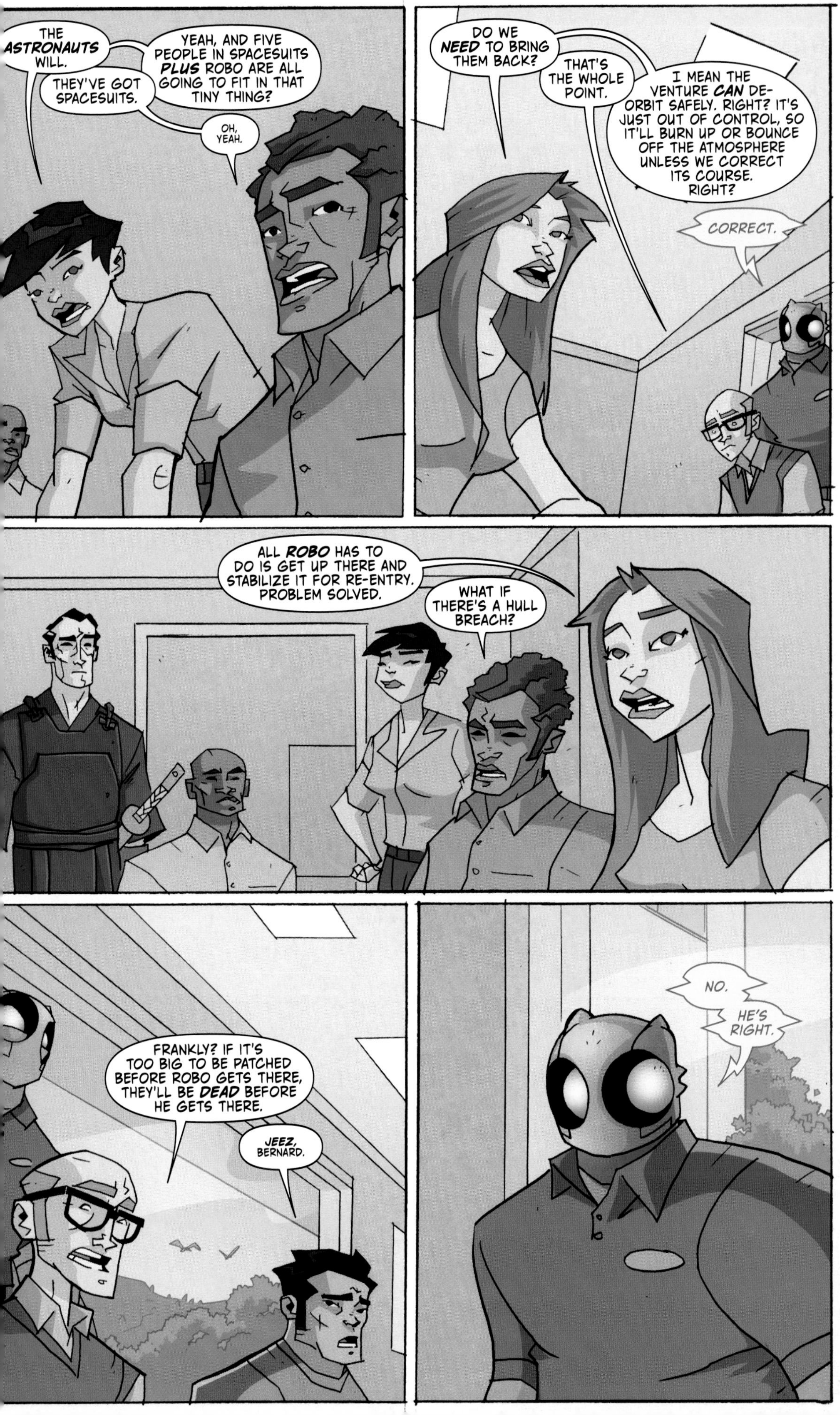
THE **ASTRONAUTS** WILL.
THEY'VE GOT SPACESUITS.
YEAH, AND FIVE PEOPLE IN SPACESUITS **PLUS** ROBO ARE ALL GOING TO FIT IN THAT TINY THING?
OH, YEAH.
DO WE **NEED** TO BRING THEM BACK?
THAT'S THE WHOLE POINT.
I MEAN THE VENTURE **CAN** DE-ORBIT SAFELY. RIGHT? IT'S JUST OUT OF CONTROL, SO IT'LL BURN UP OR BOUNCE OFF THE ATMOSPHERE UNLESS WE CORRECT ITS COURSE. RIGHT?
CORRECT.
ALL **ROBO** HAS TO DO IS GET UP THERE AND STABILIZE IT FOR RE-ENTRY. PROBLEM SOLVED.
WHAT IF THERE'S A HULL BREACH?
FRANKLY? IF IT'S TOO BIG TO BE PATCHED BEFORE ROBO GETS THERE, THEY'LL BE **DEAD** BEFORE HE GETS THERE.
JEEZ, BERNARD.
NO.
HE'S RIGHT.

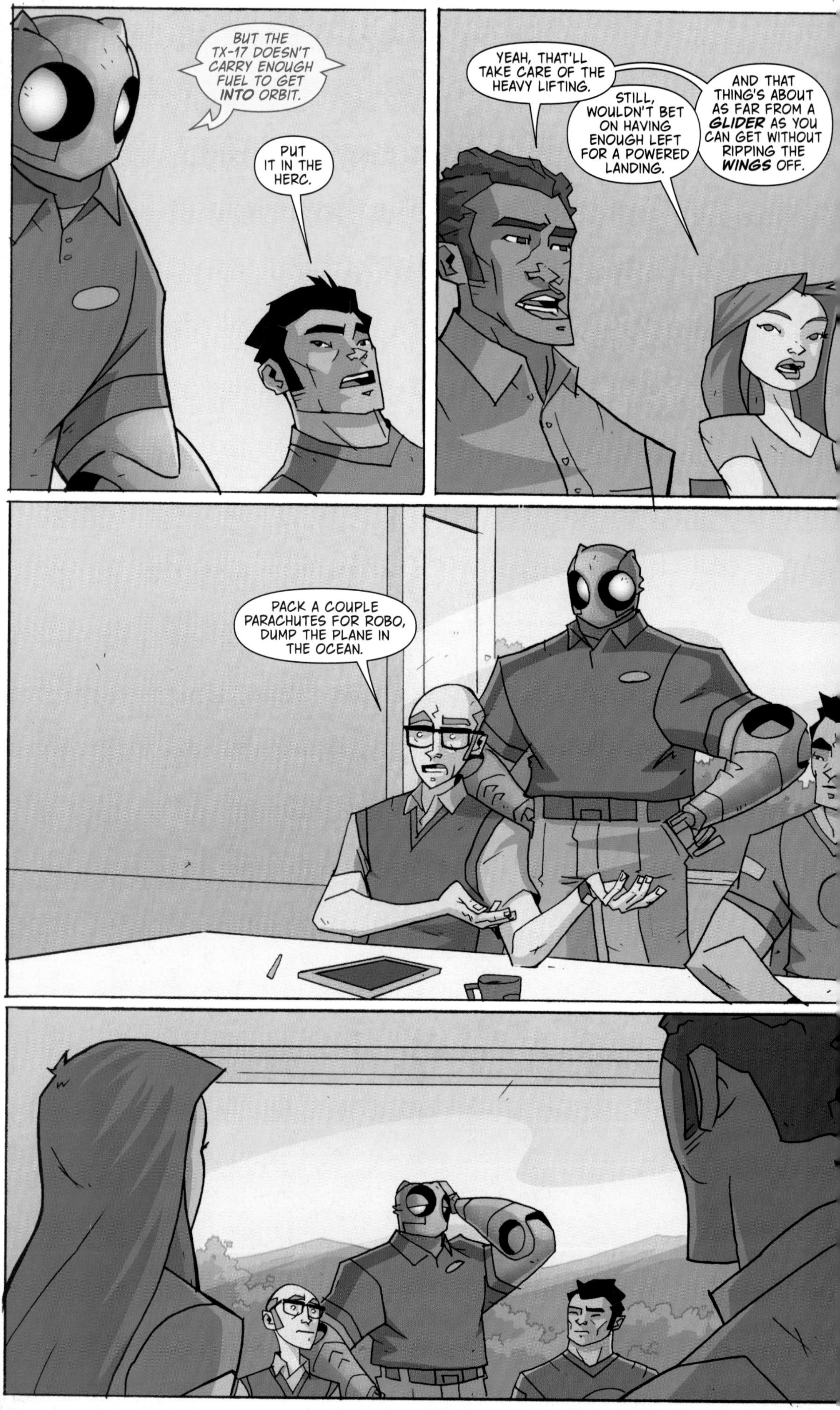

BUT THE TX-17 DOESN'T CARRY ENOUGH FUEL TO GET INTO ORBIT.
PUT IT IN THE HERC.
YEAH, THAT'LL TAKE CARE OF THE HEAVY LIFTING.
STILL, WOULDN'T BET ON HAVING ENOUGH LEFT FOR A POWERED LANDING.
AND THAT THING'S ABOUT AS FAR FROM A GLIDER AS YOU CAN GET WITHOUT RIPPING THE WINGS OFF.
PACK A COUPLE PARACHUTES FOR ROBO, DUMP THE PLANE IN THE OCEAN.

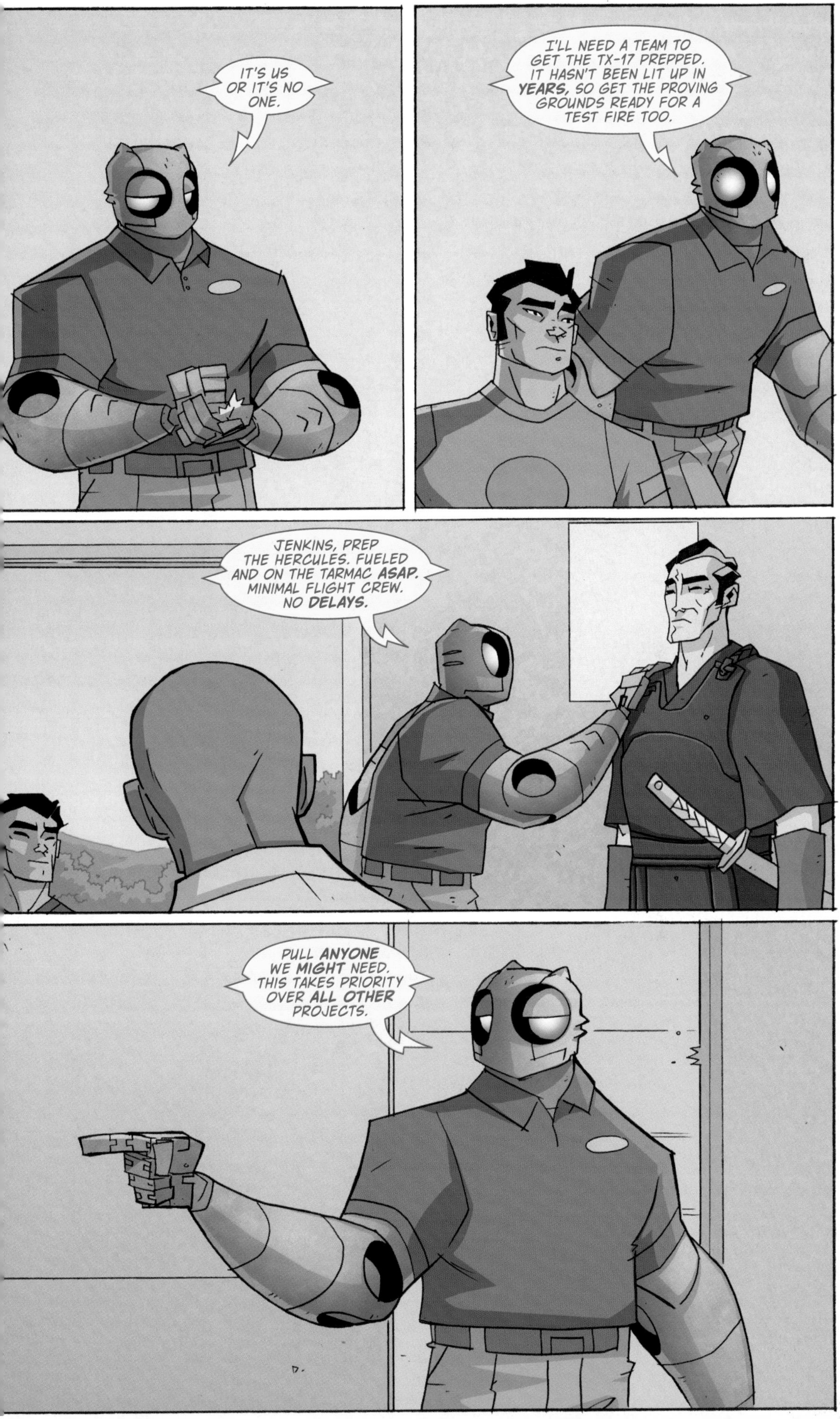
IT'S US OR IT'S NO ONE.
I'LL NEED A TEAM TO GET THE TX-17 PREPPED. IT HASN'T BEEN LIT UP IN **YEARS,** SO GET THE PROVING GROUNDS READY FOR A TEST FIRE TOO.
JENKINS, PREP THE HERCULES. FUELED AND ON THE TARMAC **ASAP.** MINIMAL FLIGHT CREW. NO **DELAYS.**
PULL **ANYONE** WE **MIGHT** NEED. THIS TAKES PRIORITY OVER **ALL OTHER** PROJECTS.

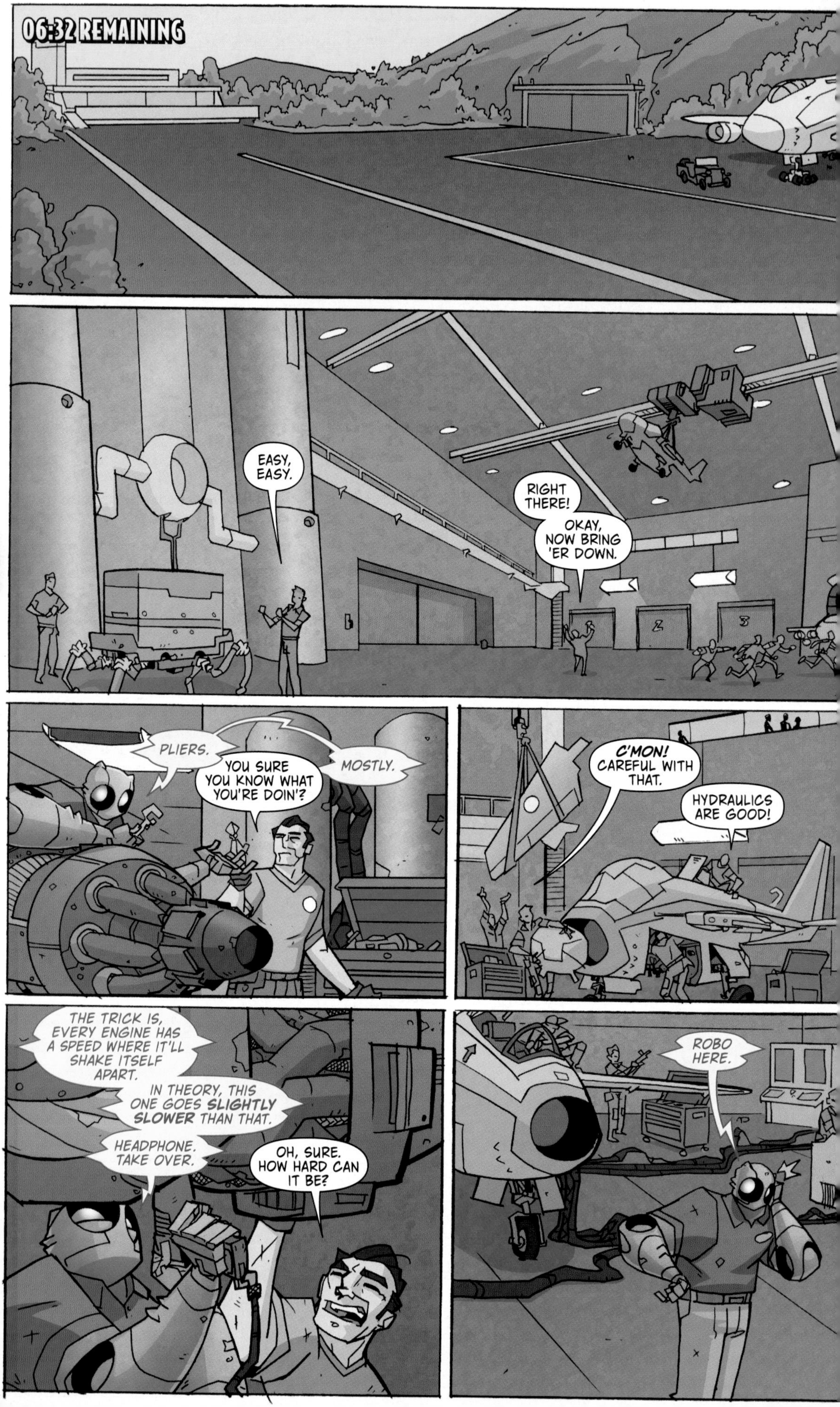
06:32 REMAINING
EASY, EASY.
RIGHT THERE!
OKAY, NOW BRING 'ER DOWN.
PLIERS.
YOU SURE YOU KNOW WHAT YOU'RE DOIN'?
MOSTLY.
C'MON! CAREFUL WITH THAT.
HYDRAULICS ARE GOOD!
THE TRICK IS, EVERY ENGINE HAS A SPEED WHERE IT'LL SHAKE ITSELF APART.
IN THEORY, THIS ONE GOES SLIGHTLY SLOWER THAN THAT.
HEADPHONE. TAKE OVER.
OH, SURE. HOW HARD CAN IT BE?
ROBO HERE.

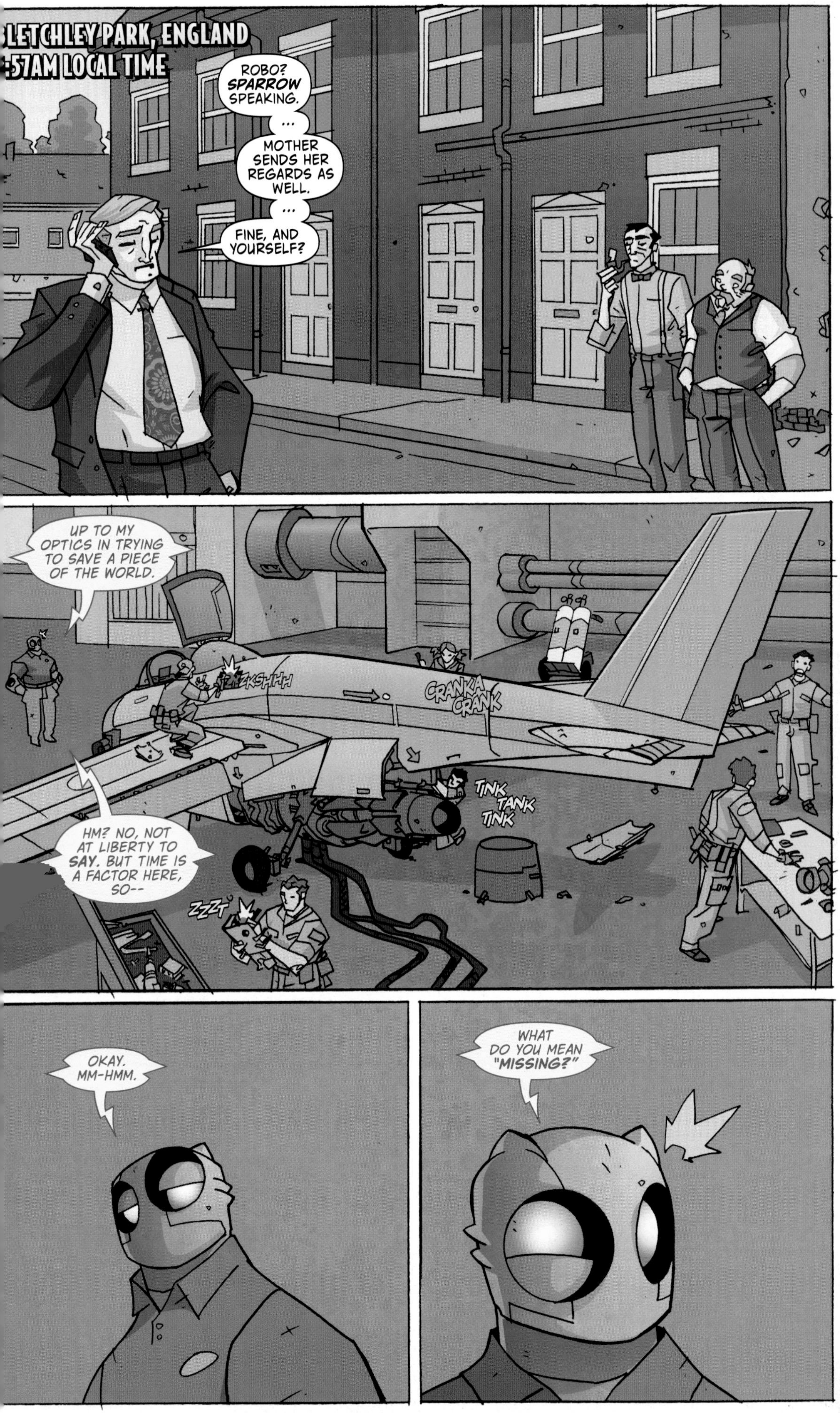

LETCHLEY PARK, ENGLAND
57AM LOCAL TIME
ROBO? SPARROW SPEAKING.
...
MOTHER SENDS HER REGARDS AS WELL.
...
FINE, AND YOURSELF?
UP TO MY OPTICS IN TRYING TO SAVE A PIECE OF THE WORLD.
KSHHH
CRANKA CRANK
TINK TANK TINK
HM? NO, NOT AT LIBERTY TO SAY. BUT TIME IS A FACTOR HERE, SO--
ZZZT
OKAY. MM-HMM.
WHAT DO YOU MEAN "MISSING?"

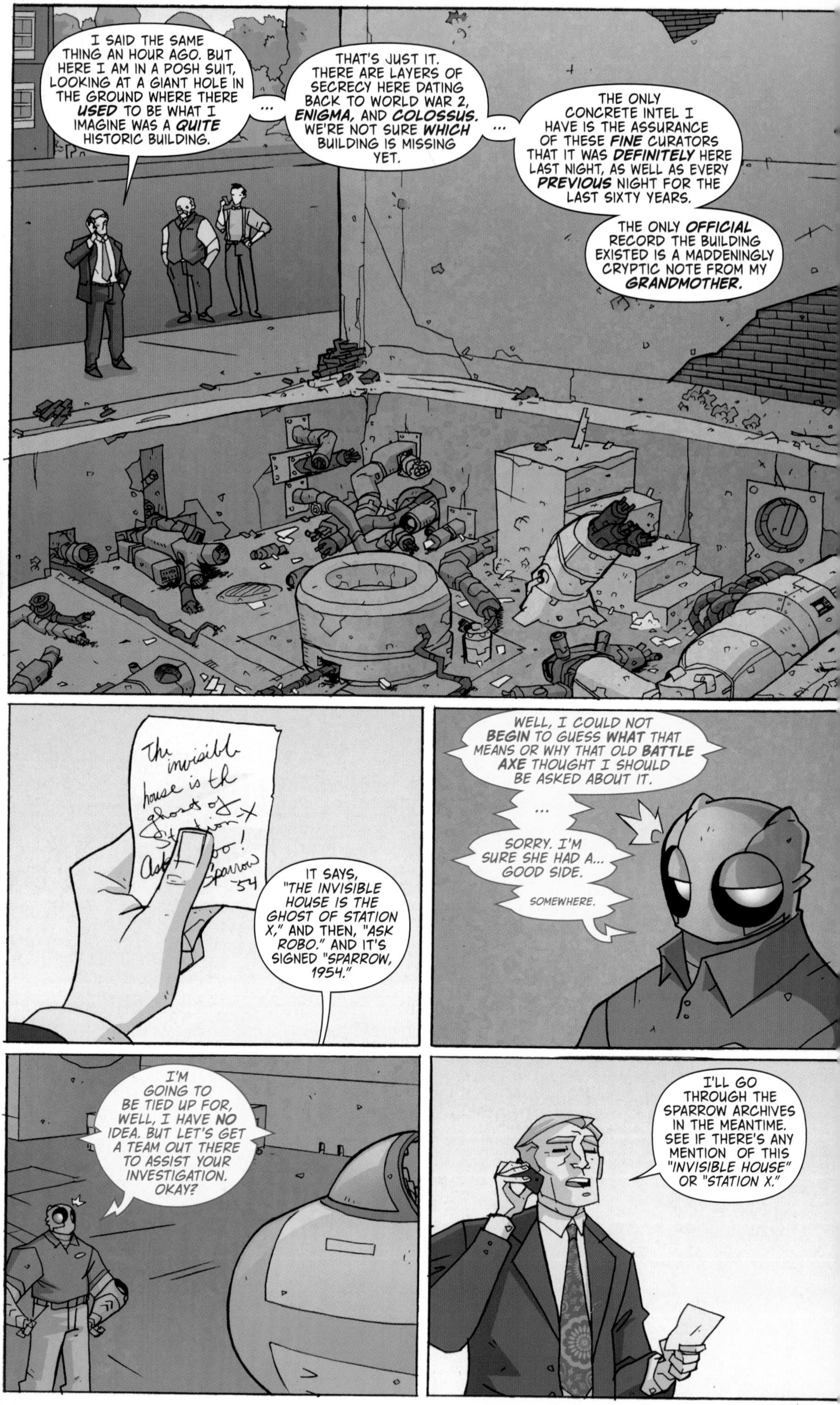
I SAID THE SAME THING AN HOUR AGO. BUT HERE I AM IN A POSH SUIT, LOOKING AT A GIANT HOLE IN THE GROUND WHERE THERE USED TO BE WHAT I IMAGINE WAS A QUITE HISTORIC BUILDING.
...
THAT'S JUST IT. THERE ARE LAYERS OF SECRECY HERE DATING BACK TO WORLD WAR 2, ENIGMA, AND COLOSSUS. WE'RE NOT SURE WHICH BUILDING IS MISSING YET.
...
THE ONLY CONCRETE INTEL I HAVE IS THE ASSURANCE OF THESE FINE CURATORS THAT IT WAS DEFINITELY HERE LAST NIGHT, AS WELL AS EVERY PREVIOUS NIGHT FOR THE LAST SIXTY YEARS.
THE ONLY OFFICIAL RECORD THE BUILDING EXISTED IS A MADDENINGLY CRYPTIC NOTE FROM MY GRANDMOTHER.
The invisibl house is th ghost of Station-X
Sparrow '54
IT SAYS, "THE INVISIBLE HOUSE IS THE GHOST OF STATION X," AND THEN, "ASK ROBO." AND IT'S SIGNED "SPARROW, 1954."
WELL, I COULD NOT BEGIN TO GUESS WHAT THAT MEANS OR WHY THAT OLD BATTLE AXE THOUGHT I SHOULD BE ASKED ABOUT IT.
...
SORRY. I'M SURE SHE HAD A... GOOD SIDE.
SOMEWHERE.
I'M GOING TO BE TIED UP FOR, WELL, I HAVE NO IDEA. BUT LET'S GET A TEAM OUT THERE TO ASSIST YOUR INVESTIGATION. OKAY?
I'LL GO THROUGH THE SPARROW ARCHIVES IN THE MEANTIME. SEE IF THERE'S ANY MENTION OF THIS "INVISIBLE HOUSE" OR "STATION X."

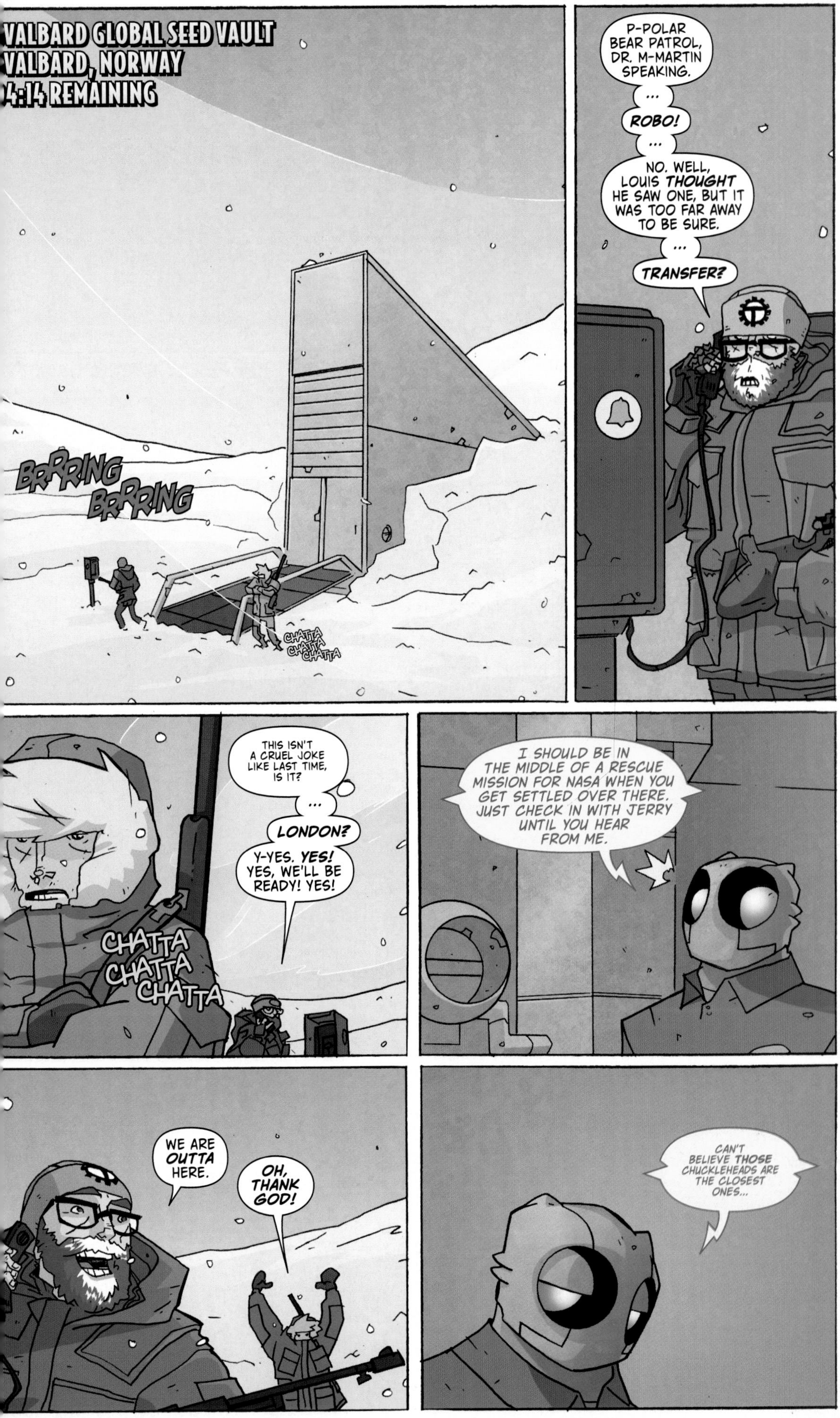

VALBARD GLOBAL SEED VAULT
VALBARD, NORWAY
4:14 REMAINING
BRRRING BRRRING
CHATTA CHATTA CHATTA
P-POLAR BEAR PATROL, DR. M-MARTIN SPEAKING.
...
ROBO!
...
NO. WELL, LOUIS THOUGHT HE SAW ONE, BUT IT WAS TOO FAR AWAY TO BE SURE.
...
TRANSFER?
CHATTA CHATTA CHATTA
THIS ISN'T A CRUEL JOKE LIKE LAST TIME, IS IT?
...
LONDON?
Y-YES. YES! YES, WE'LL BE READY! YES!
I SHOULD BE IN THE MIDDLE OF A RESCUE MISSION FOR NASA WHEN YOU GET SETTLED OVER THERE. JUST CHECK IN WITH JERRY UNTIL YOU HEAR FROM ME.
WE ARE OUTTA HERE.
OH, THANK GOD!
CAN'T BELIEVE THOSE CHUCKLEHEADS ARE THE CLOSEST ONES...

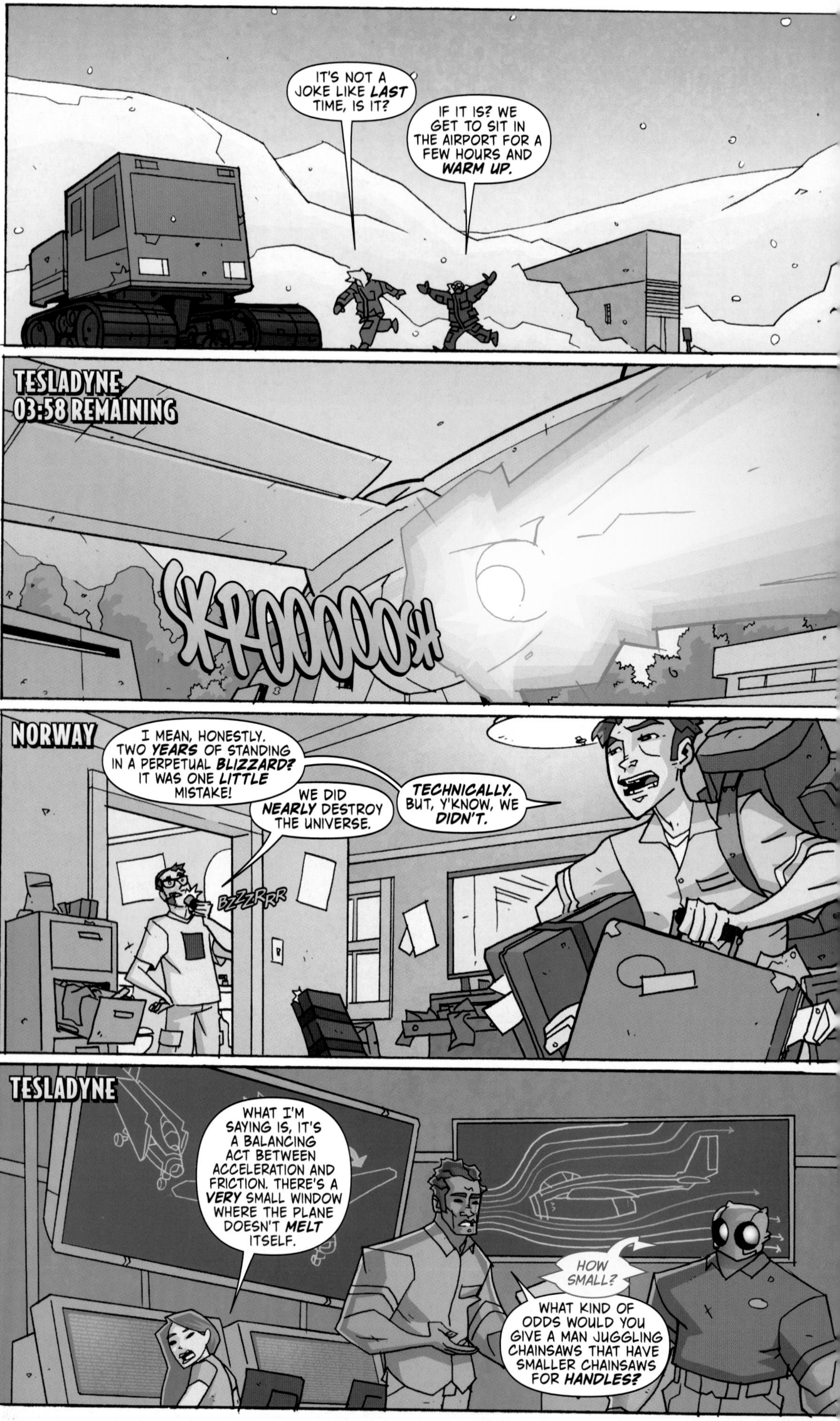

IT'S NOT A JOKE LIKE LAST TIME, IS IT?
IF IT IS? WE GET TO SIT IN THE AIRPORT FOR A FEW HOURS AND WARM UP.
TESLADYNE 03:58 REMAINING
SKROOOOOSH
NORWAY
I MEAN, HONESTLY. TWO YEARS OF STANDING IN A PERPETUAL BLIZZARD? IT WAS ONE LITTLE MISTAKE!
WE DID NEARLY DESTROY THE UNIVERSE.
TECHNICALLY. BUT, Y'KNOW, WE DIDN'T.
BZZZRRR
TESLADYNE
WHAT I'M SAYING IS, IT'S A BALANCING ACT BETWEEN ACCELERATION AND FRICTION. THERE'S A VERY SMALL WINDOW WHERE THE PLANE DOESN'T MELT ITSELF.
HOW SMALL?
WHAT KIND OF ODDS WOULD YOU GIVE A MAN JUGGLING CHAINSAWS THAT HAVE SMALLER CHAINSAWS FOR HANDLES?

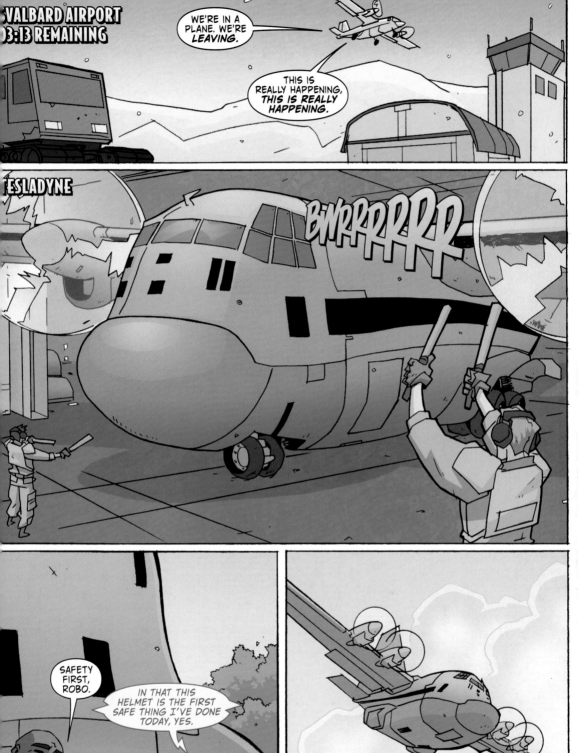

SVALBARD AIRPORT
3:13 REMAINING

WE'RE IN A PLANE. WE'RE *LEAVING.*

THIS IS *REALLY HAPPENING, THIS IS REALLY HAPPENING.*

TESLADYNE

BWRRRRRR

SAFETY FIRST, ROBO.

IN THAT THIS HELMET IS THE FIRST *SAFE* THING I'VE DONE TODAY, YES.

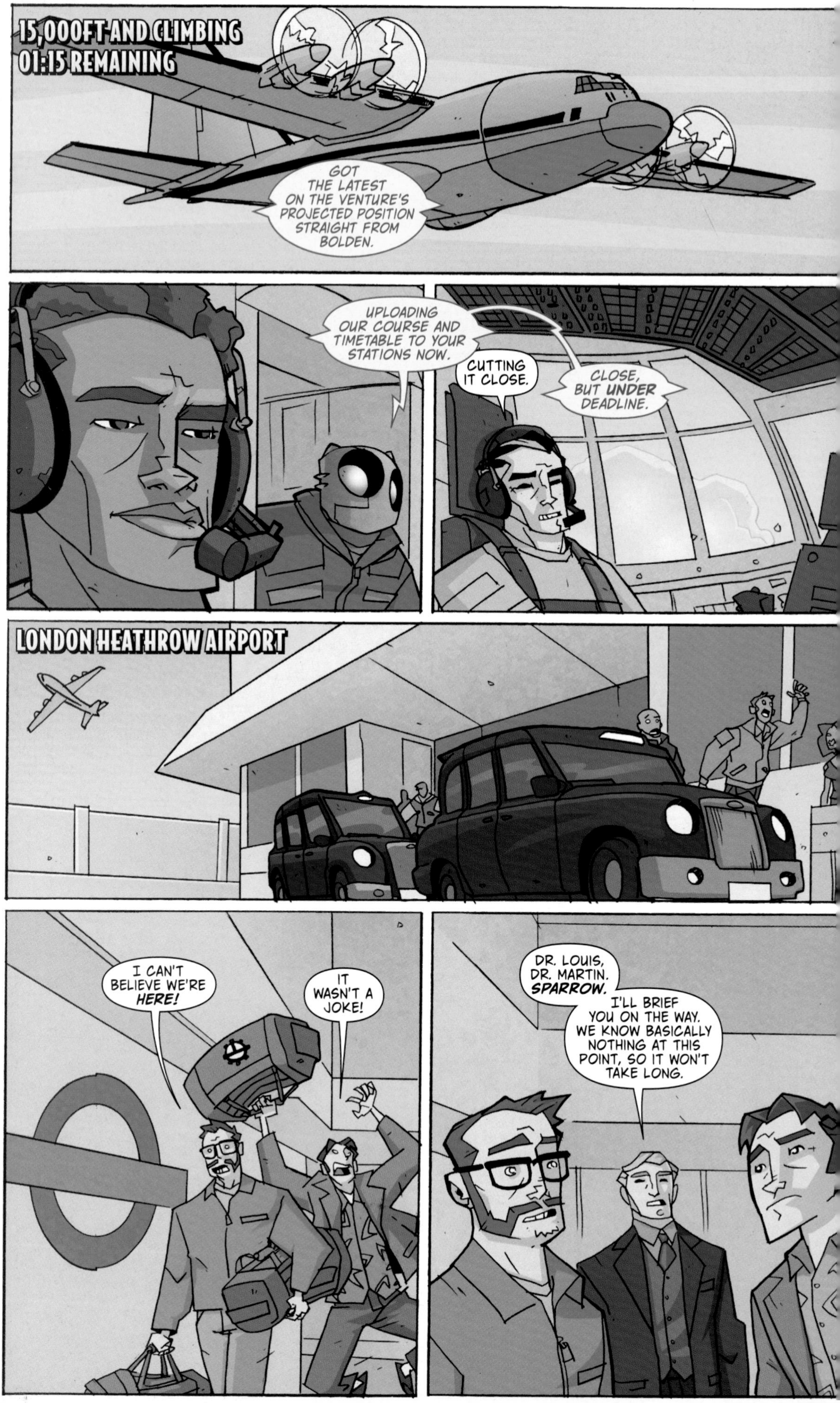
15,000FT AND CLIMBING
01:15 REMAINING
GOT THE LATEST ON THE VENTURE'S PROJECTED POSITION STRAIGHT FROM BOLDEN.
UPLOADING OUR COURSE AND TIMETABLE TO YOUR STATIONS NOW.
CUTTING IT CLOSE.
CLOSE, BUT **UNDER** DEADLINE.
LONDON HEATHROW AIRPORT
I CAN'T BELIEVE WE'RE ***HERE!***
IT WASN'T A JOKE!
DR. LOUIS, DR. MARTIN. ***SPARROW.***
I'LL BRIEF YOU ON THE WAY. WE KNOW BASICALLY NOTHING AT THIS POINT, SO IT WON'T TAKE LONG.

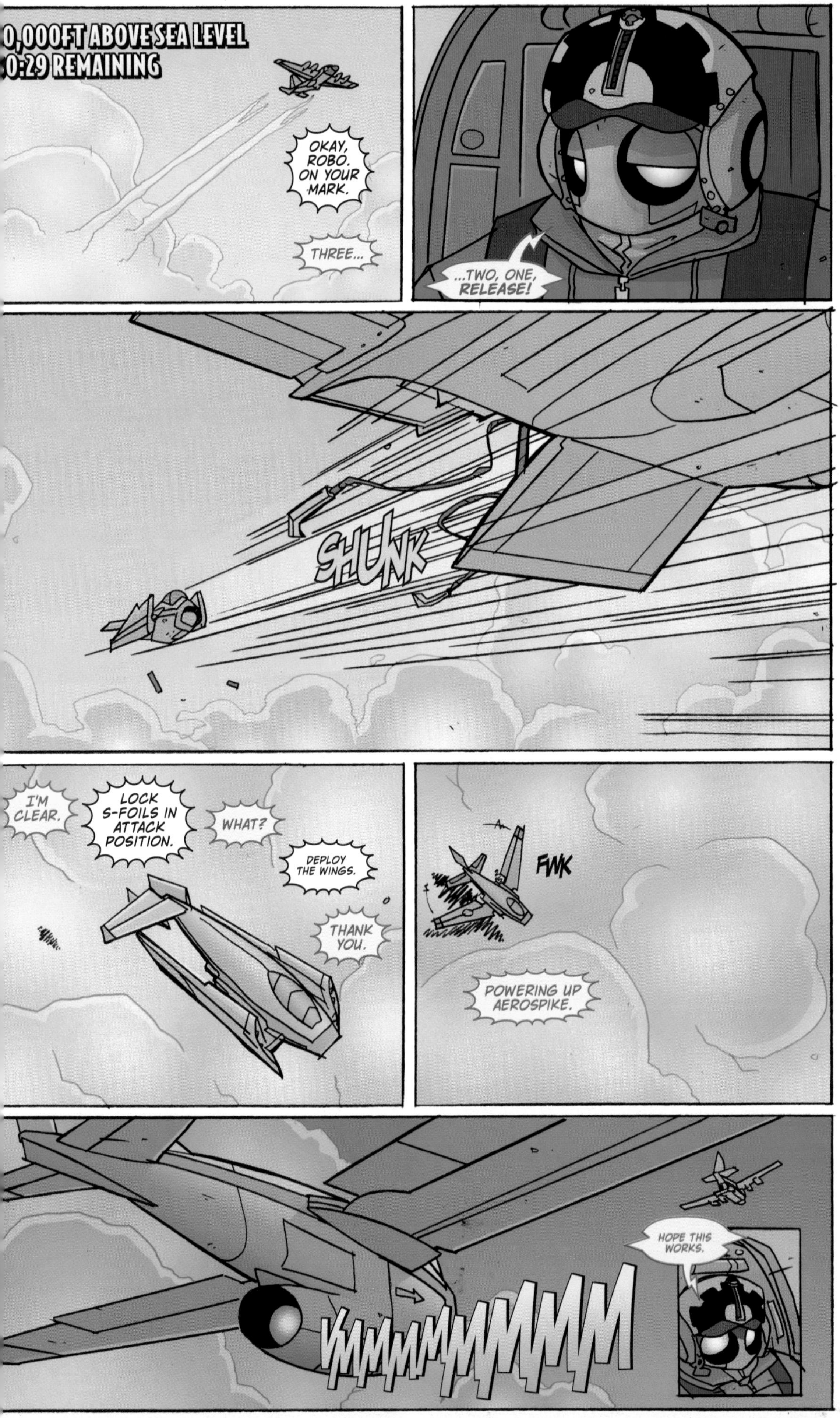
0,000FT ABOVE SEA LEVEL
0:29 REMAINING
OKAY, ROBO. ON YOUR MARK.
THREE...
...TWO, ONE, RELEASE!
SHUNK
I'M CLEAR.
LOCK S-FOILS IN ATTACK POSITION.
WHAT?
DEPLOY THE WINGS.
THANK YOU.
FWK
POWERING UP AEROSPIKE.
VMMMMMMMMM
HOPE THIS WORKS.

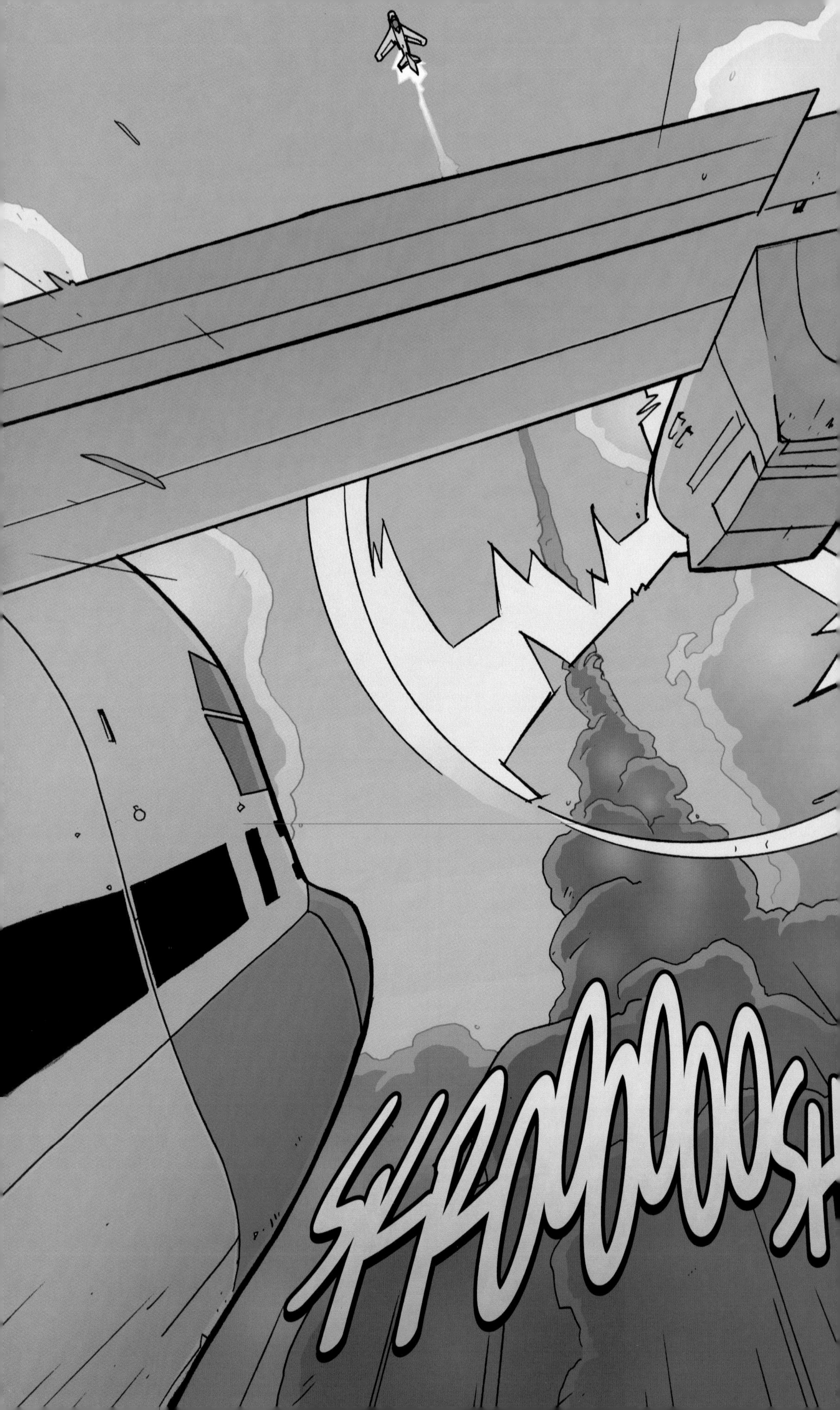
SHOOOOOSH

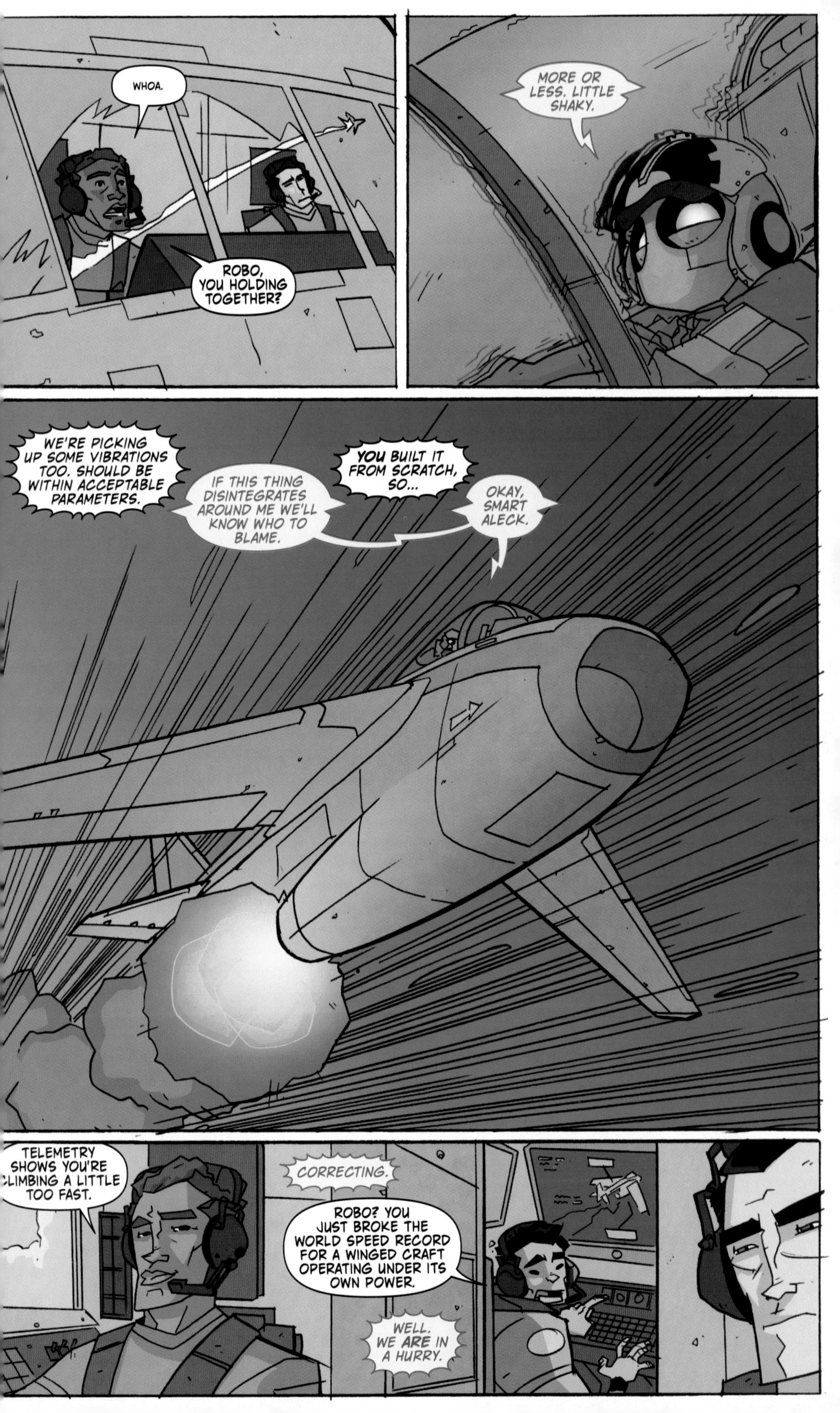
WHOA.
ROBO, YOU HOLDING TOGETHER?
MORE OR LESS. LITTLE SHAKY.
WE'RE PICKING UP SOME VIBRATIONS TOO. SHOULD BE WITHIN ACCEPTABLE PARAMETERS.
IF THIS THING DISINTEGRATES AROUND ME WE'LL KNOW WHO TO BLAME.
YOU BUILT IT FROM SCRATCH, SO...
OKAY, SMART ALECK.
TELEMETRY SHOWS YOU'RE CLIMBING A LITTLE TOO FAST.
CORRECTING.
ROBO? YOU JUST BROKE THE WORLD SPEED RECORD FOR A WINGED CRAFT OPERATING UNDER ITS OWN POWER.
WELL. WE ARE IN A HURRY.

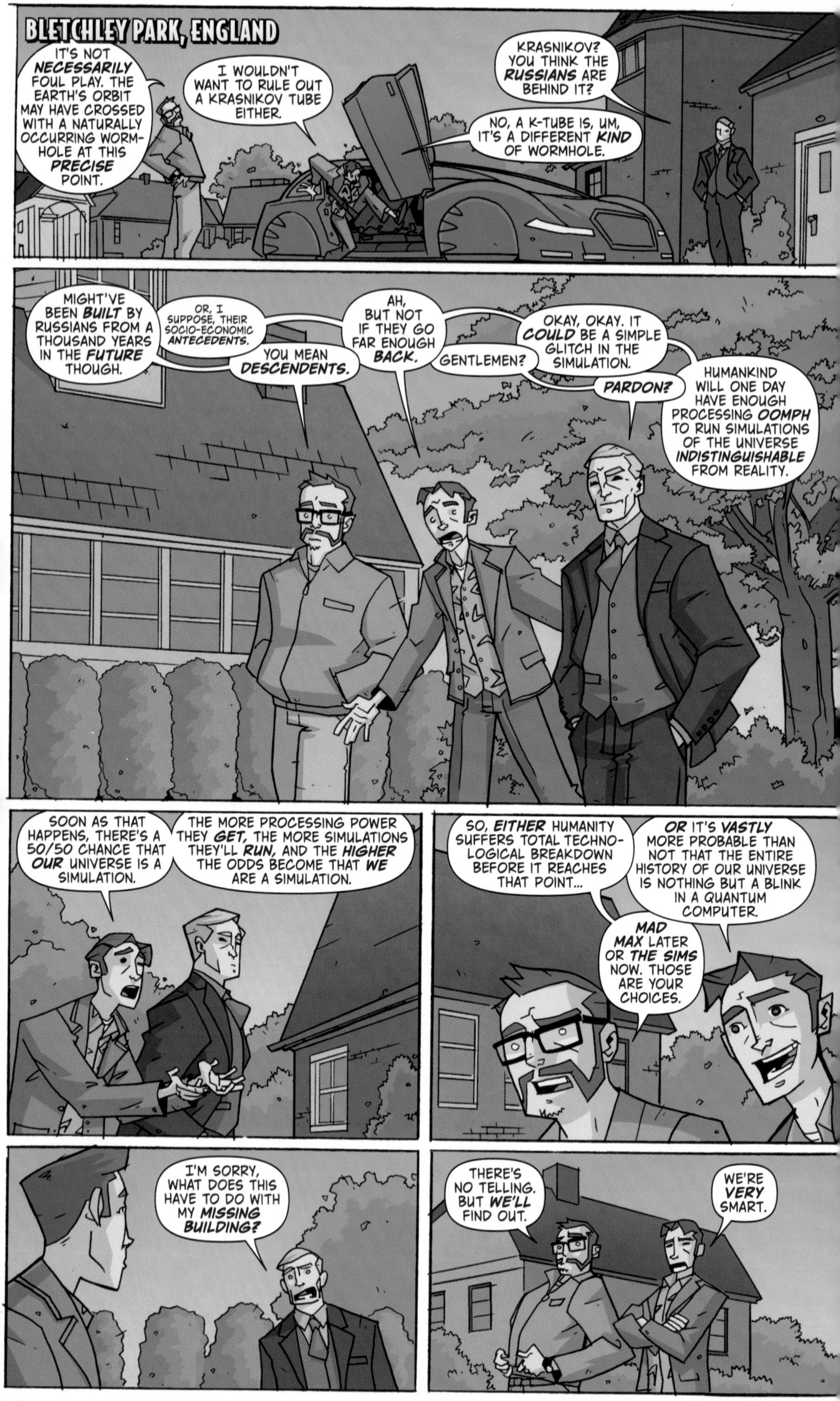
BLETCHLEY PARK, ENGLAND
IT'S NOT NECESSARILY FOUL PLAY. THE EARTH'S ORBIT MAY HAVE CROSSED WITH A NATURALLY OCCURRING WORMHOLE AT THIS PRECISE POINT.
I WOULDN'T WANT TO RULE OUT A KRASNIKOV TUBE EITHER.
KRASNIKOV? YOU THINK THE RUSSIANS ARE BEHIND IT?
NO, A K-TUBE IS, UM, IT'S A DIFFERENT KIND OF WORMHOLE.
MIGHT'VE BEEN BUILT BY RUSSIANS FROM A THOUSAND YEARS IN THE FUTURE THOUGH.
OR, I SUPPOSE, THEIR SOCIO-ECONOMIC ANTECEDENTS.
YOU MEAN DESCENDENTS.
AH, BUT NOT IF THEY GO FAR ENOUGH BACK.
GENTLEMEN?
OKAY, OKAY. IT COULD BE A SIMPLE GLITCH IN THE SIMULATION.
PARDON?
HUMANKIND WILL ONE DAY HAVE ENOUGH PROCESSING OOMPH TO RUN SIMULATIONS OF THE UNIVERSE INDISTINGUISHABLE FROM REALITY.
SOON AS THAT HAPPENS, THERE'S A 50/50 CHANCE THAT OUR UNIVERSE IS A SIMULATION.
THE MORE PROCESSING POWER THEY GET, THE MORE SIMULATIONS THEY'LL RUN, AND THE HIGHER THE ODDS BECOME THAT WE ARE A SIMULATION.
SO, EITHER HUMANITY SUFFERS TOTAL TECHNO-LOGICAL BREAKDOWN BEFORE IT REACHES THAT POINT...
OR IT'S VASTLY MORE PROBABLE THAN NOT THAT THE ENTIRE HISTORY OF OUR UNIVERSE IS NOTHING BUT A BLINK IN A QUANTUM COMPUTER.
MAD MAX LATER OR THE SIMS NOW. THOSE ARE YOUR CHOICES.
I'M SORRY, WHAT DOES THIS HAVE TO DO WITH MY MISSING BUILDING?
THERE'S NO TELLING. BUT WE'LL FIND OUT.
WE'RE VERY SMART.

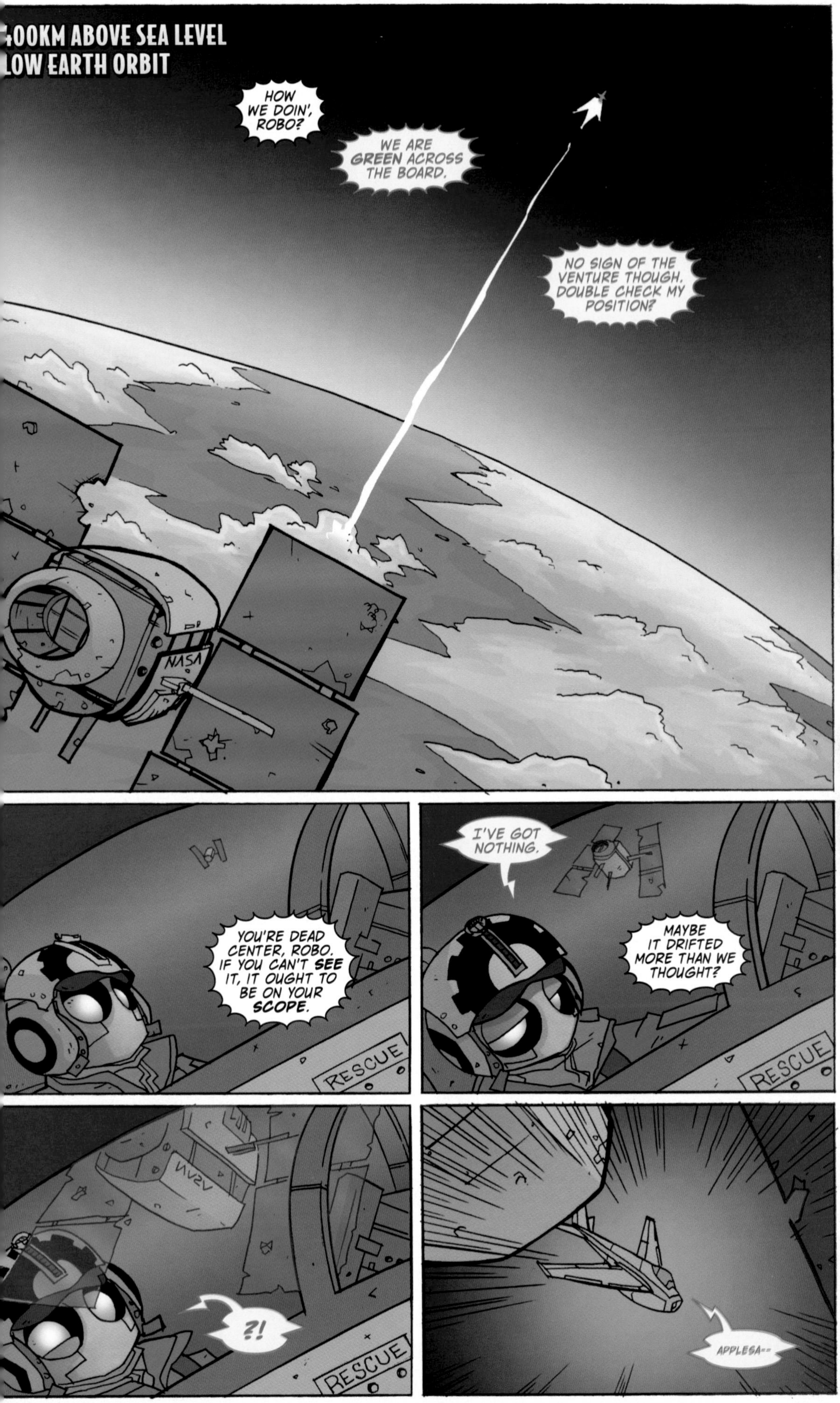
400KM ABOVE SEA LEVEL
LOW EARTH ORBIT
HOW WE DOIN', ROBO?
WE ARE GREEN ACROSS THE BOARD.
NO SIGN OF THE VENTURE THOUGH. DOUBLE CHECK MY POSITION?
NASA
YOU'RE DEAD CENTER, ROBO. IF YOU CAN'T SEE IT, IT OUGHT TO BE ON YOUR SCOPE.
RESCUE
I'VE GOT NOTHING.
MAYBE IT DRIFTED MORE THAN WE THOUGHT?
RESCUE
NASA
?!
RESCUE
APPLESA==

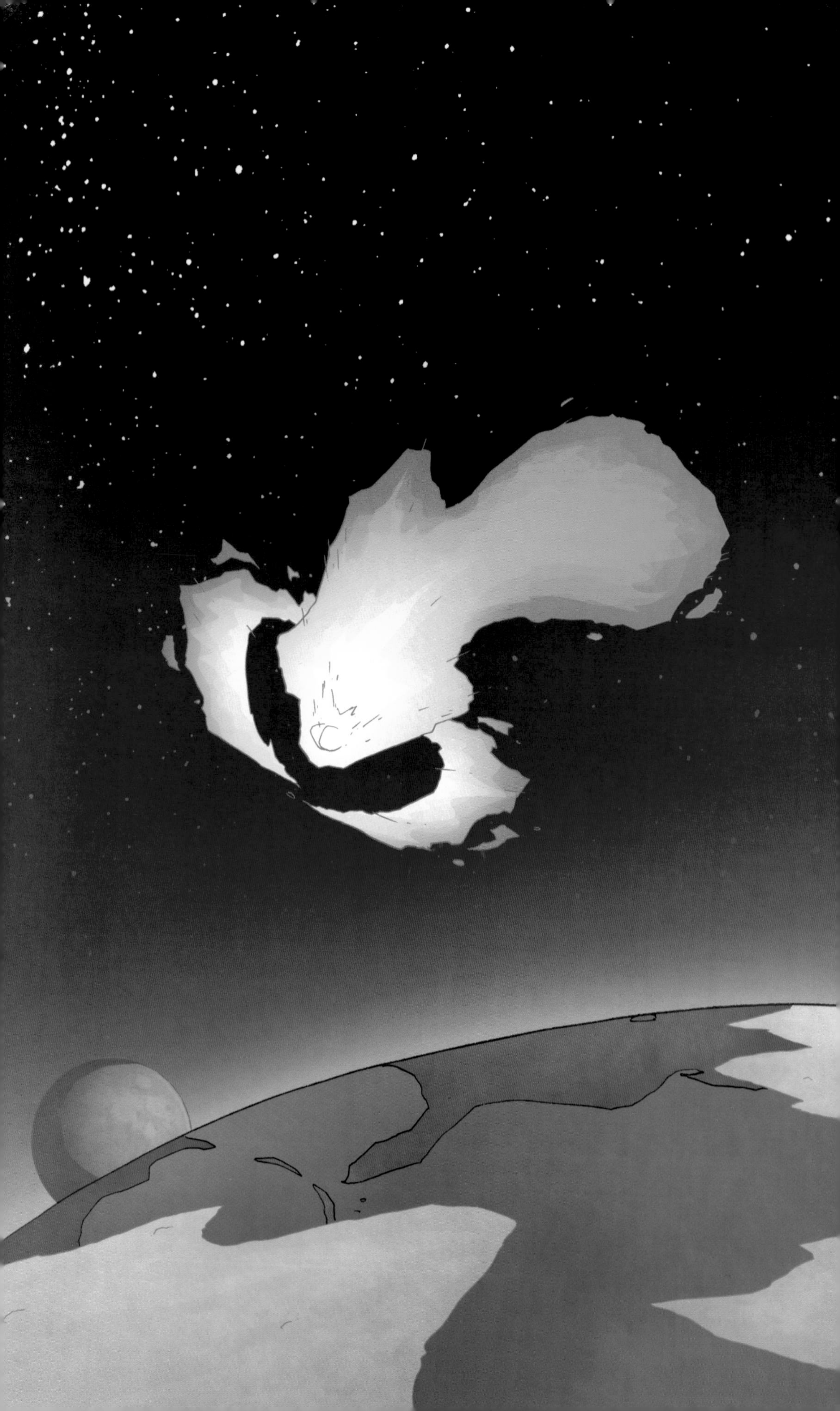

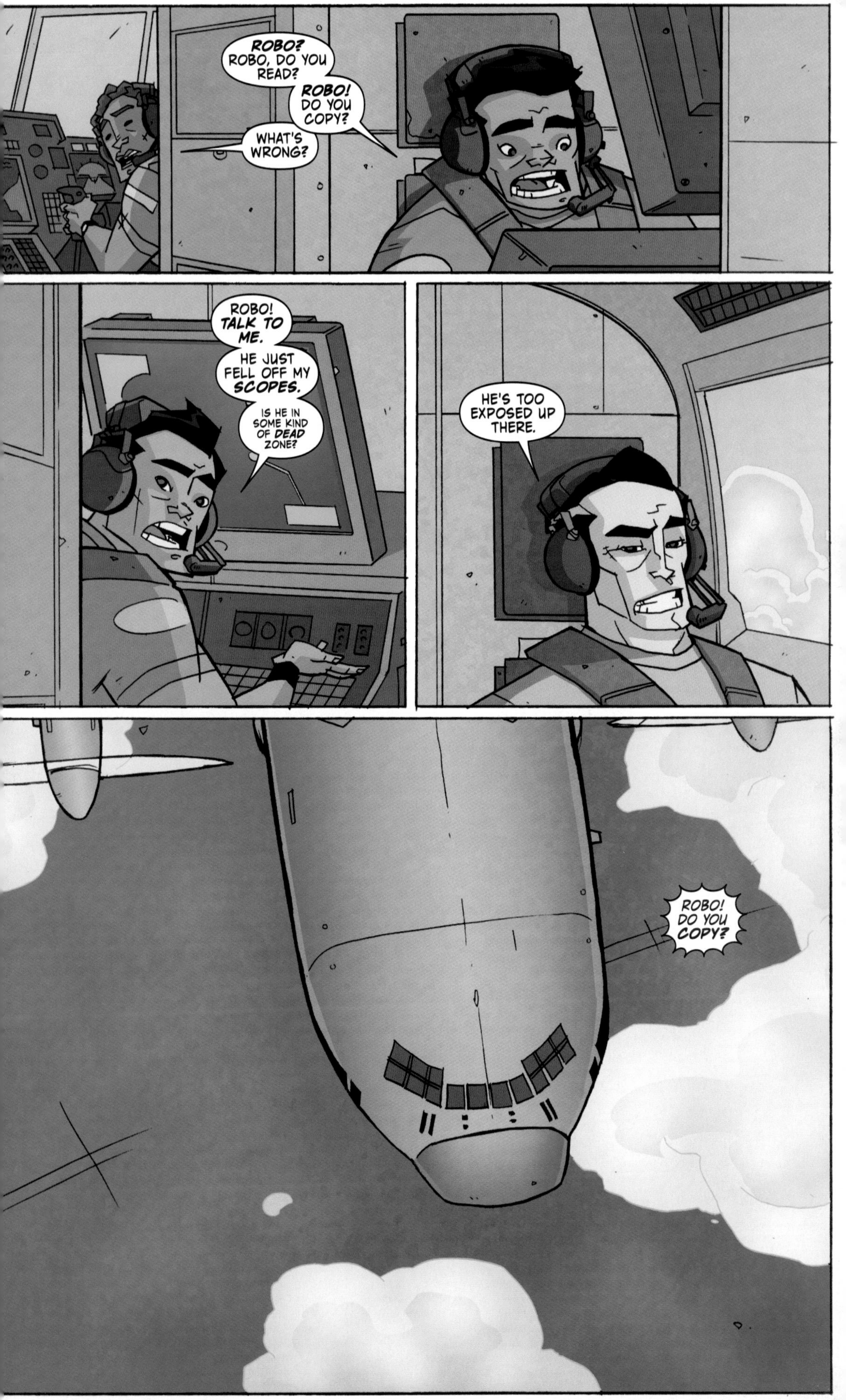

ROBO? ROBO, DO YOU READ?
ROBO! DO YOU COPY?
WHAT'S WRONG?
ROBO! TALK TO ME.
HE JUST FELL OFF MY SCOPES.
IS HE IN SOME KIND OF DEAD ZONE?
HE'S TOO EXPOSED UP THERE.
ROBO! DO YOU COPY?

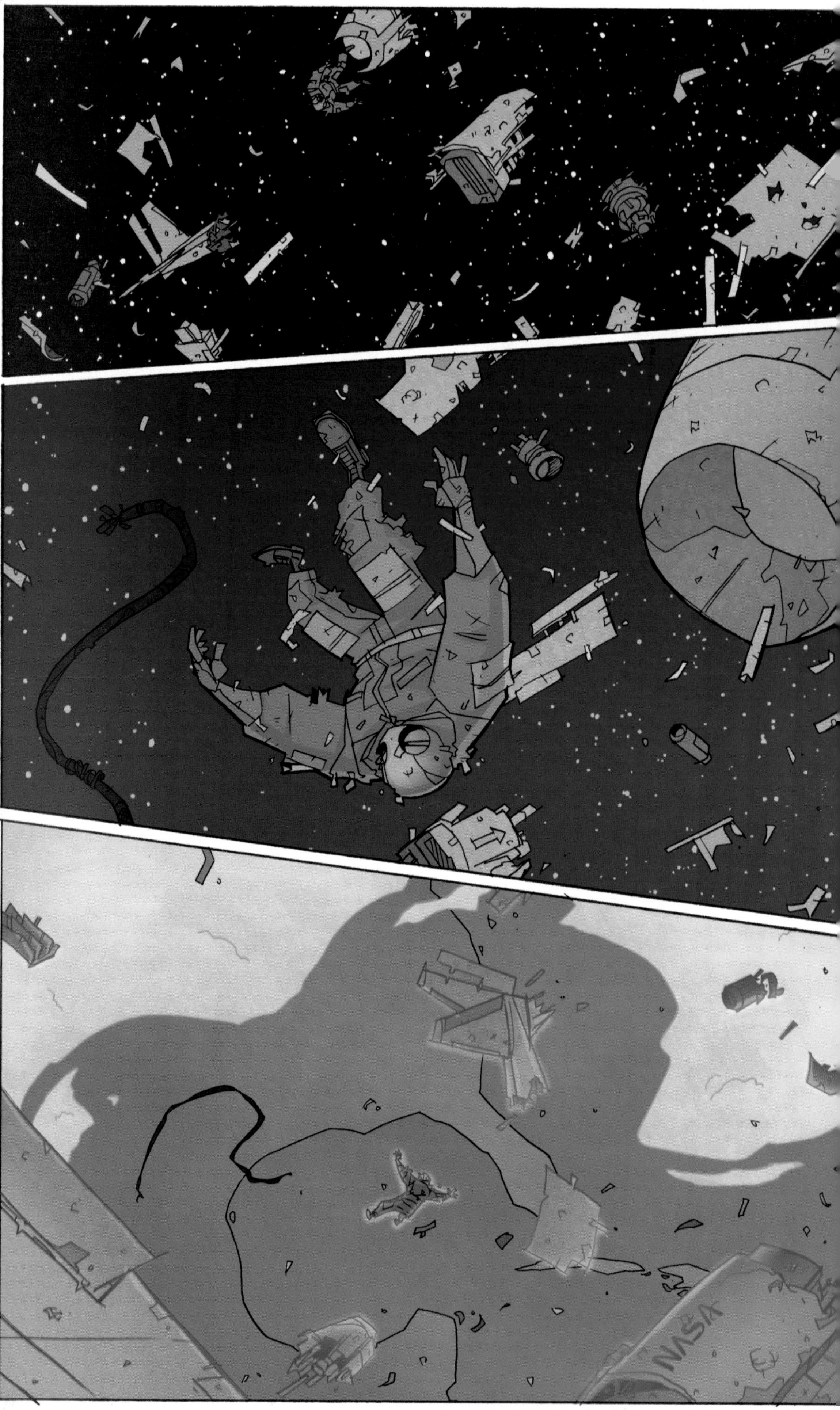
NASA

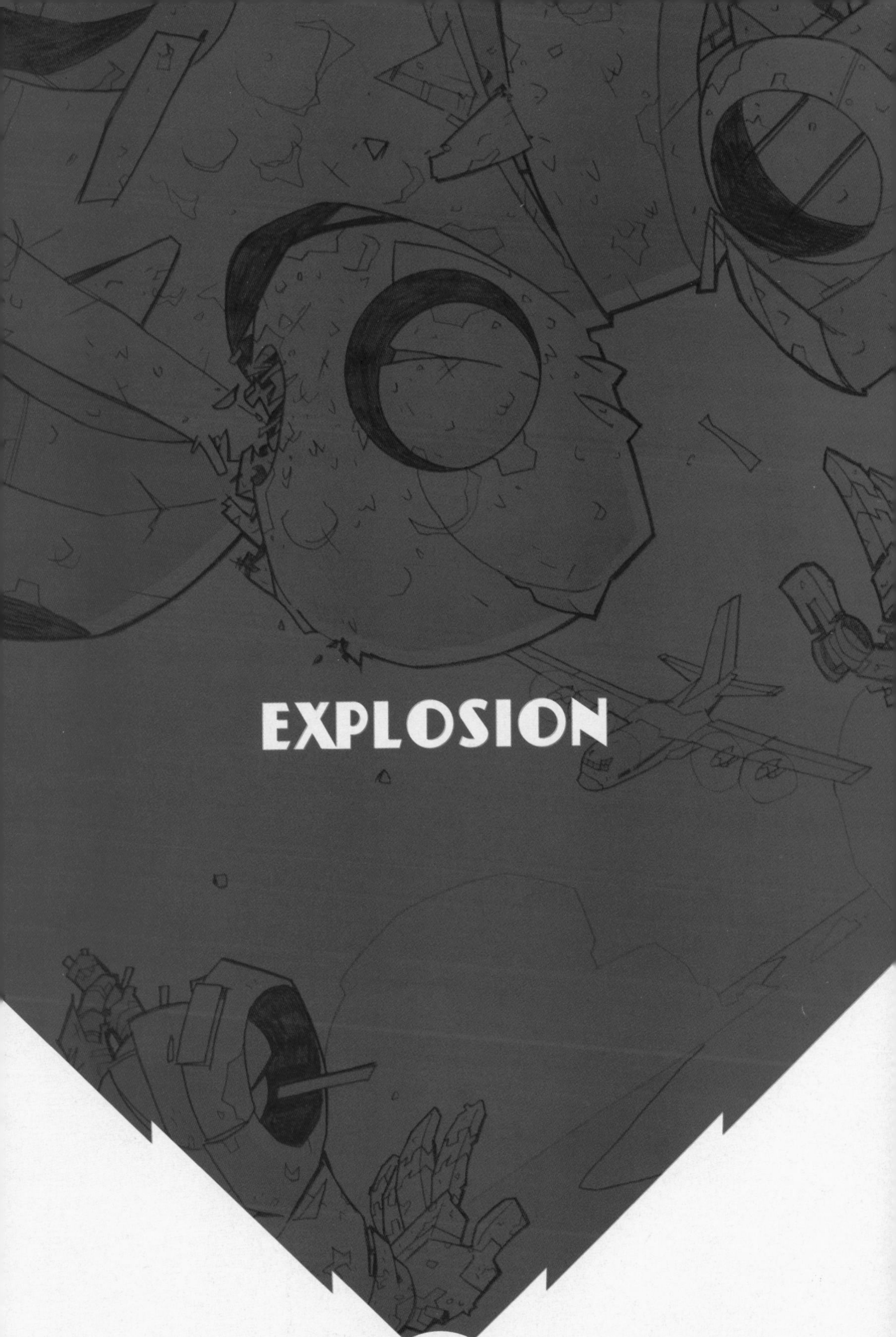

EXPLOSION

2

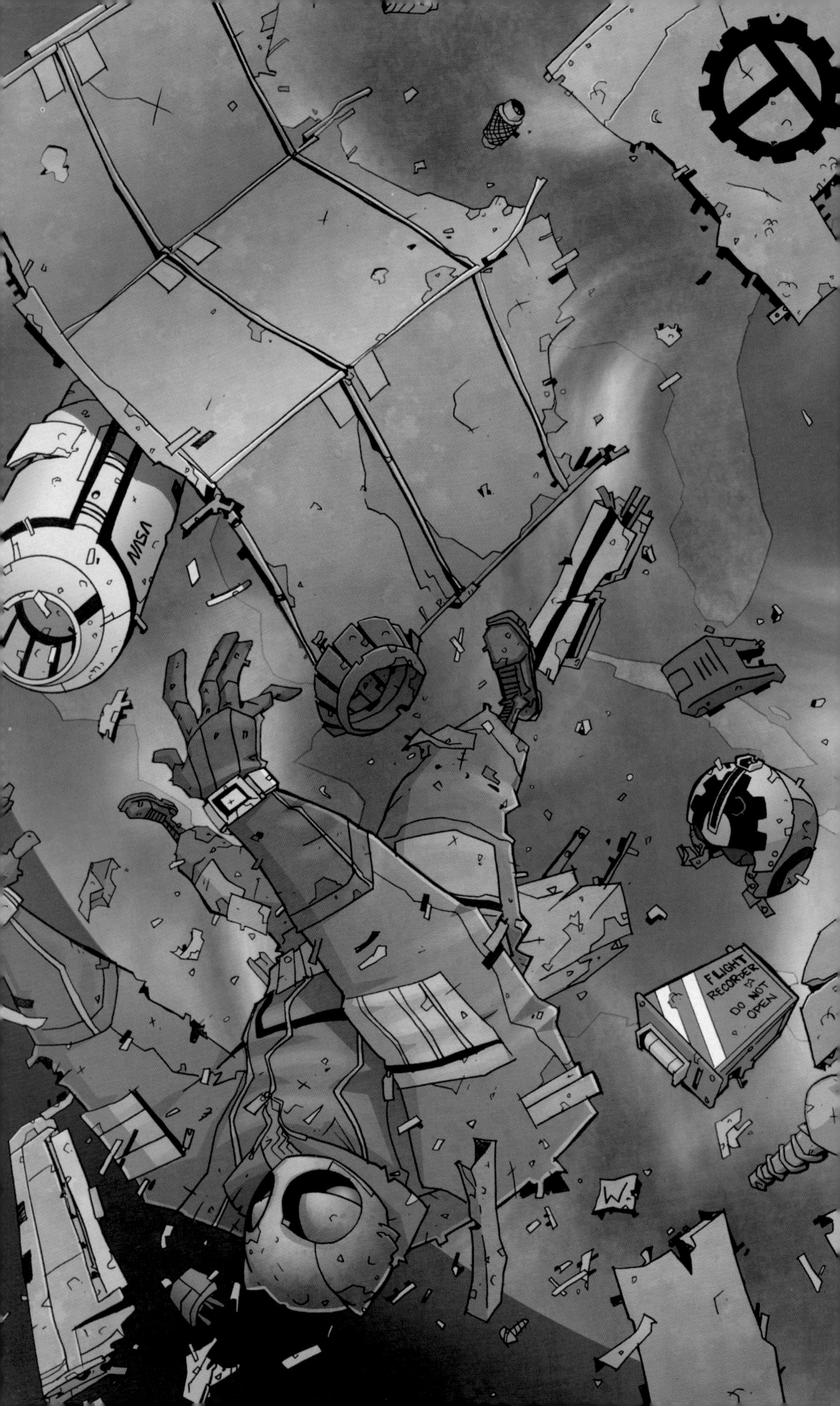
NASA
FLIGHT RECORDER
DO NOT OPEN

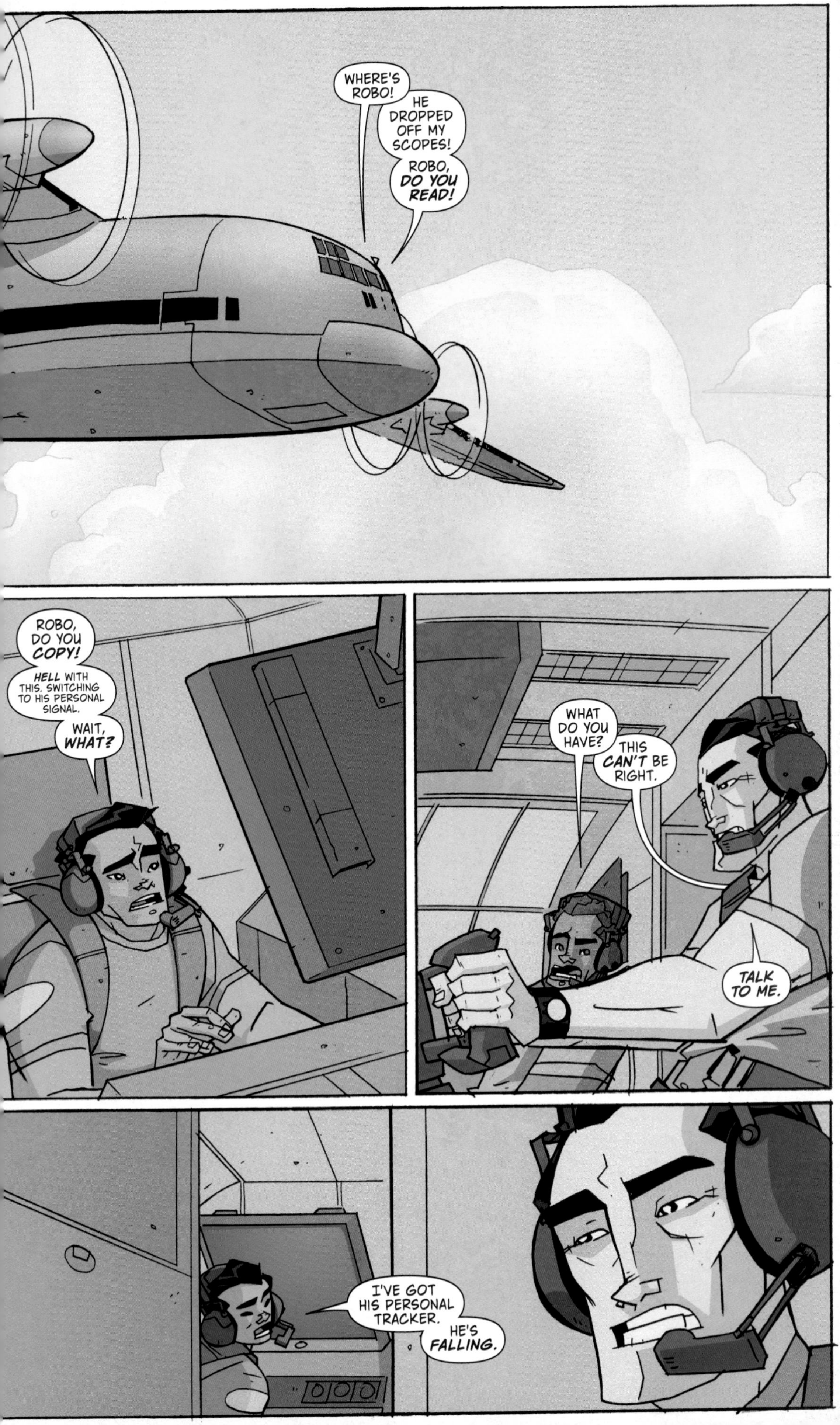
WHERE'S ROBO!
HE DROPPED OFF MY SCOPES!
ROBO, DO YOU READ!
ROBO, DO YOU COPY!
HELL WITH THIS. SWITCHING TO HIS PERSONAL SIGNAL.
WAIT, WHAT?
WHAT DO YOU HAVE?
THIS CAN'T BE RIGHT.
TALK TO ME.
I'VE GOT HIS PERSONAL TRACKER.
HE'S FALLING.

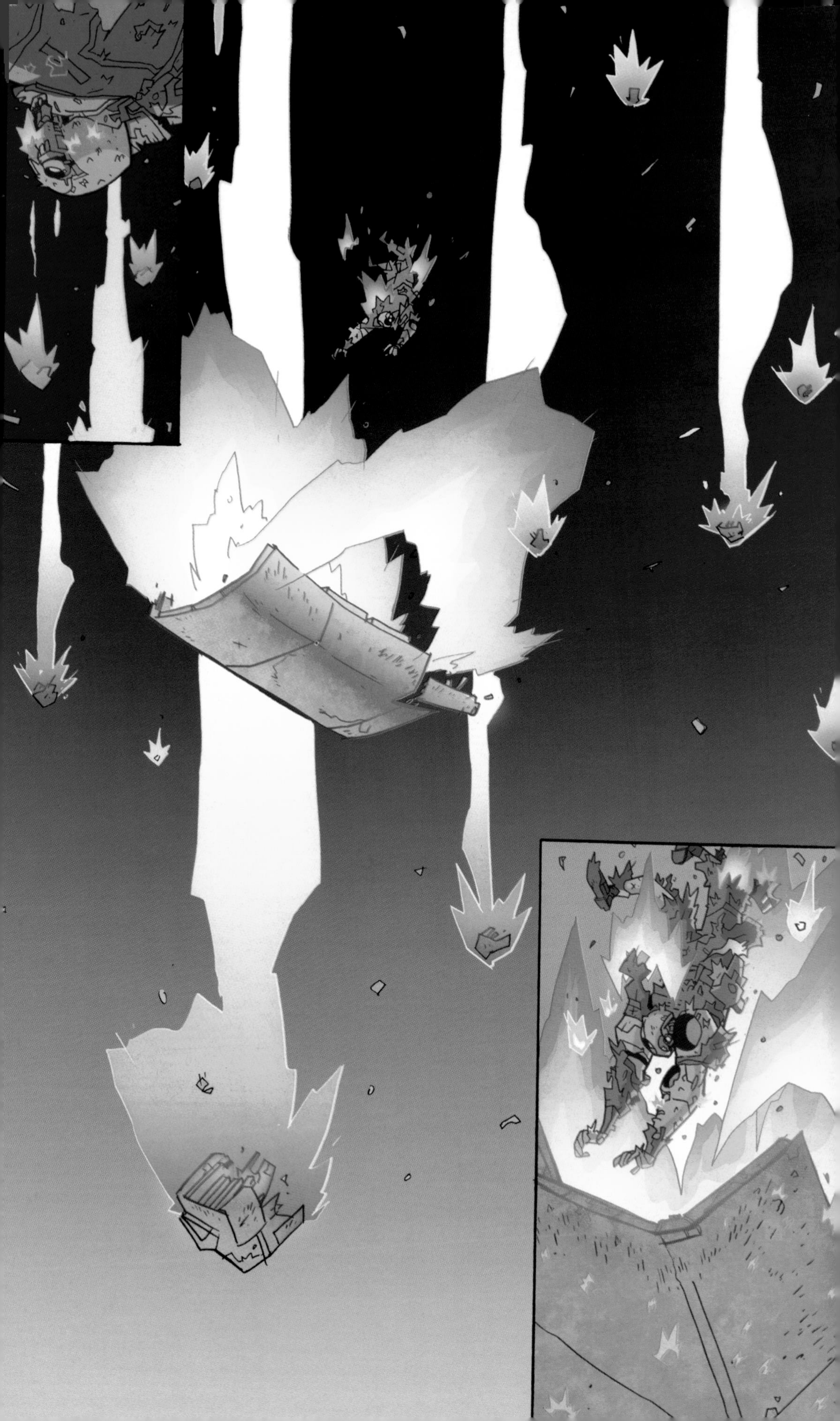

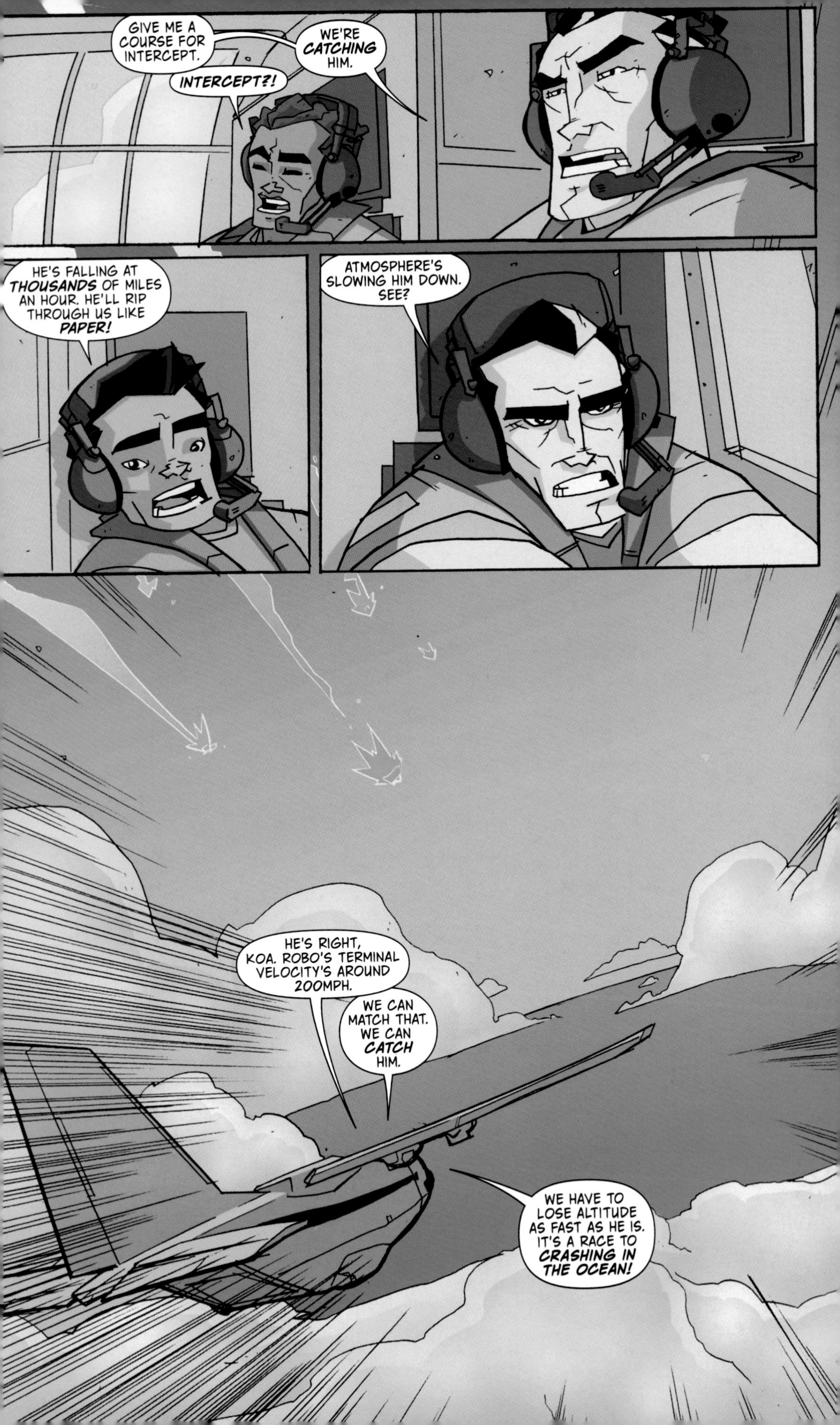
GIVE ME A COURSE FOR INTERCEPT.
INTERCEPT?!
WE'RE CATCHING HIM.
HE'S FALLING AT THOUSANDS OF MILES AN HOUR. HE'LL RIP THROUGH US LIKE PAPER!
ATMOSPHERE'S SLOWING HIM DOWN. SEE?
HE'S RIGHT, KOA. ROBO'S TERMINAL VELOCITY'S AROUND 200MPH.
WE CAN MATCH THAT. WE CAN CATCH HIM.
WE HAVE TO LOSE ALTITUDE AS FAST AS HE IS. IT'S A RACE TO CRASHING IN THE OCEAN!

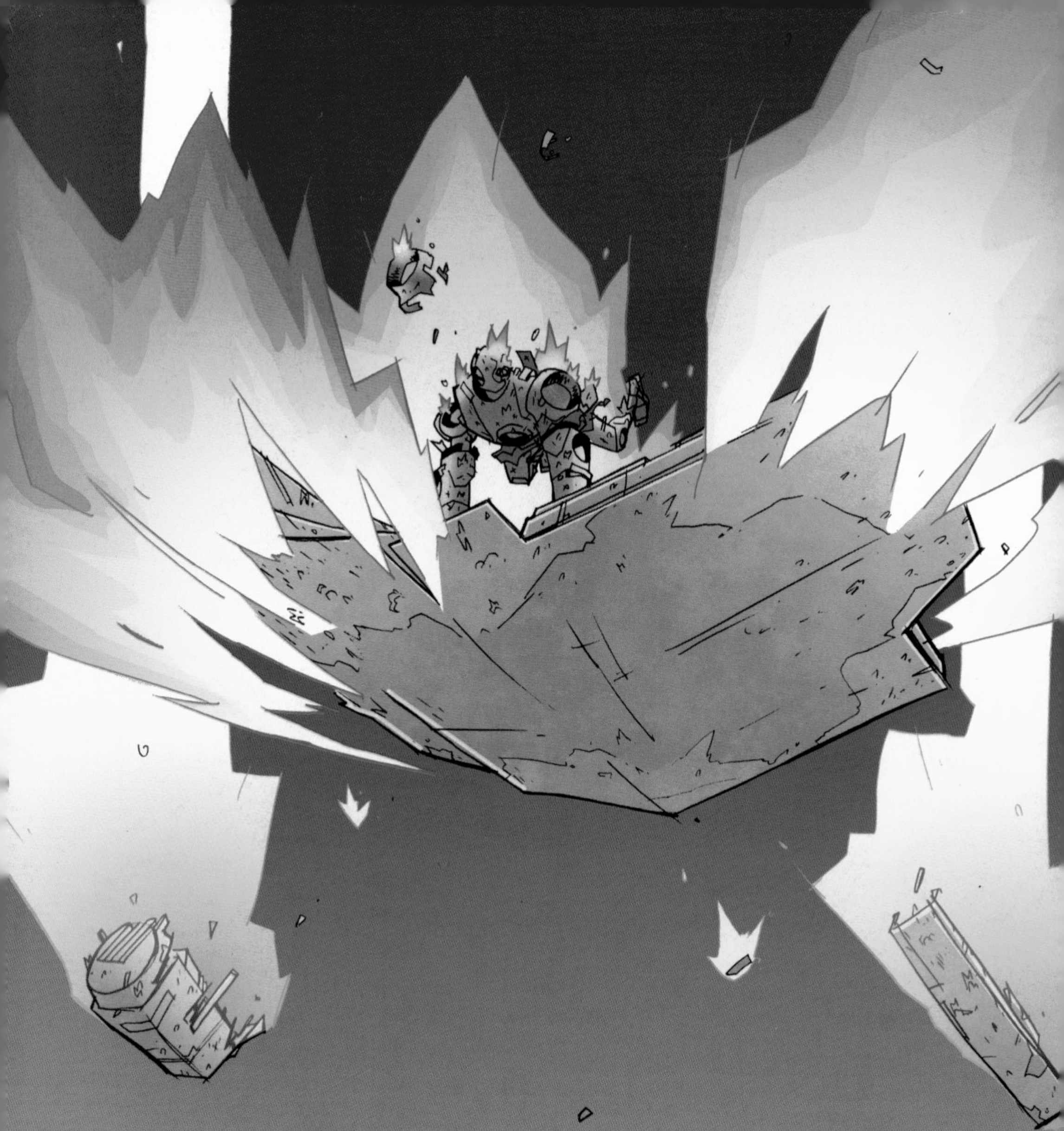

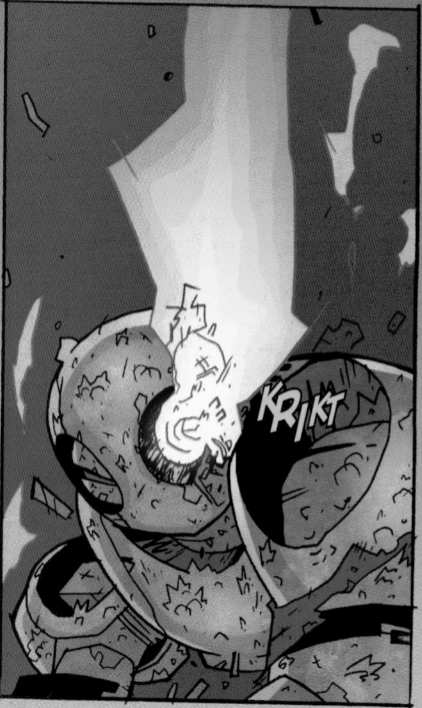
KRIKT

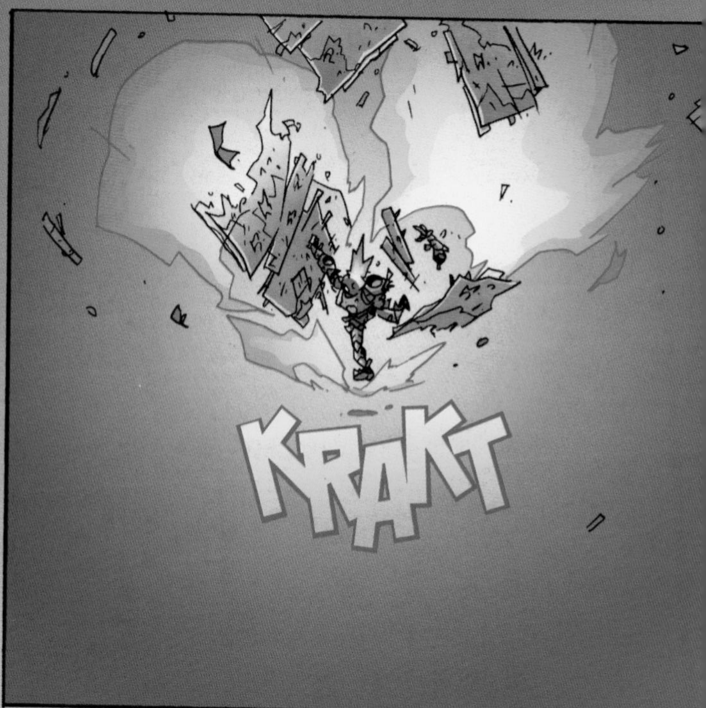
KRAKT

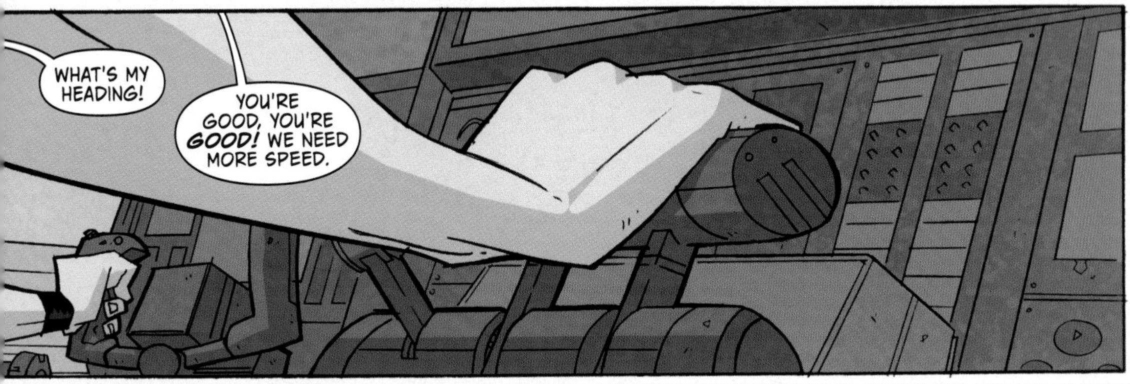
WHAT'S MY HEADING!
YOU'RE GOOD, YOU'RE **GOOD!** WE NEED MORE SPEED.
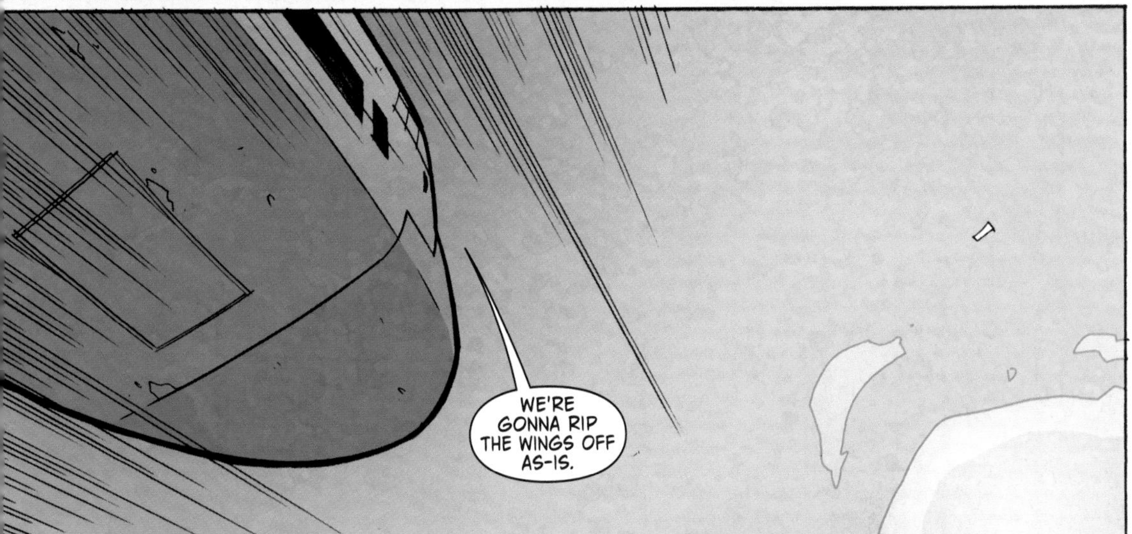
WE'RE GONNA RIP THE WINGS OFF AS-IS.
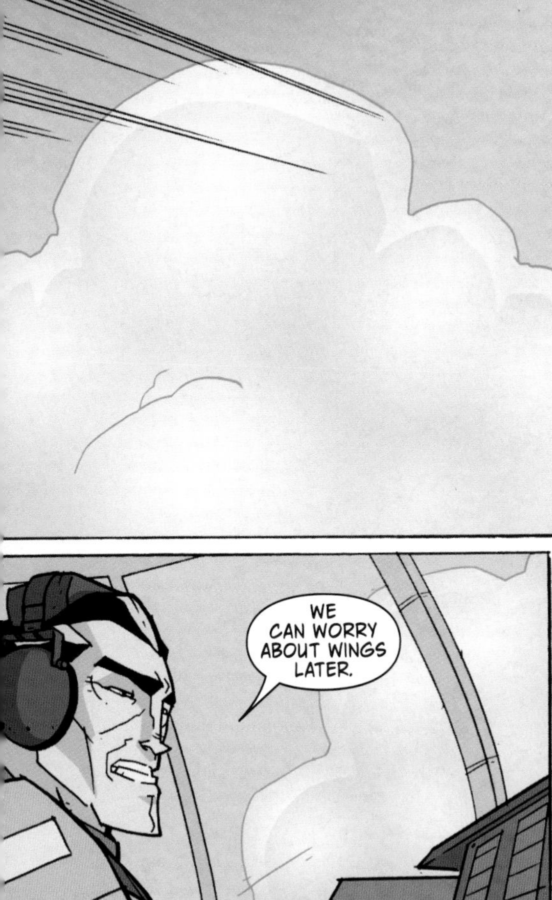
WE CAN WORRY ABOUT WINGS LATER.
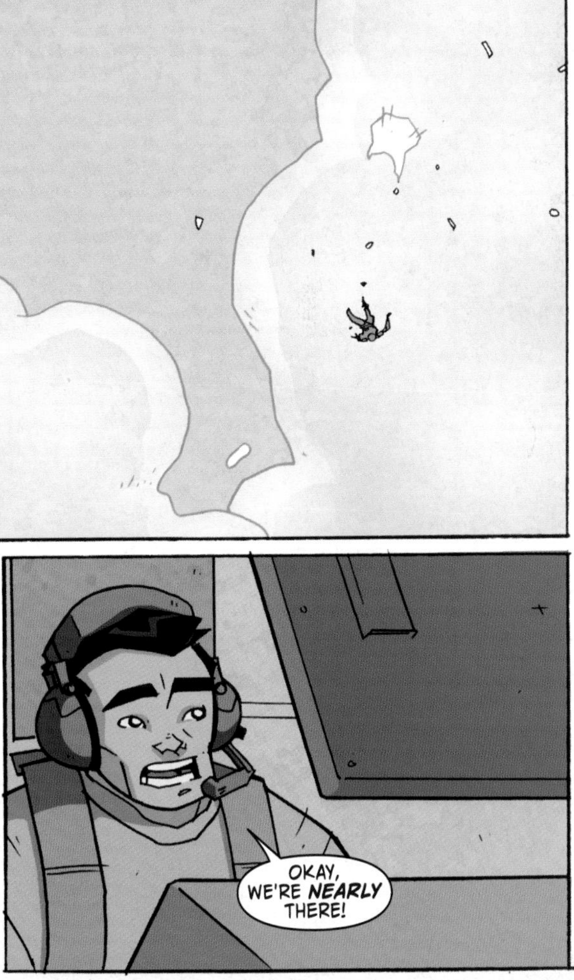
OKAY, WE'RE **NEARLY** THERE!

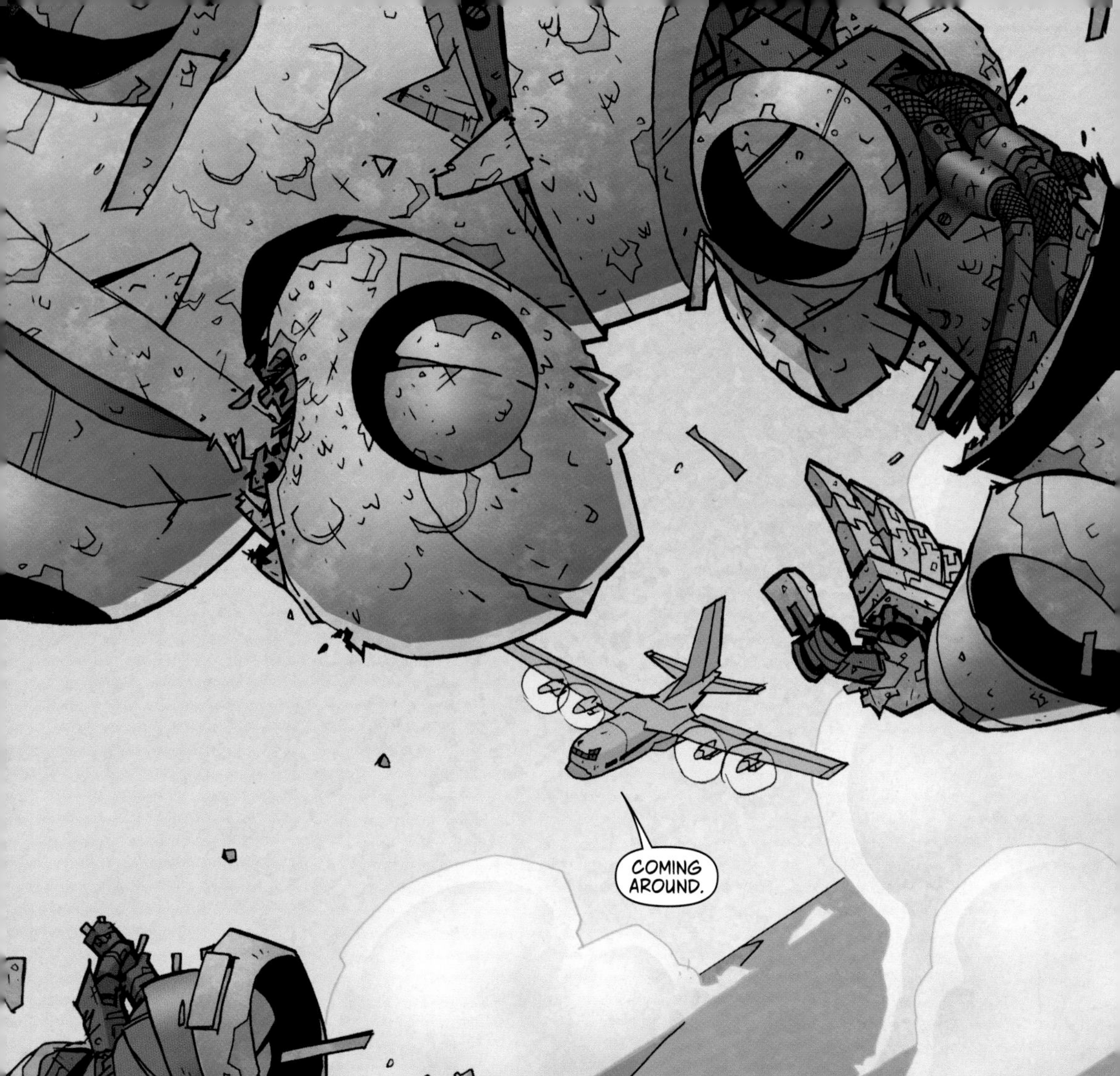
COMING AROUND.

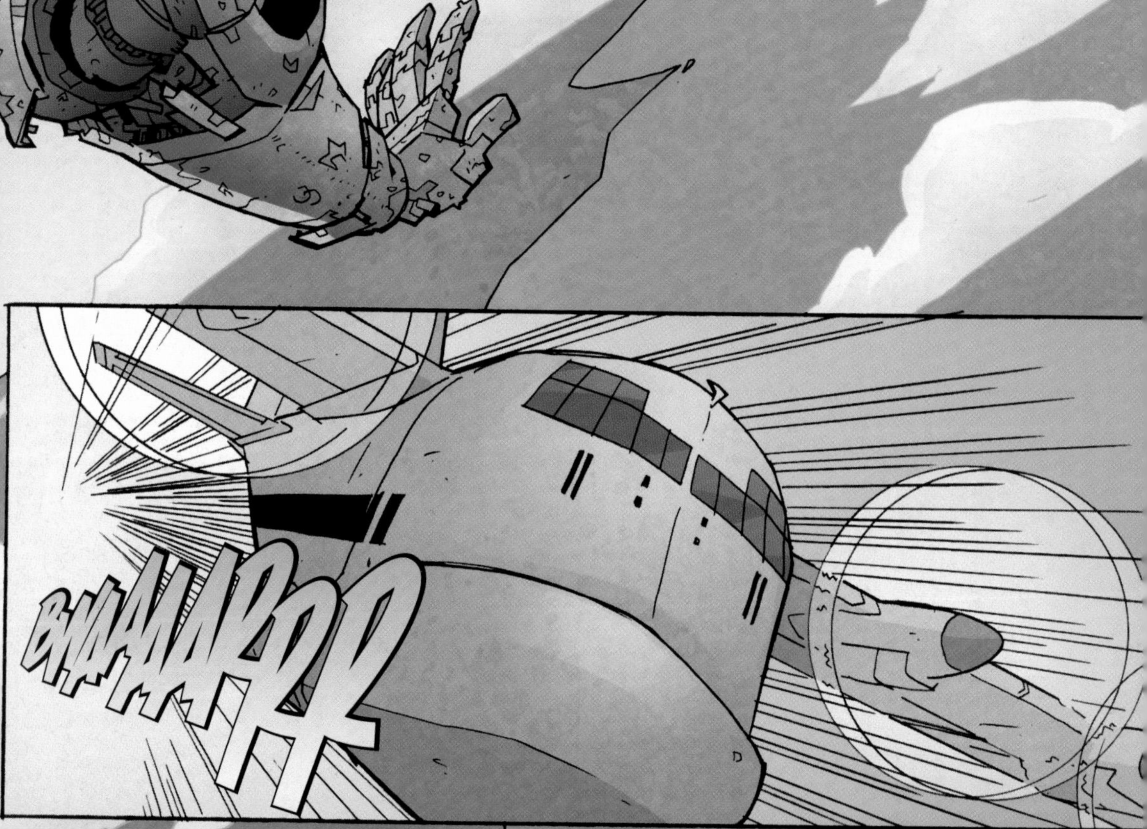
BWAAARRR

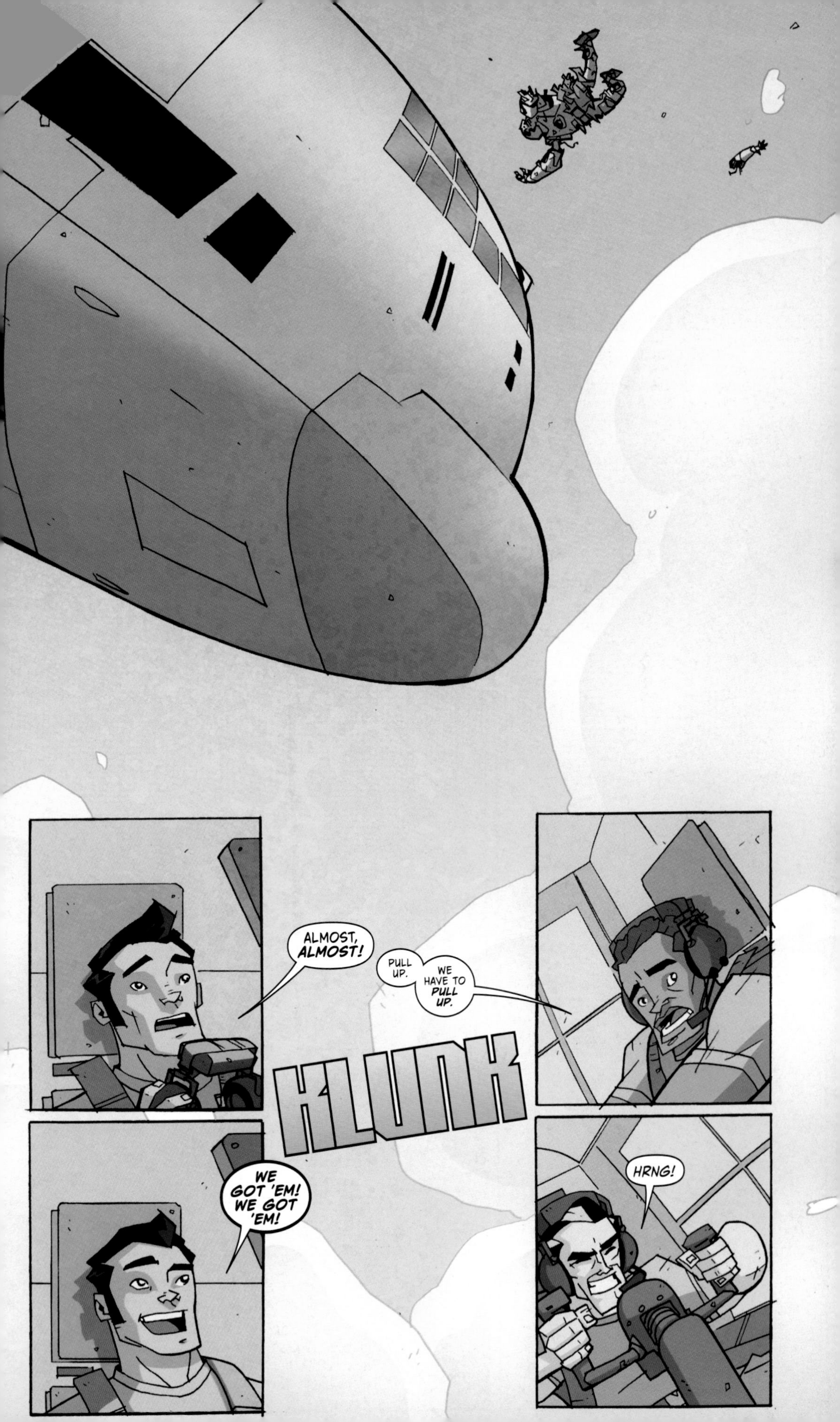
ALMOST, ALMOST!
PULL UP.
WE HAVE TO PULL UP.
KLUNK
WE GOT 'EM! WE GOT 'EM!
HRNG!

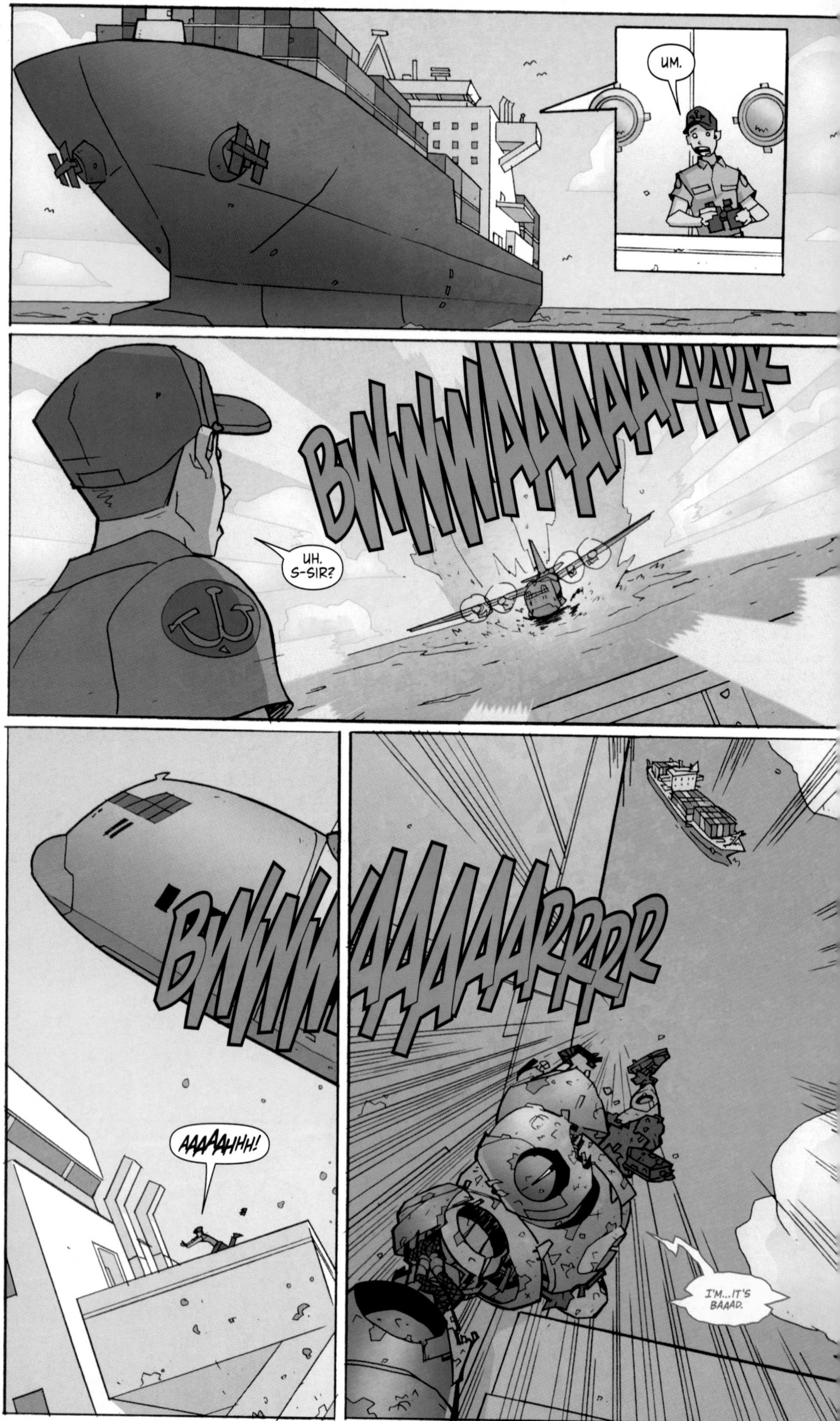
UM.
BWWWAAAAARRRR
UH. S-SIR?
BWWWAAAAARRRR
AAAAAHHH!
I'M...IT'S BAAAD.

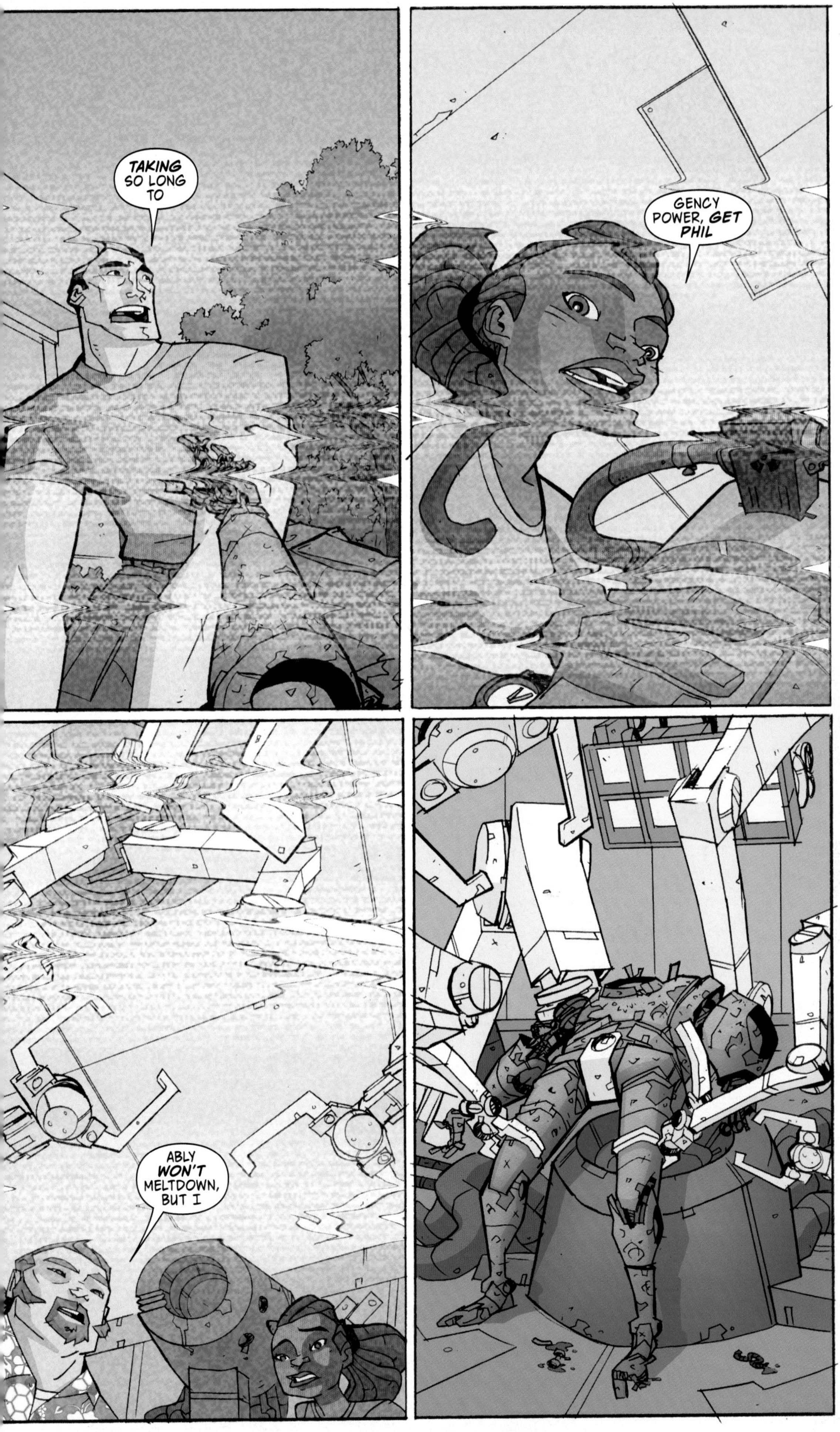
TAKING SO LONG TO
GENCY POWER, GET PHIL
ABLY WON'T MELTDOWN, BUT I

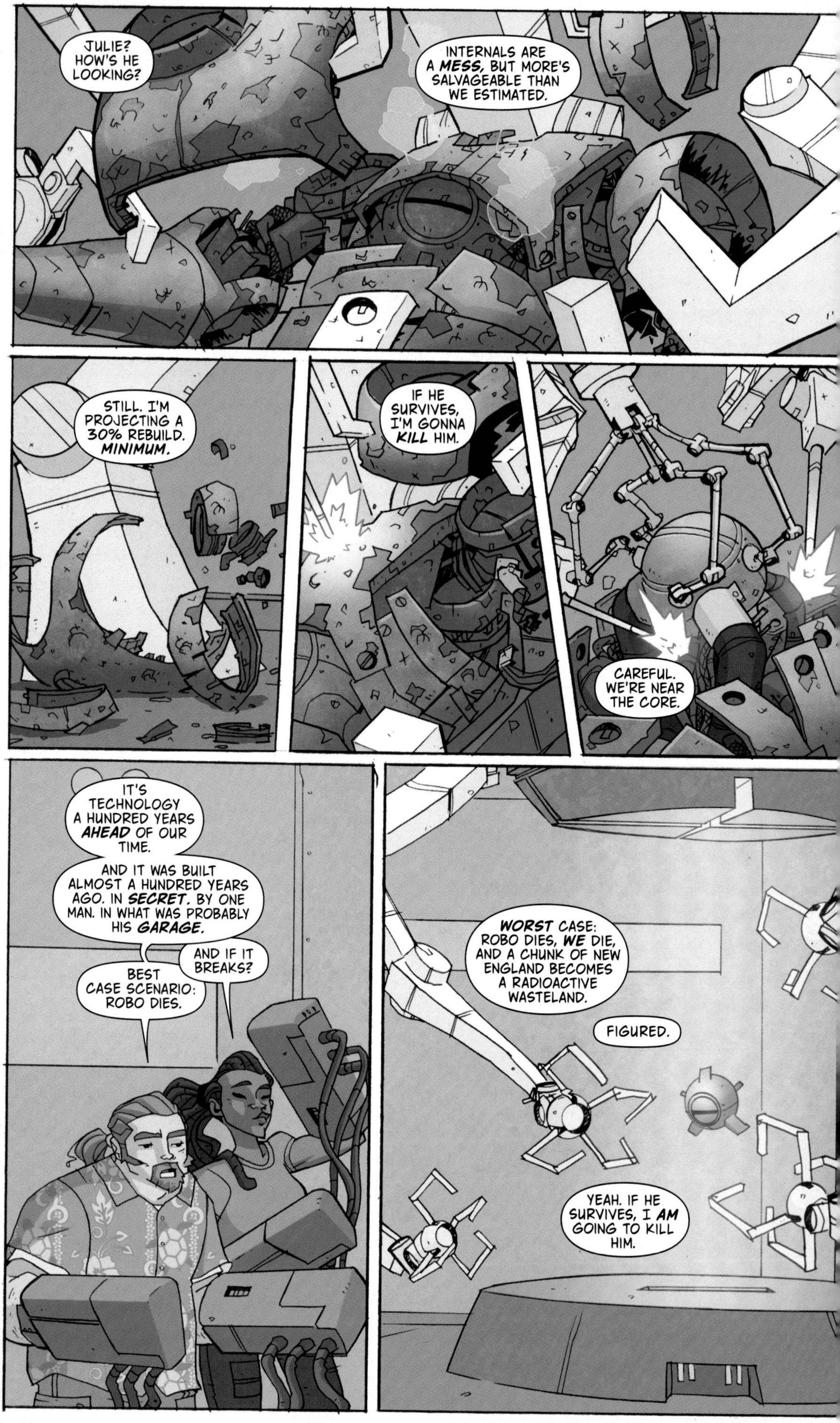
JULIE? HOW'S HE LOOKING?
INTERNALS ARE A MESS, BUT MORE'S SALVAGEABLE THAN WE ESTIMATED.
STILL. I'M PROJECTING A 30% REBUILD. MINIMUM.
IF HE SURVIVES, I'M GONNA KILL HIM.
CAREFUL. WE'RE NEAR THE CORE.
IT'S TECHNOLOGY A HUNDRED YEARS AHEAD OF OUR TIME.
AND IT WAS BUILT ALMOST A HUNDRED YEARS AGO. IN SECRET. BY ONE MAN. IN WHAT WAS PROBABLY HIS GARAGE.
AND IF IT BREAKS?
BEST CASE SCENARIO: ROBO DIES.
WORST CASE: ROBO DIES, WE DIE, AND A CHUNK OF NEW ENGLAND BECOMES A RADIOACTIVE WASTELAND.
FIGURED.
YEAH. IF HE SURVIVES, I AM GOING TO KILL HIM.

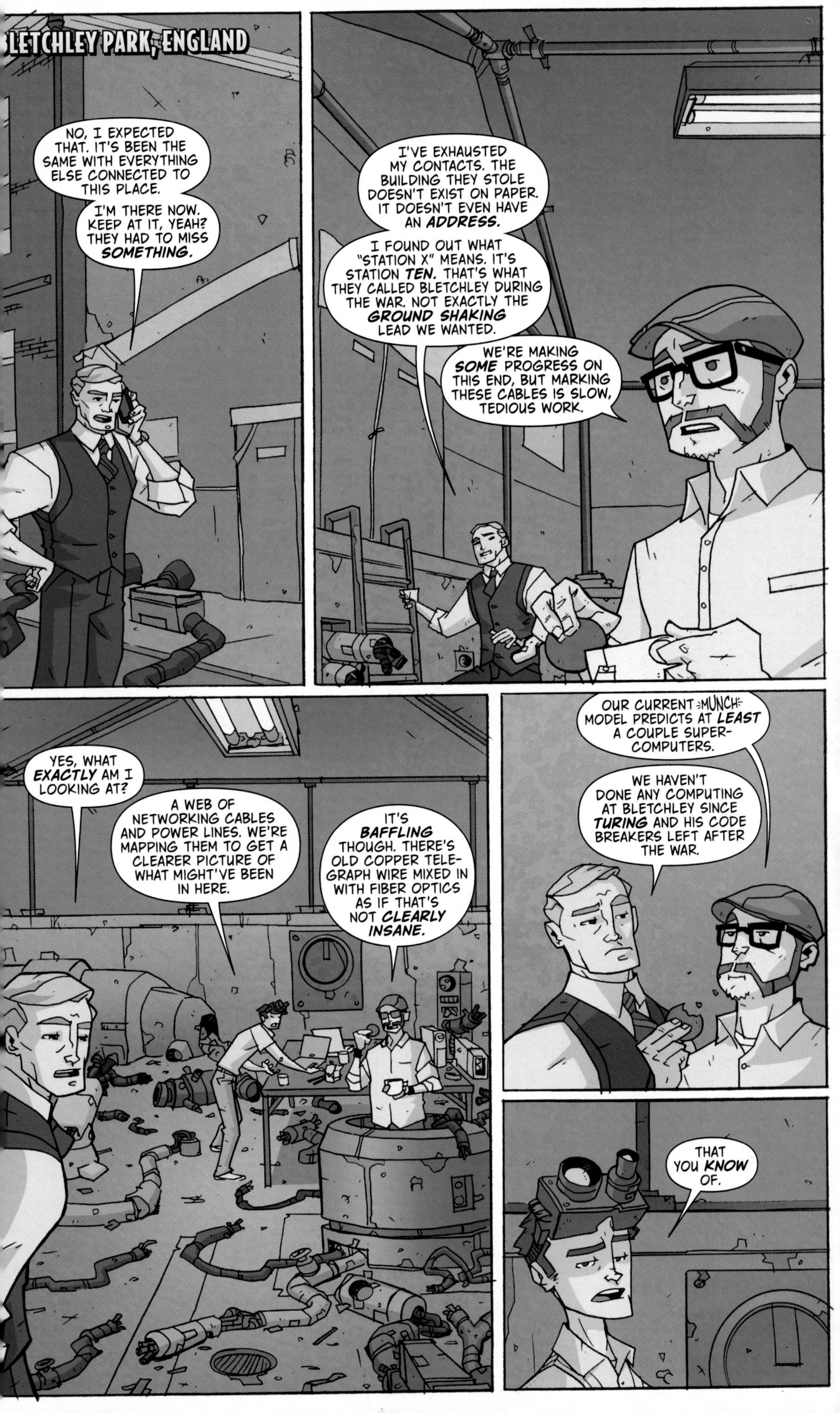
LETCHLEY PARK, ENGLAND
NO, I EXPECTED THAT. IT'S BEEN THE SAME WITH EVERYTHING ELSE CONNECTED TO THIS PLACE.
I'M THERE NOW. KEEP AT IT, YEAH? THEY HAD TO MISS SOMETHING.
I'VE EXHAUSTED MY CONTACTS. THE BUILDING THEY STOLE DOESN'T EXIST ON PAPER. IT DOESN'T EVEN HAVE AN ADDRESS.
I FOUND OUT WHAT "STATION X" MEANS. IT'S STATION TEN. THAT'S WHAT THEY CALLED BLETCHLEY DURING THE WAR. NOT EXACTLY THE GROUND SHAKING LEAD WE WANTED.
WE'RE MAKING SOME PROGRESS ON THIS END, BUT MARKING THESE CABLES IS SLOW, TEDIOUS WORK.
YES, WHAT EXACTLY AM I LOOKING AT?
A WEB OF NETWORKING CABLES AND POWER LINES. WE'RE MAPPING THEM TO GET A CLEARER PICTURE OF WHAT MIGHT'VE BEEN IN HERE.
IT'S BAFFLING THOUGH. THERE'S OLD COPPER TELE-GRAPH WIRE MIXED IN WITH FIBER OPTICS AS IF THAT'S NOT CLEARLY INSANE.
OUR CURRENT MUNCH MODEL PREDICTS AT LEAST A COUPLE SUPER-COMPUTERS.
WE HAVEN'T DONE ANY COMPUTING AT BLETCHLEY SINCE TURING AND HIS CODE BREAKERS LEFT AFTER THE WAR.
THAT YOU KNOW OF.

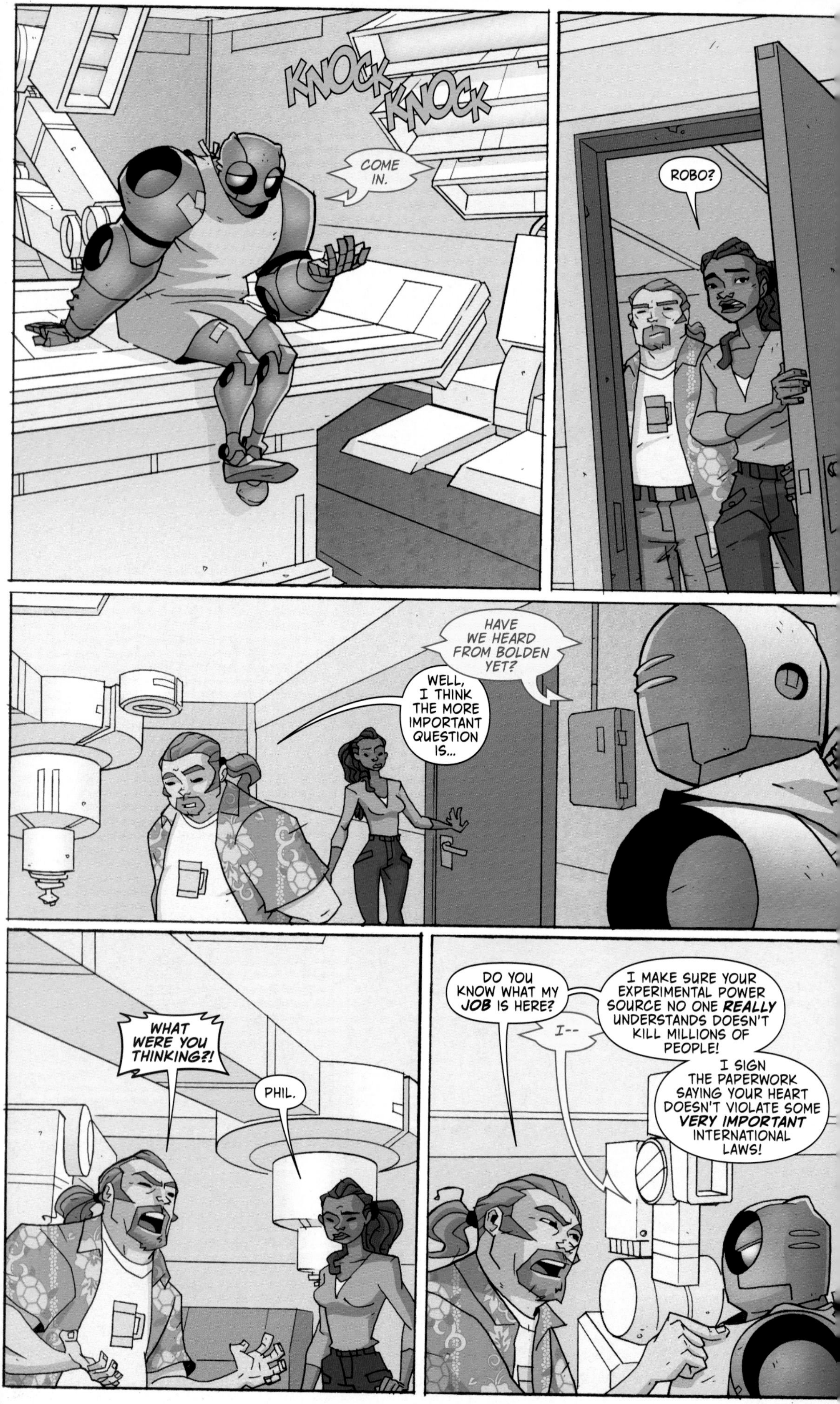

KNOCK KNOCK
COME IN.
ROBO?
HAVE WE HEARD FROM BOLDEN YET?
WELL, I THINK THE MORE IMPORTANT QUESTION IS...
WHAT WERE YOU THINKING?!
PHIL.
DO YOU KNOW WHAT MY JOB IS HERE?
I--
I MAKE SURE YOUR EXPERIMENTAL POWER SOURCE NO ONE REALLY UNDERSTANDS DOESN'T KILL MILLIONS OF PEOPLE!
I SIGN THE PAPERWORK SAYING YOUR HEART DOESN'T VIOLATE SOME VERY IMPORTANT INTERNATIONAL LAWS!

AND *I'M* THE ONE WHO GOES TO *WAR CRIMINAL JAIL* IF YOU DO SOMETHING *RECKLESS* AND *STUPID* AND START LEAKING RADIATION!

DO YOU *KNOW* HOW CLOSE YOU WERE TO MELTING DOWN?

I--

SHUT UP, NO YOU *DON'T!*

NEITHER DO I! BECAUSE YOUR TEMP GAUGE *MELTED!*

PHIL!

ALL *RIGHT,* OKAY!

HE GETS IT, *OKAY?*

SORRY, I KNOW. IT'S JUST--

JUST *WHAT?*

JUST THAT I SPENT *TWENTY-EIGHT HOURS* PUTTING HUMPTY DUMPTY BACK TOGETHER AGAIN--

HEY!

--BECAUSE HE'S SO DAMN *DUMB* HE FELL *FOUR HUNDRED KILO-METERS* AND DAMN NEAR *KILLED HIMSELF!*

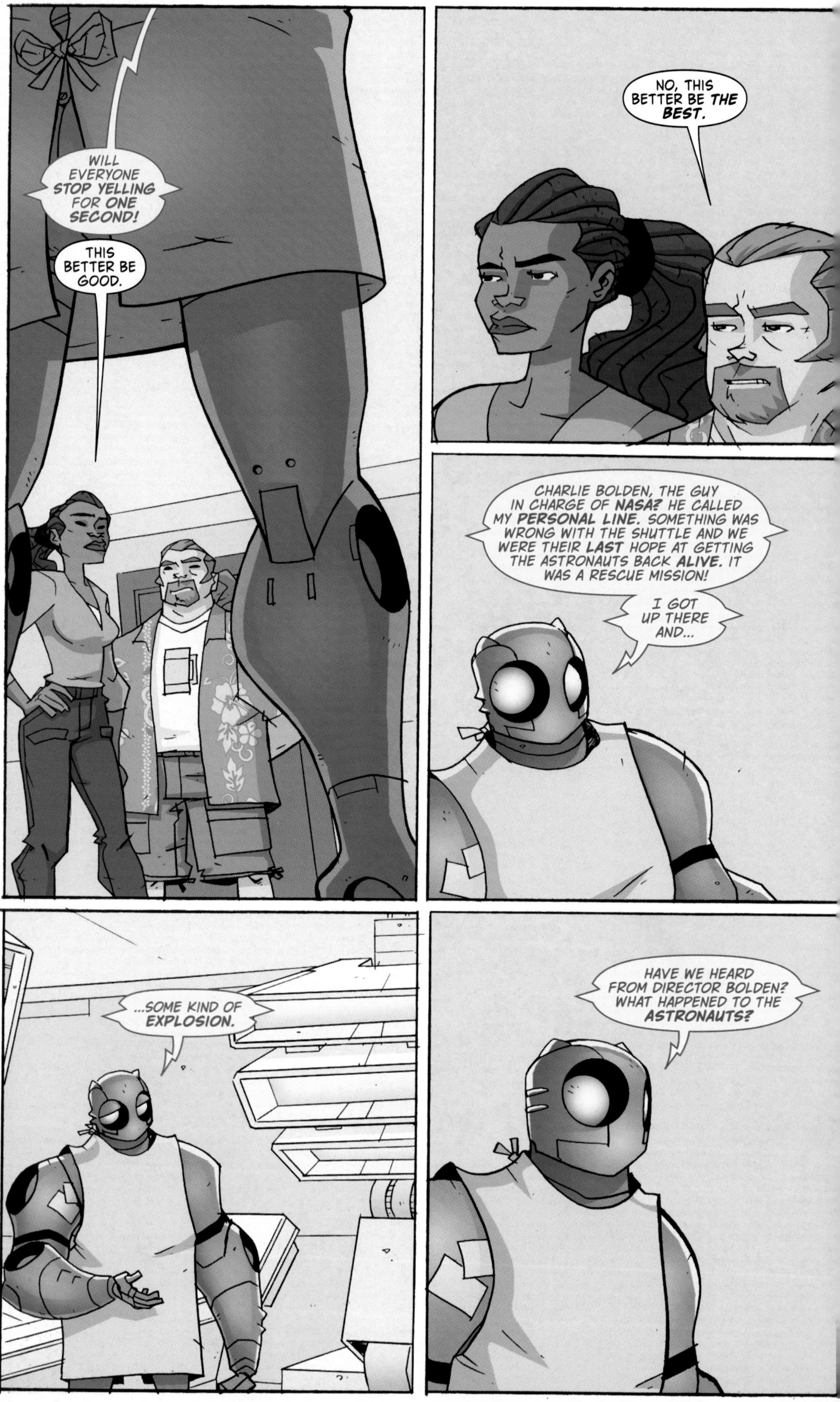
WILL EVERYONE STOP YELLING FOR ONE SECOND!
THIS BETTER BE GOOD.
NO, THIS BETTER BE THE BEST.
CHARLIE BOLDEN, THE GUY IN CHARGE OF NASA? HE CALLED MY PERSONAL LINE. SOMETHING WAS WRONG WITH THE SHUTTLE AND WE WERE THEIR LAST HOPE AT GETTING THE ASTRONAUTS BACK ALIVE. IT WAS A RESCUE MISSION!
I GOT UP THERE AND...
...SOME KIND OF EXPLOSION.
HAVE WE HEARD FROM DIRECTOR BOLDEN? WHAT HAPPENED TO THE ASTRONAUTS?

ROBO? I'VE GOT DIRECTOR BOLDEN ON THE LINE.

PATCH HIM THROUGH TO MY HEAD.

DIRECTOR BOLDEN!

ROBO, YOUR PEOPLE GOT IN TOUCH WITH ME MINUTES AFTER YOU LANDED. YOU HAD US WORRIED FOR A COUPLE OF DAYS.

IT WAS NOTHING.

NOTHING?! NOTHING?!

LET ME GET STRAIGHT TO IT.

ROBO, I DID NOT PLACE THAT CALL.

SPACE

IT'S OUT THERE

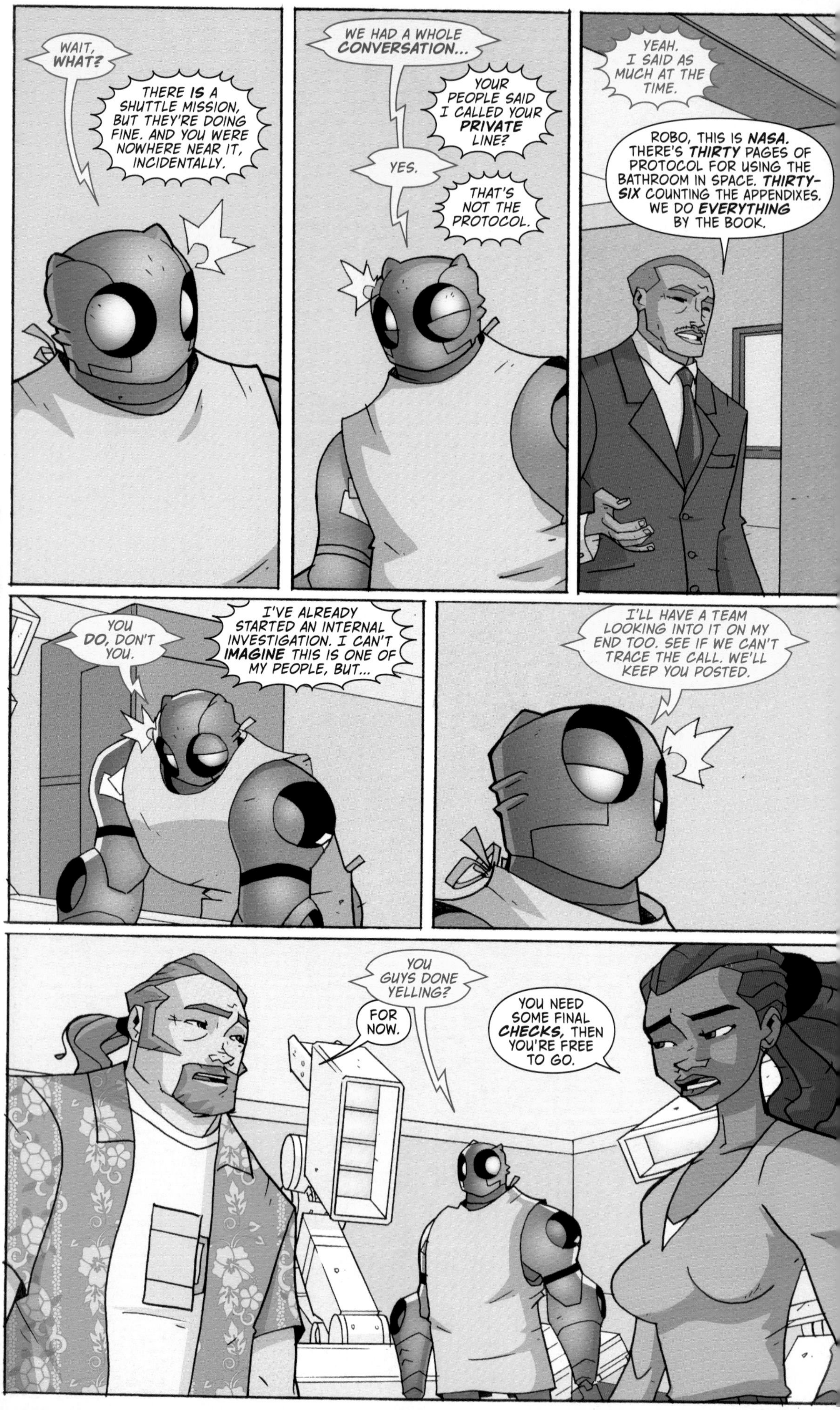
WAIT, WHAT?
THERE IS A SHUTTLE MISSION, BUT THEY'RE DOING FINE. AND YOU WERE NOWHERE NEAR IT, INCIDENTALLY.
WE HAD A WHOLE CONVERSATION...
YOUR PEOPLE SAID I CALLED YOUR PRIVATE LINE?
YES.
THAT'S NOT THE PROTOCOL.
YEAH. I SAID AS MUCH AT THE TIME.
ROBO, THIS IS NASA. THERE'S THIRTY PAGES OF PROTOCOL FOR USING THE BATHROOM IN SPACE. THIRTY-SIX COUNTING THE APPENDIXES. WE DO EVERYTHING BY THE BOOK.
YOU DO, DON'T YOU.
I'VE ALREADY STARTED AN INTERNAL INVESTIGATION. I CAN'T IMAGINE THIS IS ONE OF MY PEOPLE, BUT...
I'LL HAVE A TEAM LOOKING INTO IT ON MY END TOO. SEE IF WE CAN'T TRACE THE CALL. WE'LL KEEP YOU POSTED.
YOU GUYS DONE YELLING?
FOR NOW.
YOU NEED SOME FINAL CHECKS, THEN YOU'RE FREE TO GO.

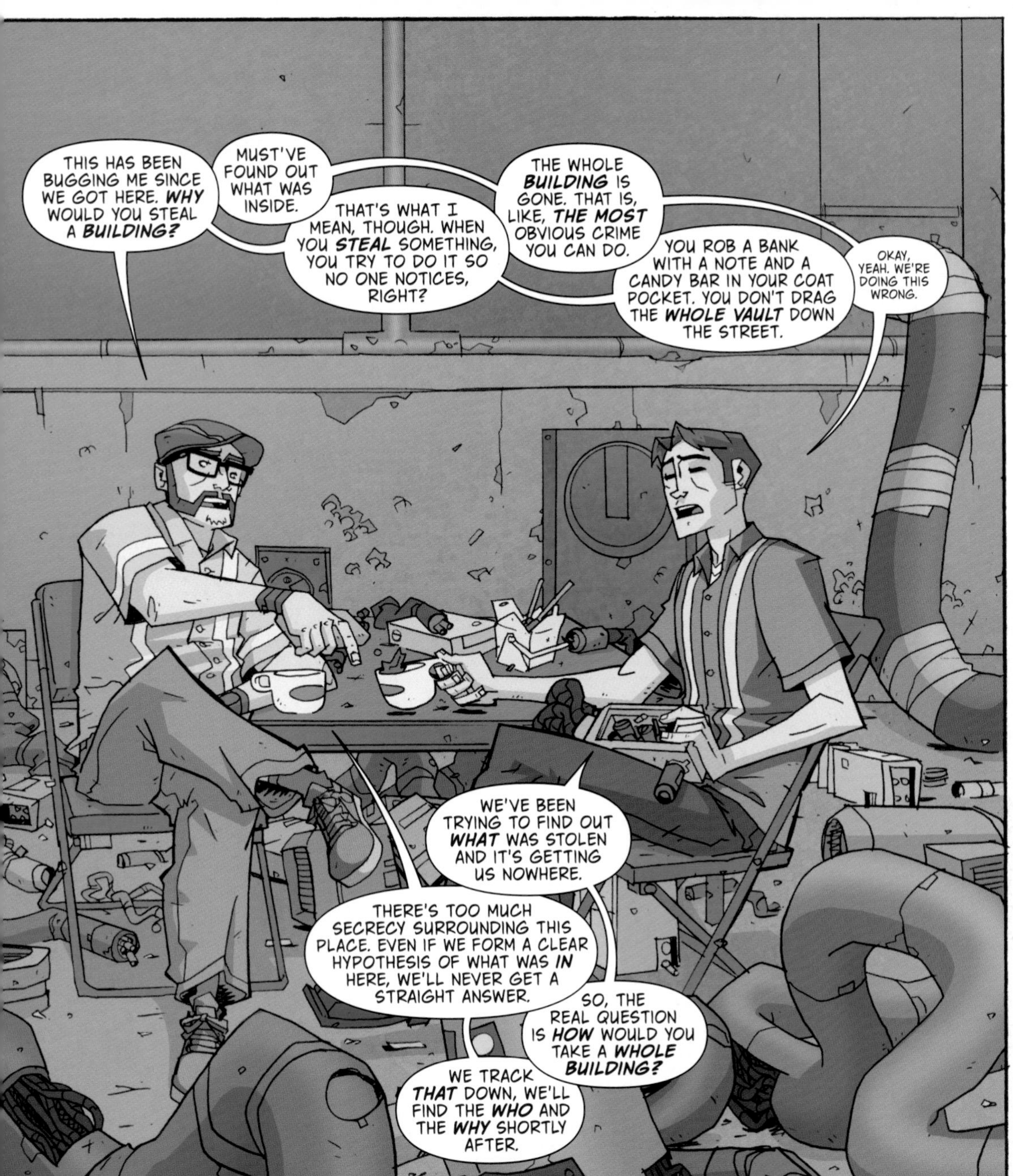
THIS HAS BEEN BUGGING ME SINCE WE GOT HERE. **WHY** WOULD YOU STEAL A **BUILDING?**
MUST'VE FOUND OUT WHAT WAS INSIDE.
THAT'S WHAT I MEAN, THOUGH. WHEN YOU **STEAL** SOMETHING, YOU TRY TO DO IT SO NO ONE NOTICES, RIGHT?
THE WHOLE **BUILDING** IS GONE. THAT IS, LIKE, **THE MOST** OBVIOUS CRIME YOU CAN DO.
YOU ROB A BANK WITH A NOTE AND A CANDY BAR IN YOUR COAT POCKET. YOU DON'T DRAG THE **WHOLE VAULT** DOWN THE STREET.
OKAY, YEAH. WE'RE DOING THIS WRONG.
WE'VE BEEN TRYING TO FIND OUT **WHAT** WAS STOLEN AND IT'S GETTING US NOWHERE.
THERE'S TOO MUCH SECRECY SURROUNDING THIS PLACE. EVEN IF WE FORM A CLEAR HYPOTHESIS OF WHAT WAS **IN** HERE, WE'LL NEVER GET A STRAIGHT ANSWER.
SO, THE REAL QUESTION IS **HOW** WOULD YOU TAKE A **WHOLE BUILDING?**
WE TRACK **THAT** DOWN, WE'LL FIND THE **WHO** AND THE **WHY** SHORTLY AFTER.

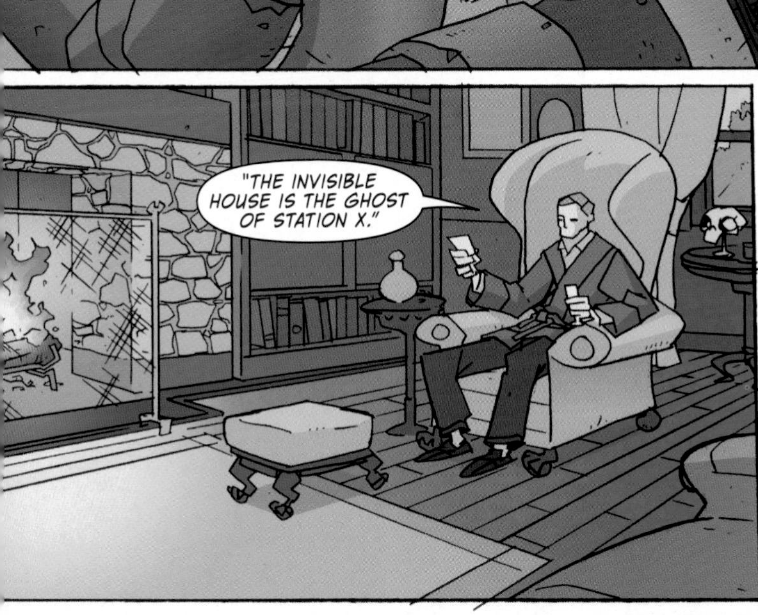
"THE INVISIBLE HOUSE IS THE GHOST OF STATION X."

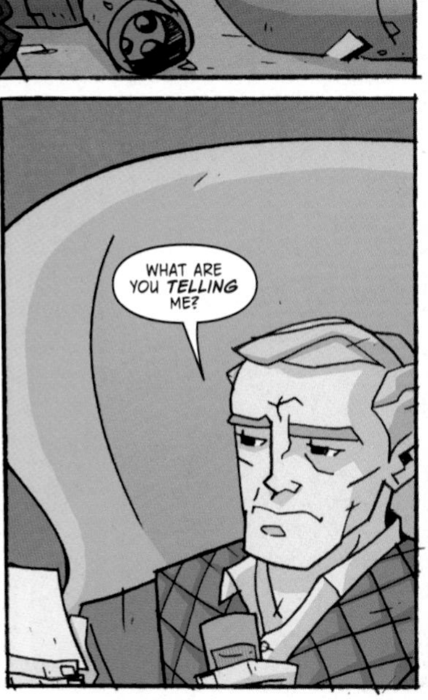
WHAT ARE YOU **TELLING** ME?

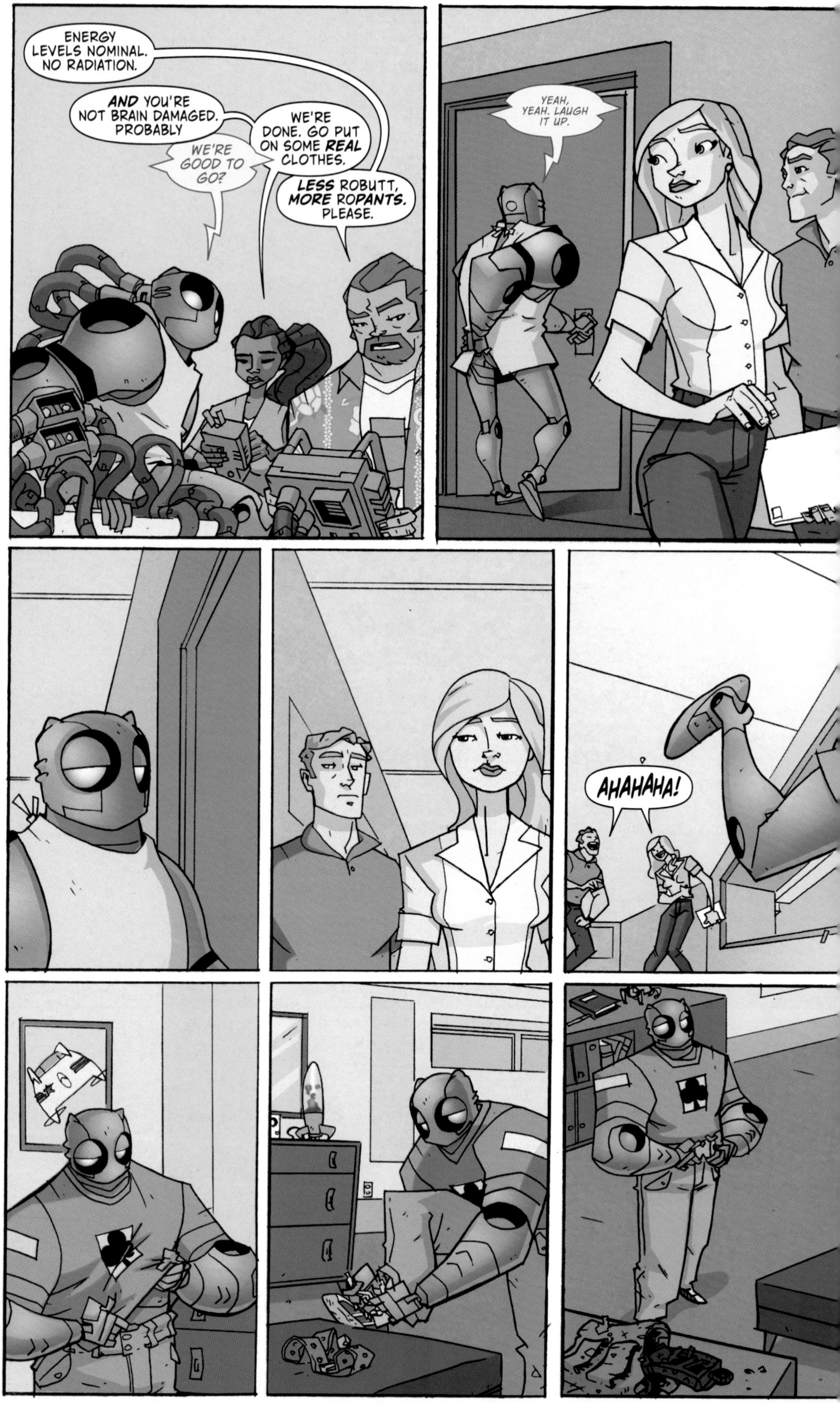
ENERGY LEVELS NOMINAL. NO RADIATION.
AND YOU'RE NOT BRAIN DAMAGED. PROBABLY
WE'RE GOOD TO GO?
WE'RE DONE. GO PUT ON SOME REAL CLOTHES.
LESS ROBUTT, MORE ROPANTS. PLEASE.
YEAH, YEAH. LAUGH IT UP.
AHAHAHA!

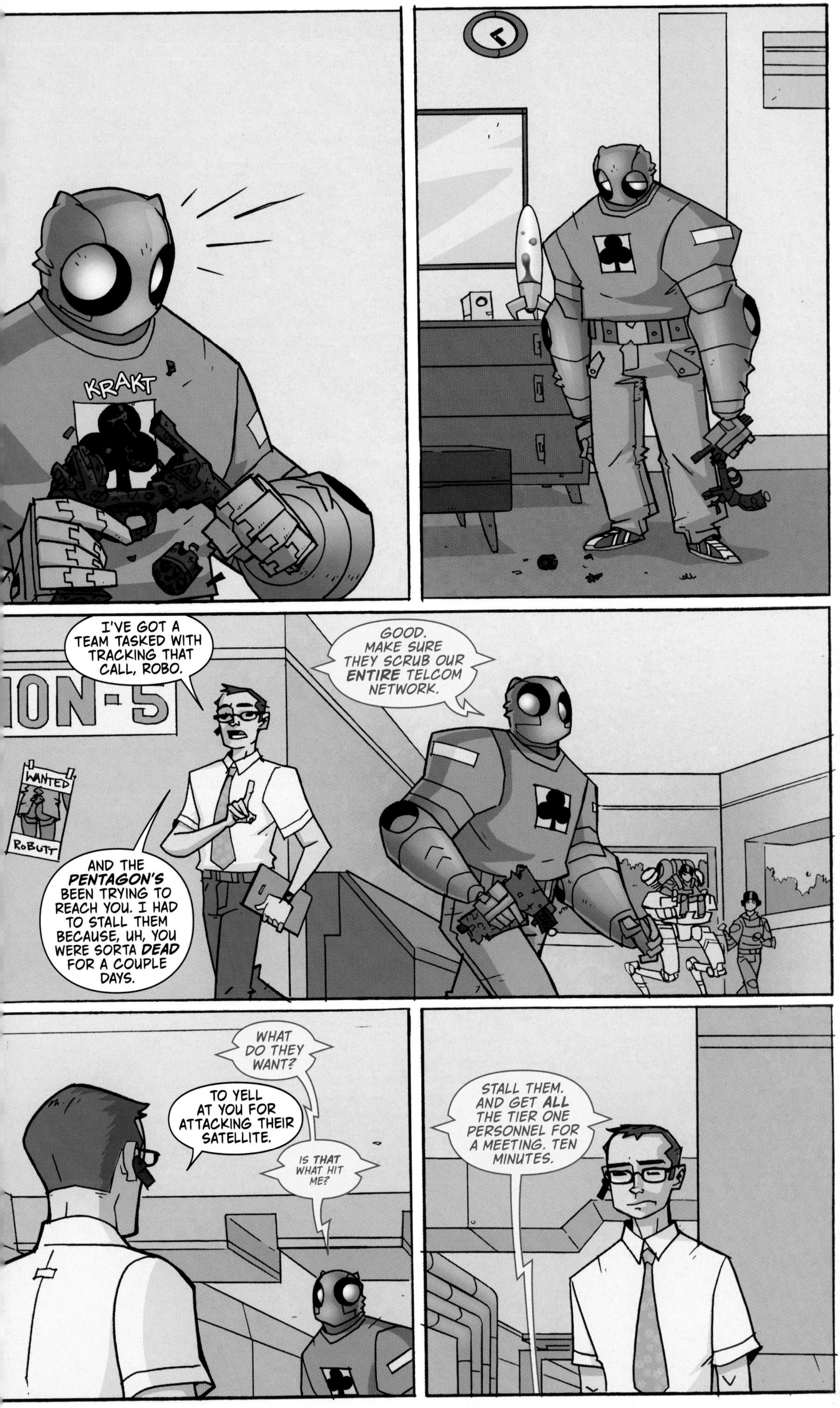

KRAKT
I'VE GOT A TEAM TASKED WITH TRACKING THAT CALL, ROBO.
GOOD. MAKE SURE THEY SCRUB OUR ENTIRE TELCOM NETWORK.
ION-5
WANTED
ROBUTT
AND THE PENTAGON'S BEEN TRYING TO REACH YOU. I HAD TO STALL THEM BECAUSE, UH, YOU WERE SORTA DEAD FOR A COUPLE DAYS.
WHAT DO THEY WANT?
TO YELL AT YOU FOR ATTACKING THEIR SATELLITE.
IS THAT WHAT HIT ME?
STALL THEM. AND GET ALL THE TIER ONE PERSONNEL FOR A MEETING. TEN MINUTES.

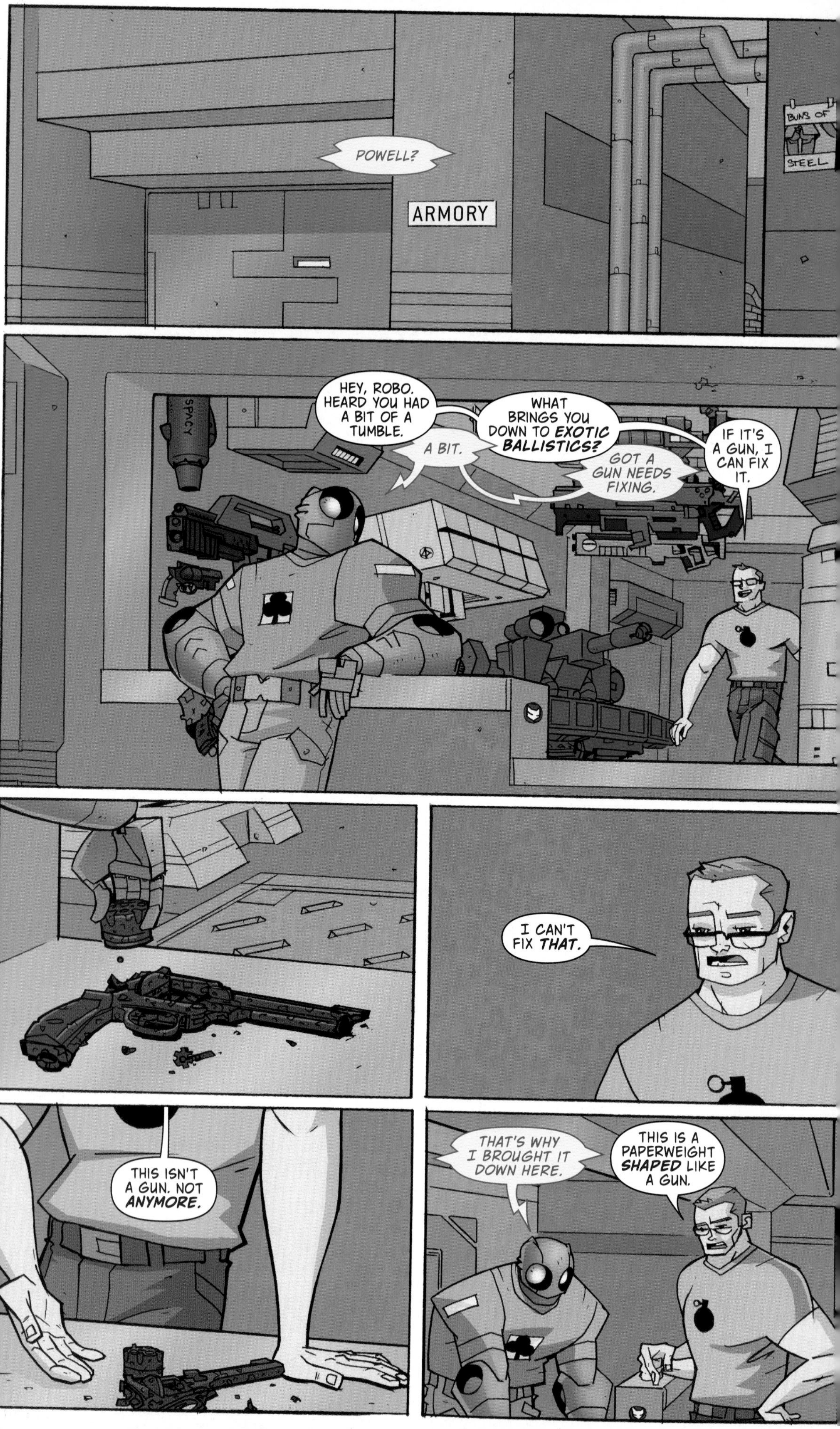
POWELL?
ARMORY
BUNS OF STEEL
SPACY
HEY, ROBO. HEARD YOU HAD A BIT OF A TUMBLE.
A BIT.
WHAT BRINGS YOU DOWN TO **EXOTIC BALLISTICS?**
GOT A GUN NEEDS FIXING.
IF IT'S A GUN, I CAN FIX IT.
I CAN'T FIX **THAT.**
THIS ISN'T A GUN. NOT **ANYMORE.**
THAT'S WHY I BROUGHT IT DOWN HERE.
THIS IS A PAPERWEIGHT **SHAPED** LIKE A GUN.

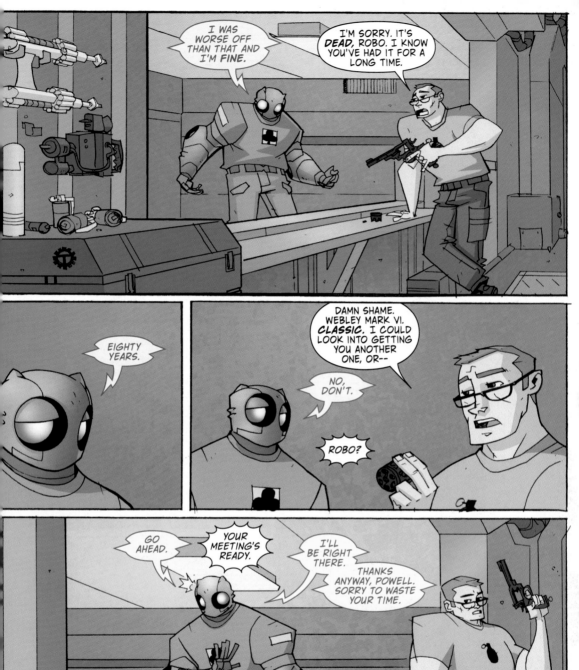

I WAS WORSE OFF THAN THAT AND I'M **FINE.**

I'M SORRY. IT'S **DEAD,** ROBO. I KNOW YOU'VE HAD IT FOR A LONG TIME.

EIGHTY YEARS.

DAMN SHAME. WEBLEY MARK VI. **CLASSIC.** I COULD LOOK INTO GETTING YOU ANOTHER ONE, OR--

NO, DON'T.

ROBO?

GO AHEAD.

YOUR MEETING'S READY.

I'LL BE RIGHT THERE. THANKS ANYWAY, POWELL. SORRY TO WASTE YOUR TIME.

HMM...

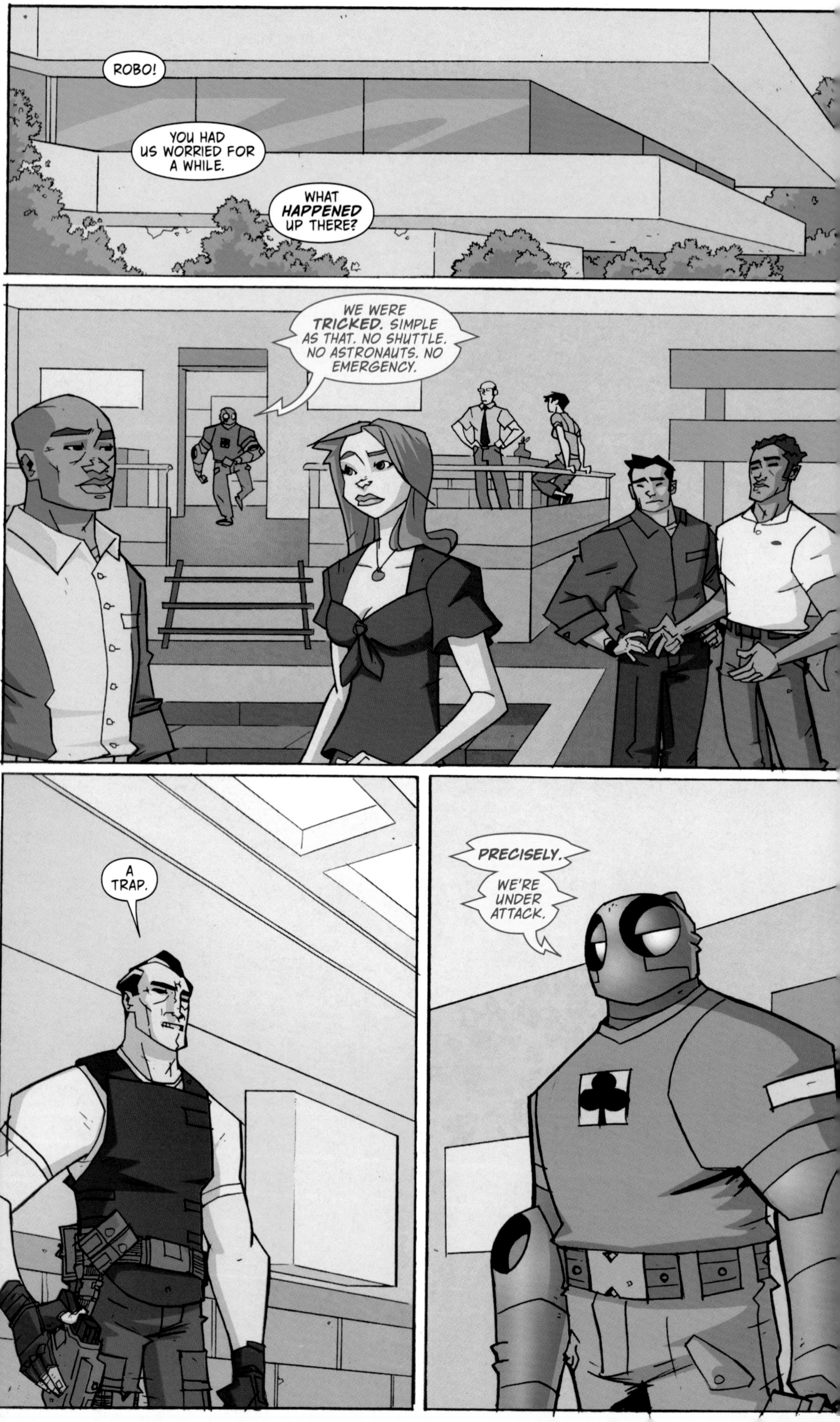
ROBO!
YOU HAD US WORRIED FOR A WHILE.
WHAT HAPPENED UP THERE?
WE WERE TRICKED. SIMPLE AS THAT. NO SHUTTLE. NO ASTRONAUTS. NO EMERGENCY.
A TRAP.
PRECISELY.
WE'RE UNDER ATTACK.

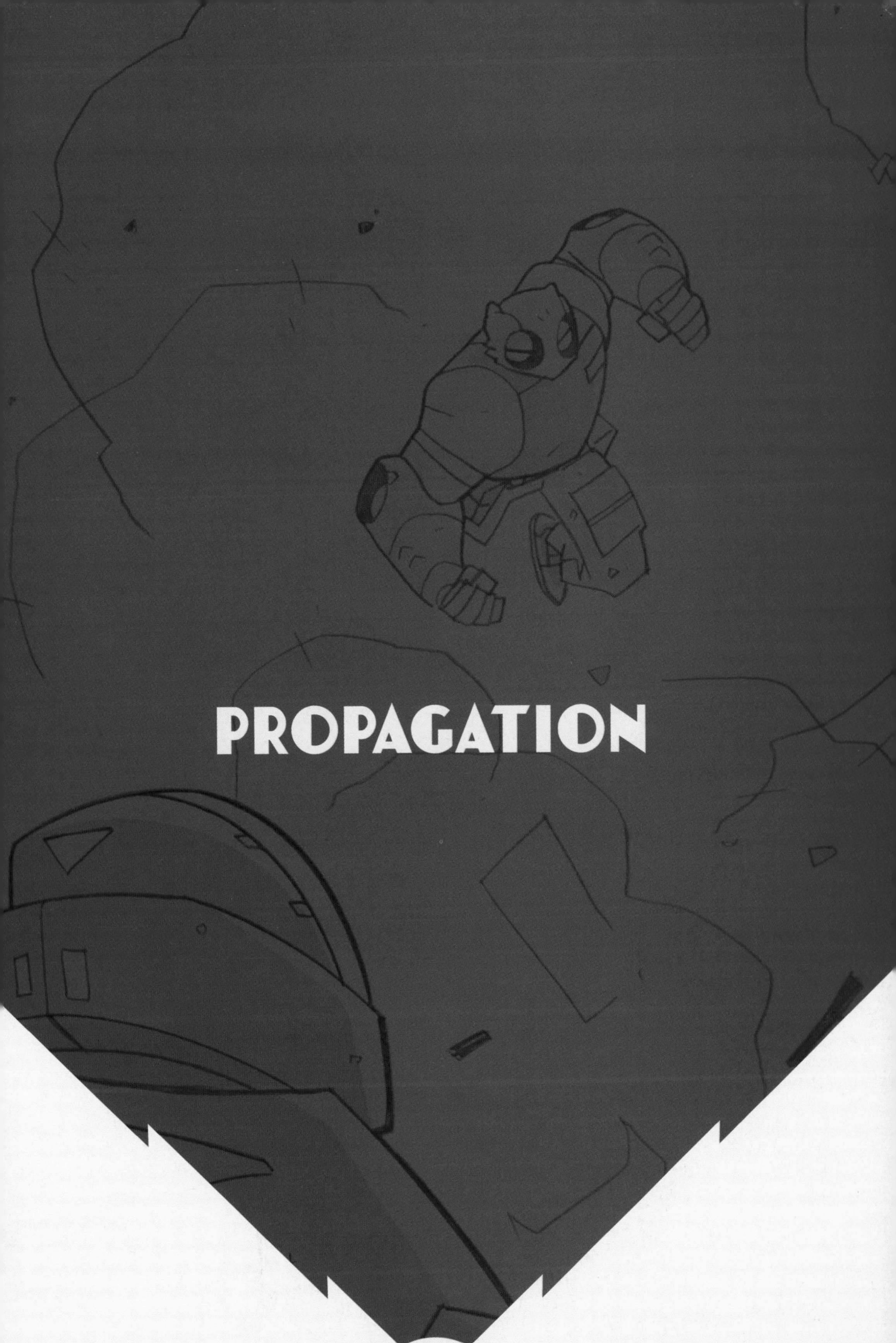

PROPAGATION

3

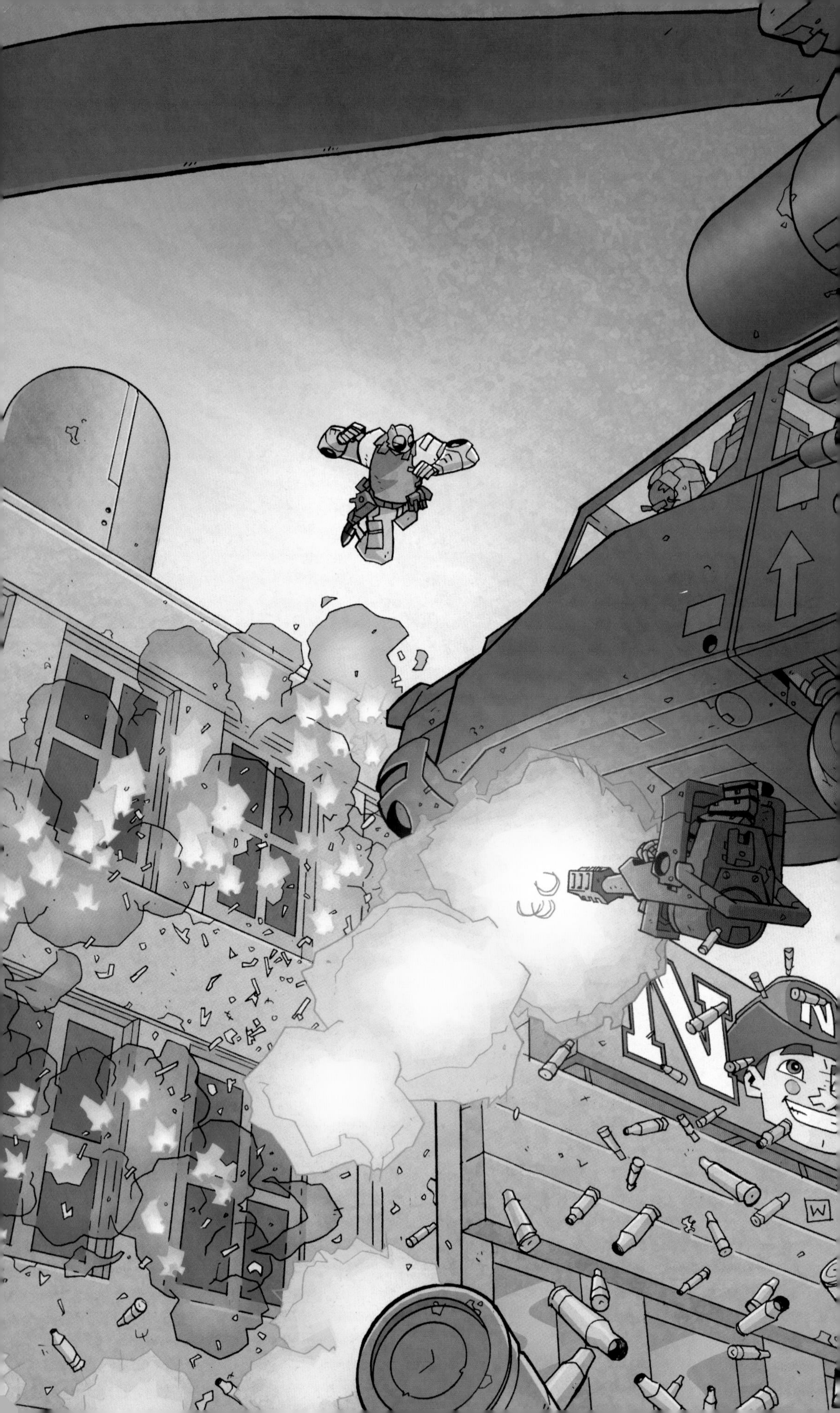

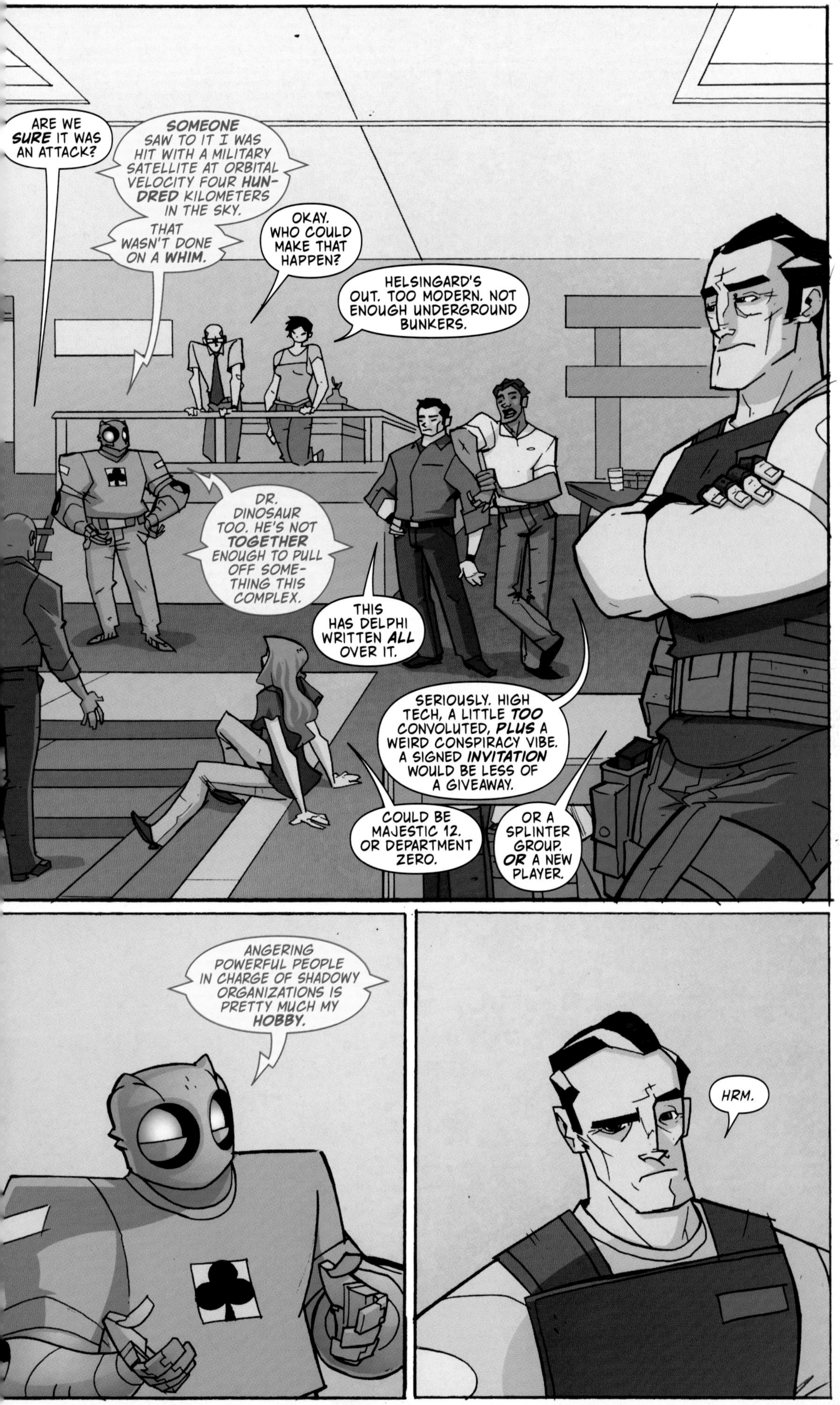
ARE WE SURE IT WAS AN ATTACK?
SOMEONE SAW TO IT I WAS HIT WITH A MILITARY SATELLITE AT ORBITAL VELOCITY FOUR HUNDRED KILOMETERS IN THE SKY.
THAT WASN'T DONE ON A WHIM.
OKAY. WHO COULD MAKE THAT HAPPEN?
HELSINGARD'S OUT. TOO MODERN. NOT ENOUGH UNDERGROUND BUNKERS.
DR. DINOSAUR TOO. HE'S NOT TOGETHER ENOUGH TO PULL OFF SOMETHING THIS COMPLEX.
THIS HAS DELPHI WRITTEN ALL OVER IT.
SERIOUSLY. HIGH TECH, A LITTLE TOO CONVOLUTED, PLUS A WEIRD CONSPIRACY VIBE. A SIGNED INVITATION WOULD BE LESS OF A GIVEAWAY.
COULD BE MAJESTIC 12. OR DEPARTMENT ZERO.
OR A SPLINTER GROUP. OR A NEW PLAYER.
ANGERING POWERFUL PEOPLE IN CHARGE OF SHADOWY ORGANIZATIONS IS PRETTY MUCH MY HOBBY.
HRM.

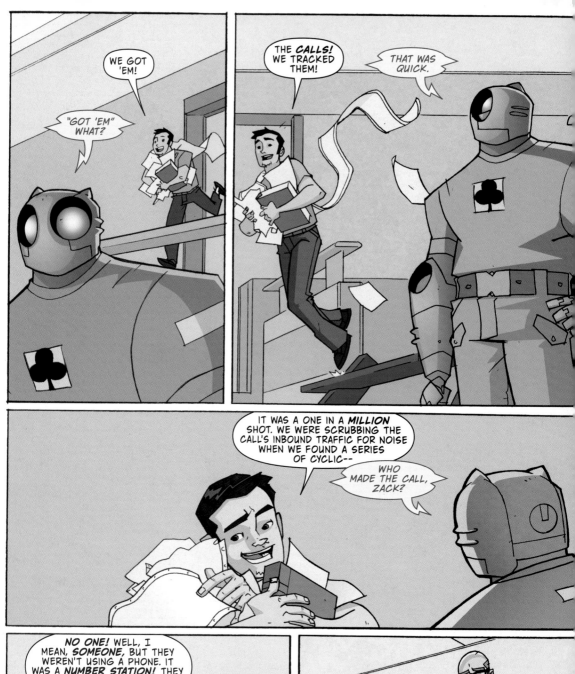

WE GOT 'EM!

"GOT 'EM" WHAT?

THE *CALLS!* WE TRACKED THEM!

THAT WAS QUICK.

IT WAS A ONE IN A *MILLION* SHOT. WE WERE SCRUBBING THE CALL'S INBOUND TRAFFIC FOR NOISE WHEN WE FOUND A SERIES OF CYCLIC--

WHO MADE THE CALL, ZACK?

NO ONE! WELL, I MEAN, *SOMEONE*, BUT THEY WEREN'T USING A PHONE. IT WAS A *NUMBER STATION!* THEY HIJACKED A TELCOM SIGNAL TO *ACT* LIKE A PHONE!

NUMBER STATION?

SECRET RADIO SIGNALS. THEY BROAD-CAST IN CODE. LOW POWER, SHORT RANGE, HARD TO FIND AND HARDER TO TRACE.

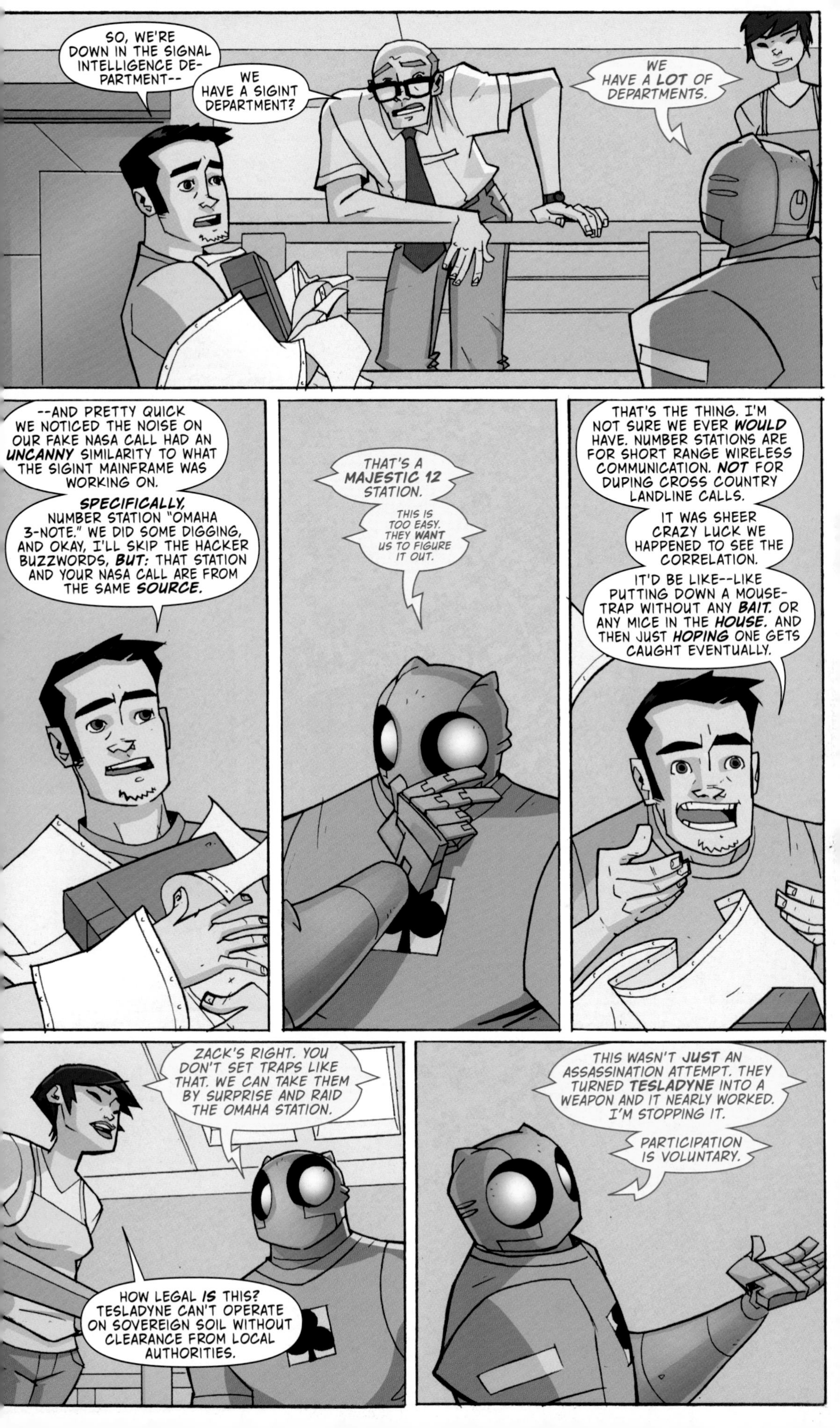
SO, WE'RE DOWN IN THE SIGNAL INTELLIGENCE DE-PARTMENT--
WE HAVE A SIGINT DEPARTMENT?
WE HAVE A LOT OF DEPARTMENTS.
--AND PRETTY QUICK WE NOTICED THE NOISE ON OUR FAKE NASA CALL HAD AN UNCANNY SIMILARITY TO WHAT THE SIGINT MAINFRAME WAS WORKING ON.
SPECIFICALLY, NUMBER STATION "OMAHA 3-NOTE." WE DID SOME DIGGING, AND OKAY, I'LL SKIP THE HACKER BUZZWORDS, BUT: THAT STATION AND YOUR NASA CALL ARE FROM THE SAME SOURCE.
THAT'S A MAJESTIC 12 STATION.
THIS IS TOO EASY. THEY WANT US TO FIGURE IT OUT.
THAT'S THE THING. I'M NOT SURE WE EVER WOULD HAVE. NUMBER STATIONS ARE FOR SHORT RANGE WIRELESS COMMUNICATION. NOT FOR DUPING CROSS COUNTRY LANDLINE CALLS.
IT WAS SHEER CRAZY LUCK WE HAPPENED TO SEE THE CORRELATION.
IT'D BE LIKE--LIKE PUTTING DOWN A MOUSE-TRAP WITHOUT ANY BAIT. OR ANY MICE IN THE HOUSE. AND THEN JUST HOPING ONE GETS CAUGHT EVENTUALLY.
ZACK'S RIGHT. YOU DON'T SET TRAPS LIKE THAT. WE CAN TAKE THEM BY SURPRISE AND RAID THE OMAHA STATION.
HOW LEGAL IS THIS? TESLADYNE CAN'T OPERATE ON SOVEREIGN SOIL WITHOUT CLEARANCE FROM LOCAL AUTHORITIES.
THIS WASN'T JUST AN ASSASSINATION ATTEMPT. THEY TURNED TESLADYNE INTO A WEAPON AND IT NEARLY WORKED. I'M STOPPING IT.
PARTICIPATION IS VOLUNTARY.

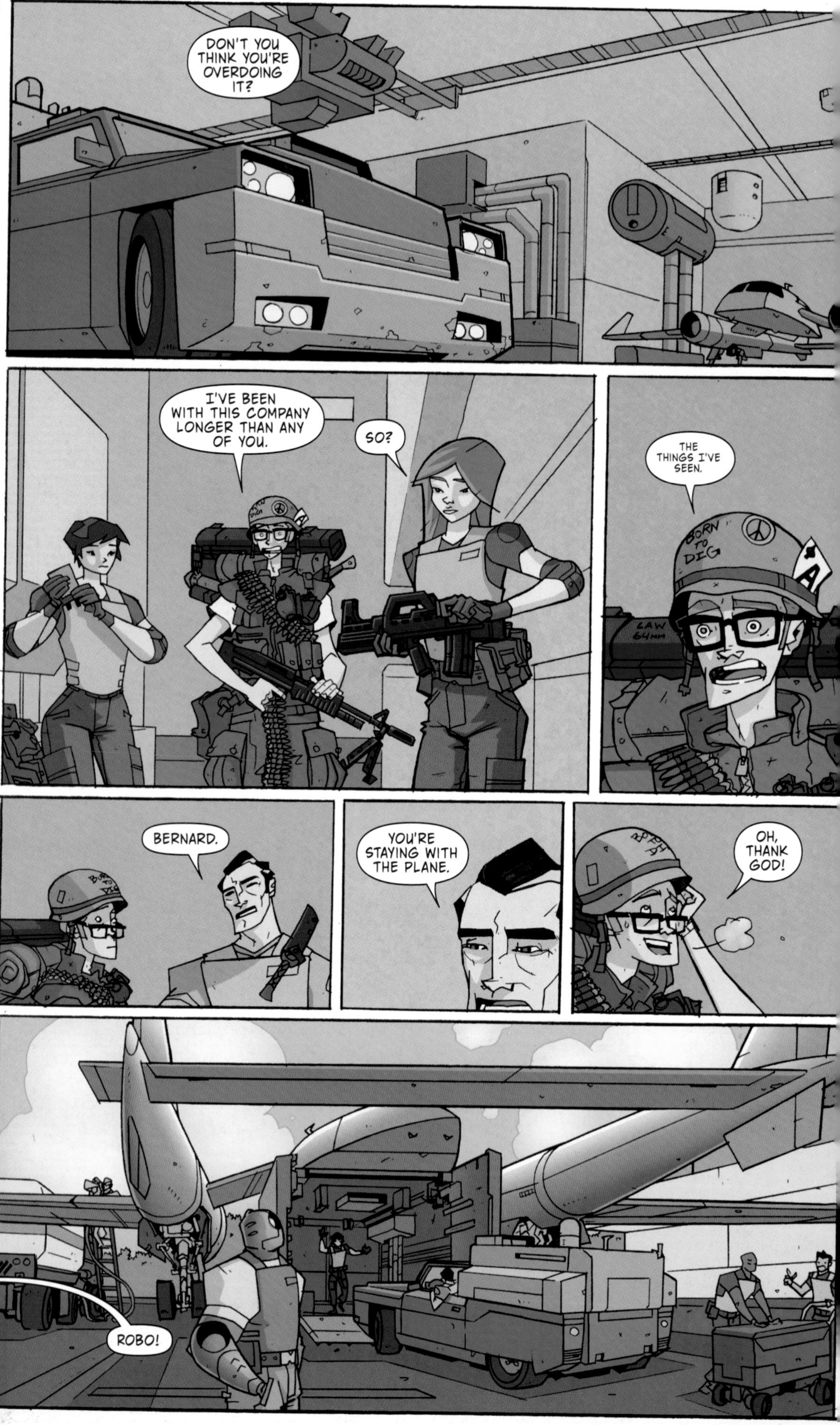
DON'T YOU THINK YOU'RE OVERDOING IT?
I'VE BEEN WITH THIS COMPANY LONGER THAN ANY OF YOU.
SO?
THE THINGS I'VE SEEN.
BORN TO DIG
LAW 64MM
BERNARD.
YOU'RE STAYING WITH THE PLANE.
OH, THANK GOD!
ROBO!

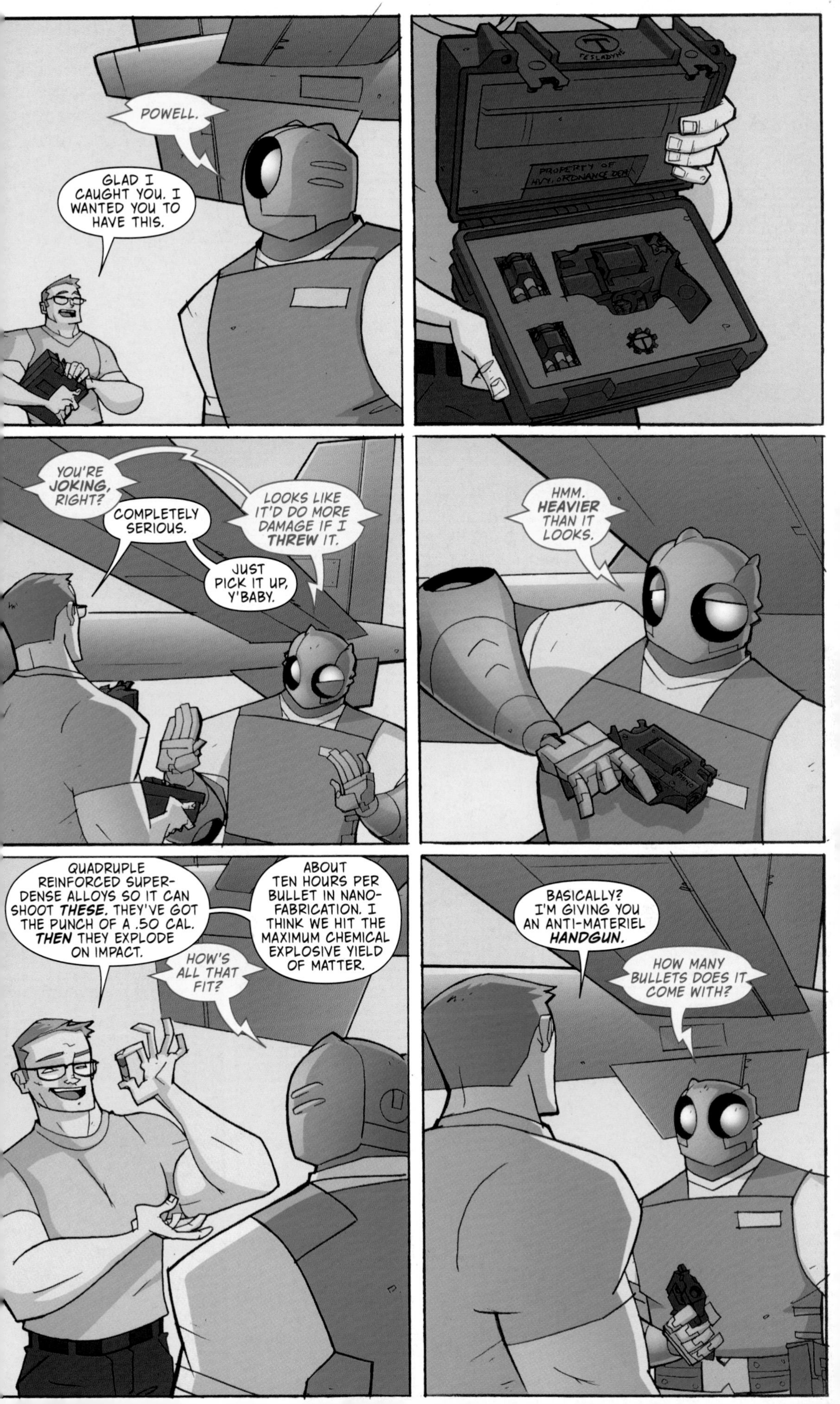
POWELL.
GLAD I CAUGHT YOU. I WANTED YOU TO HAVE THIS.
TESLADYNE
PROPERTY OF HVY. ORDNANCE DEPT.
YOU'RE **JOKING,** RIGHT?
COMPLETELY SERIOUS.
LOOKS LIKE IT'D DO MORE DAMAGE IF I **THREW** IT.
JUST PICK IT UP, Y'BABY.
HMM. **HEAVIER** THAN IT LOOKS.
QUADRUPLE REINFORCED SUPER-DENSE ALLOYS SO IT CAN SHOOT **THESE.** THEY'VE GOT THE PUNCH OF A .50 CAL. **THEN** THEY EXPLODE ON IMPACT.
HOW'S ALL THAT FIT?
ABOUT TEN HOURS PER BULLET IN NANO-FABRICATION. I THINK WE HIT THE MAXIMUM CHEMICAL EXPLOSIVE YIELD OF MATTER.
BASICALLY? I'M GIVING YOU AN ANTI-MATERIEL **HANDGUN.**
HOW MANY BULLETS DOES IT COME WITH?

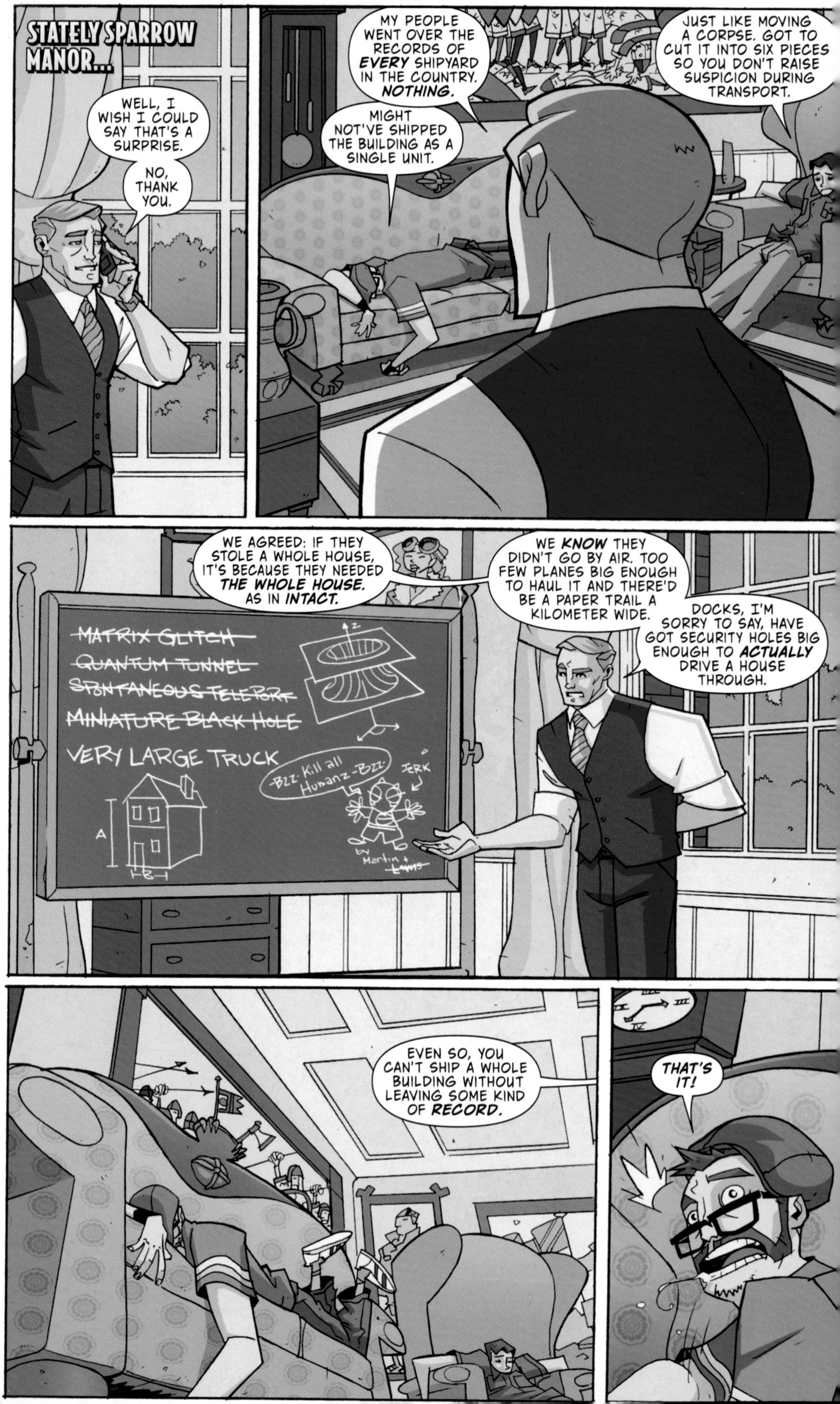
STATELY SPARROW MANOR...
WELL, I WISH I COULD SAY THAT'S A SURPRISE.
NO, THANK YOU.
MY PEOPLE WENT OVER THE RECORDS OF EVERY SHIPYARD IN THE COUNTRY. NOTHING.
MIGHT NOT'VE SHIPPED THE BUILDING AS A SINGLE UNIT.
JUST LIKE MOVING A CORPSE. GOT TO CUT IT INTO SIX PIECES SO YOU DON'T RAISE SUSPICION DURING TRANSPORT.
WE AGREED: IF THEY STOLE A WHOLE HOUSE, IT'S BECAUSE THEY NEEDED THE WHOLE HOUSE. AS IN INTACT.
WE KNOW THEY DIDN'T GO BY AIR. TOO FEW PLANES BIG ENOUGH TO HAUL IT AND THERE'D BE A PAPER TRAIL A KILOMETER WIDE.
DOCKS, I'M SORRY TO SAY, HAVE GOT SECURITY HOLES BIG ENOUGH TO ACTUALLY DRIVE A HOUSE THROUGH.
MATRIX GLITCH
QUANTUM TUNNEL
SPONTANEOUS TELEPORT
MINIATURE BLACK HOLE
VERY LARGE TRUCK
-BZZ- KILL ALL HUMANZ -BZZ-
JERK
by Martin + Lewis
EVEN SO, YOU CAN'T SHIP A WHOLE BUILDING WITHOUT LEAVING SOME KIND OF RECORD.
THAT'S IT!

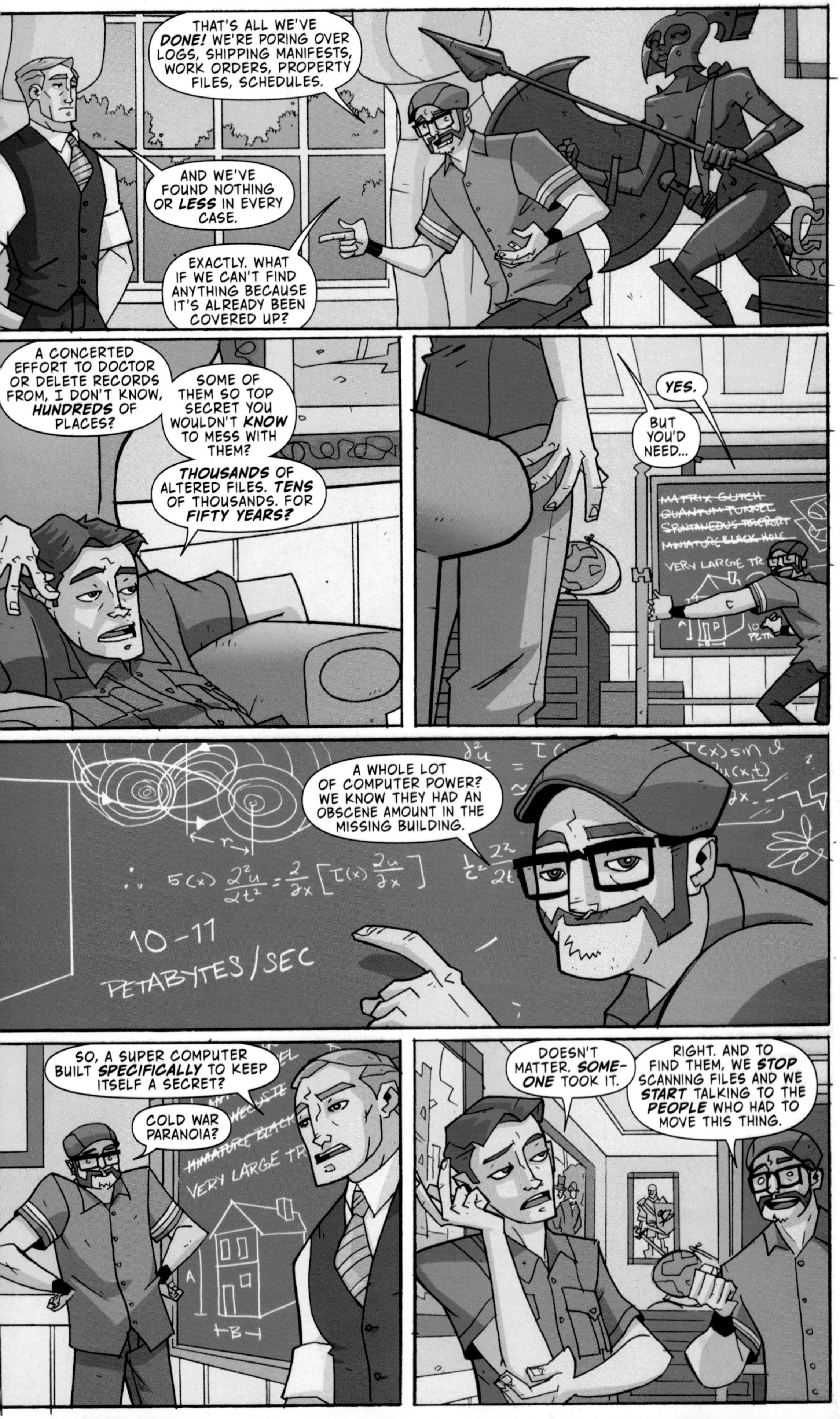

THAT'S ALL WE'VE DONE! WE'RE PORING OVER LOGS, SHIPPING MANIFESTS, WORK ORDERS, PROPERTY FILES, SCHEDULES.
AND WE'VE FOUND NOTHING OR LESS IN EVERY CASE.
EXACTLY. WHAT IF WE CAN'T FIND ANYTHING BECAUSE IT'S ALREADY BEEN COVERED UP?
A CONCERTED EFFORT TO DOCTOR OR DELETE RECORDS FROM, I DON'T KNOW, HUNDREDS OF PLACES?
SOME OF THEM SO TOP SECRET YOU WOULDN'T KNOW TO MESS WITH THEM?
THOUSANDS OF ALTERED FILES. TENS OF THOUSANDS. FOR FIFTY YEARS?
YES.
BUT YOU'D NEED...
VERY LARGE TR
A WHOLE LOT OF COMPUTER POWER? WE KNOW THEY HAD AN OBSCENE AMOUNT IN THE MISSING BUILDING.
10-11
PETABYTES/SEC
SO, A SUPER COMPUTER BUILT SPECIFICALLY TO KEEP ITSELF A SECRET?
COLD WAR PARANOIA?
VERY LARGE TR
DOESN'T MATTER. SOME-ONE TOOK IT.
RIGHT. AND TO FIND THEM, WE STOP SCANNING FILES AND WE START TALKING TO THE PEOPLE WHO HAD TO MOVE THIS THING.

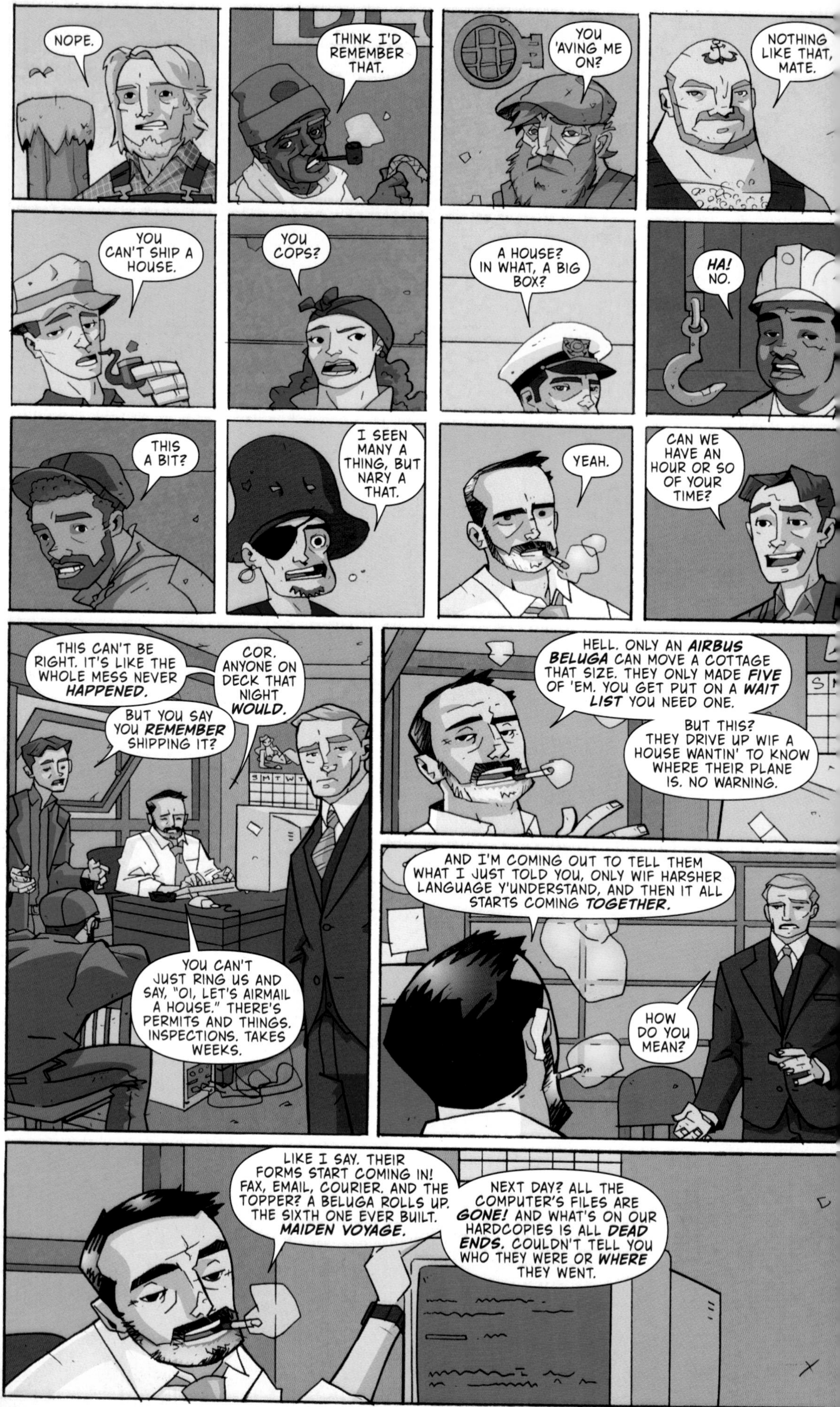
NOPE.
THINK I'D REMEMBER THAT.
YOU 'AVING ME ON?
NOTHING LIKE THAT, MATE.
YOU CAN'T SHIP A HOUSE.
YOU COPS?
A HOUSE? IN WHAT, A BIG BOX?
HA! NO.
THIS A BIT?
I SEEN MANY A THING, BUT NARY A THAT.
YEAH.
CAN WE HAVE AN HOUR OR SO OF YOUR TIME?
THIS CAN'T BE RIGHT. IT'S LIKE THE WHOLE MESS NEVER HAPPENED.
COR. ANYONE ON DECK THAT NIGHT WOULD.
BUT YOU SAY YOU REMEMBER SHIPPING IT?
YOU CAN'T JUST RING US AND SAY, "OI, LET'S AIRMAIL A HOUSE." THERE'S PERMITS AND THINGS. INSPECTIONS. TAKES WEEKS.
HELL. ONLY AN AIRBUS BELUGA CAN MOVE A COTTAGE THAT SIZE. THEY ONLY MADE FIVE OF 'EM. YOU GET PUT ON A WAIT LIST YOU NEED ONE.
BUT THIS? THEY DRIVE UP WIF A HOUSE WANTIN' TO KNOW WHERE THEIR PLANE IS. NO WARNING.
AND I'M COMING OUT TO TELL THEM WHAT I JUST TOLD YOU, ONLY WIF HARSHER LANGUAGE Y'UNDERSTAND, AND THEN IT ALL STARTS COMING TOGETHER.
HOW DO YOU MEAN?
LIKE I SAY. THEIR FORMS START COMING IN! FAX, EMAIL, COURIER. AND THE TOPPER? A BELUGA ROLLS UP. THE SIXTH ONE EVER BUILT. MAIDEN VOYAGE.
NEXT DAY? ALL THE COMPUTER'S FILES ARE GONE! AND WHAT'S ON OUR HARDCOPIES IS ALL DEAD ENDS. COULDN'T TELL YOU WHO THEY WERE OR WHERE THEY WENT.

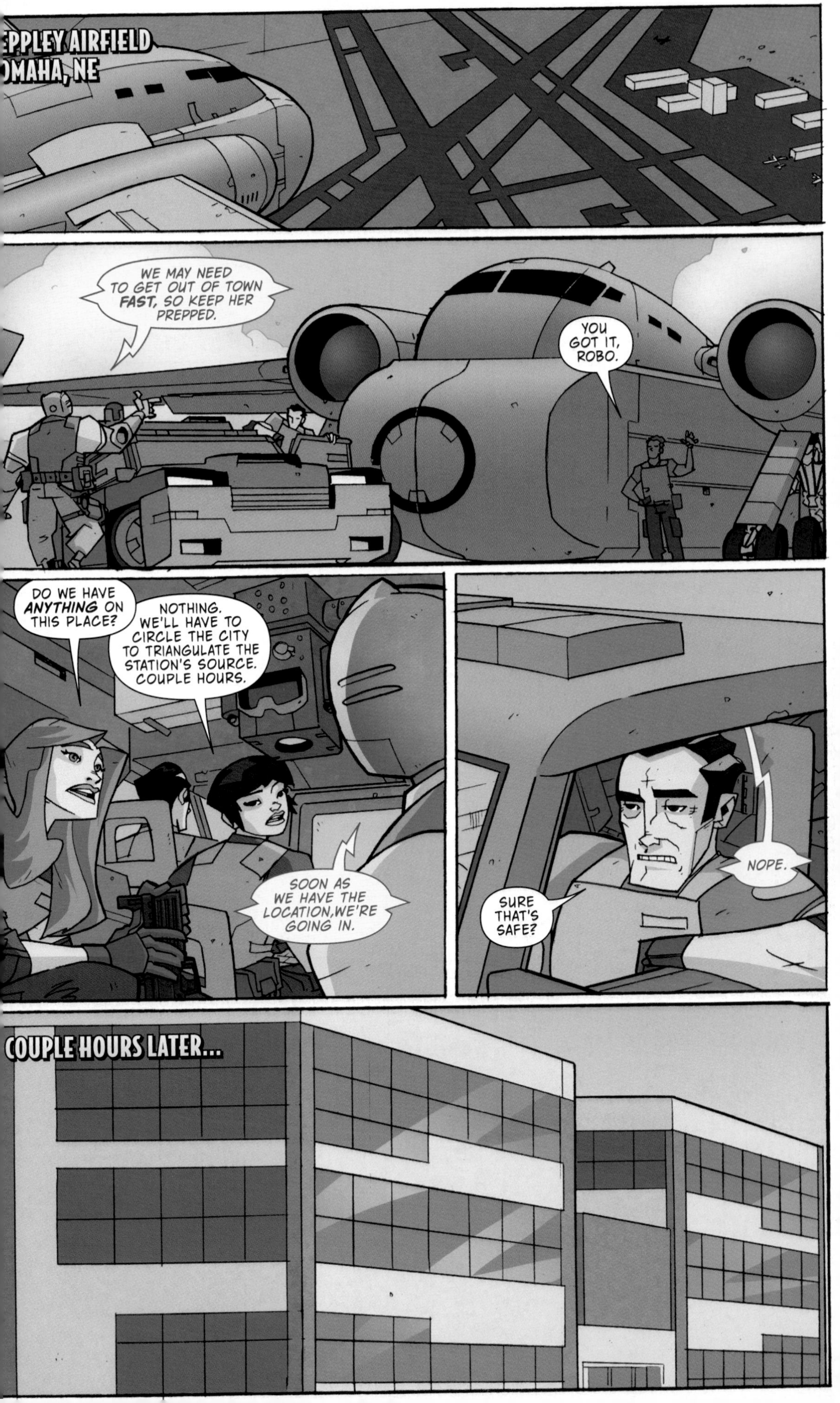
EPPLEY AIRFIELD OMAHA, NE
WE MAY NEED TO GET OUT OF TOWN FAST, SO KEEP HER PREPPED.
YOU GOT IT, ROBO.
DO WE HAVE ANYTHING ON THIS PLACE?
NOTHING. WE'LL HAVE TO CIRCLE THE CITY TO TRIANGULATE THE STATION'S SOURCE. COUPLE HOURS.
SOON AS WE HAVE THE LOCATION,WE'RE GOING IN.
SURE THAT'S SAFE?
NOPE.
COUPLE HOURS LATER...

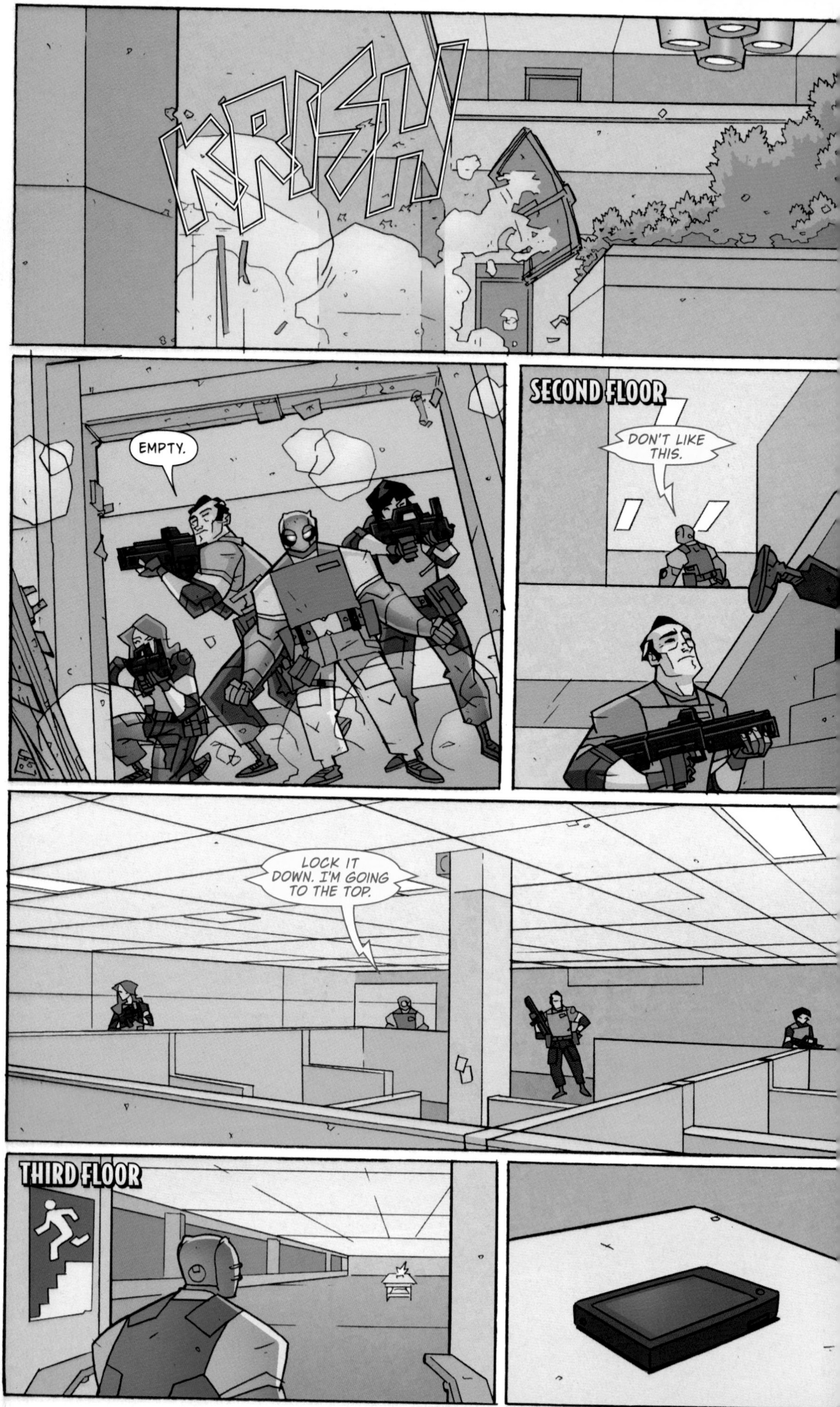
KRISH
EMPTY.
SECOND FLOOR
DON'T LIKE THIS.
LOCK IT DOWN. I'M GOING TO THE TOP.
THIRD FLOOR

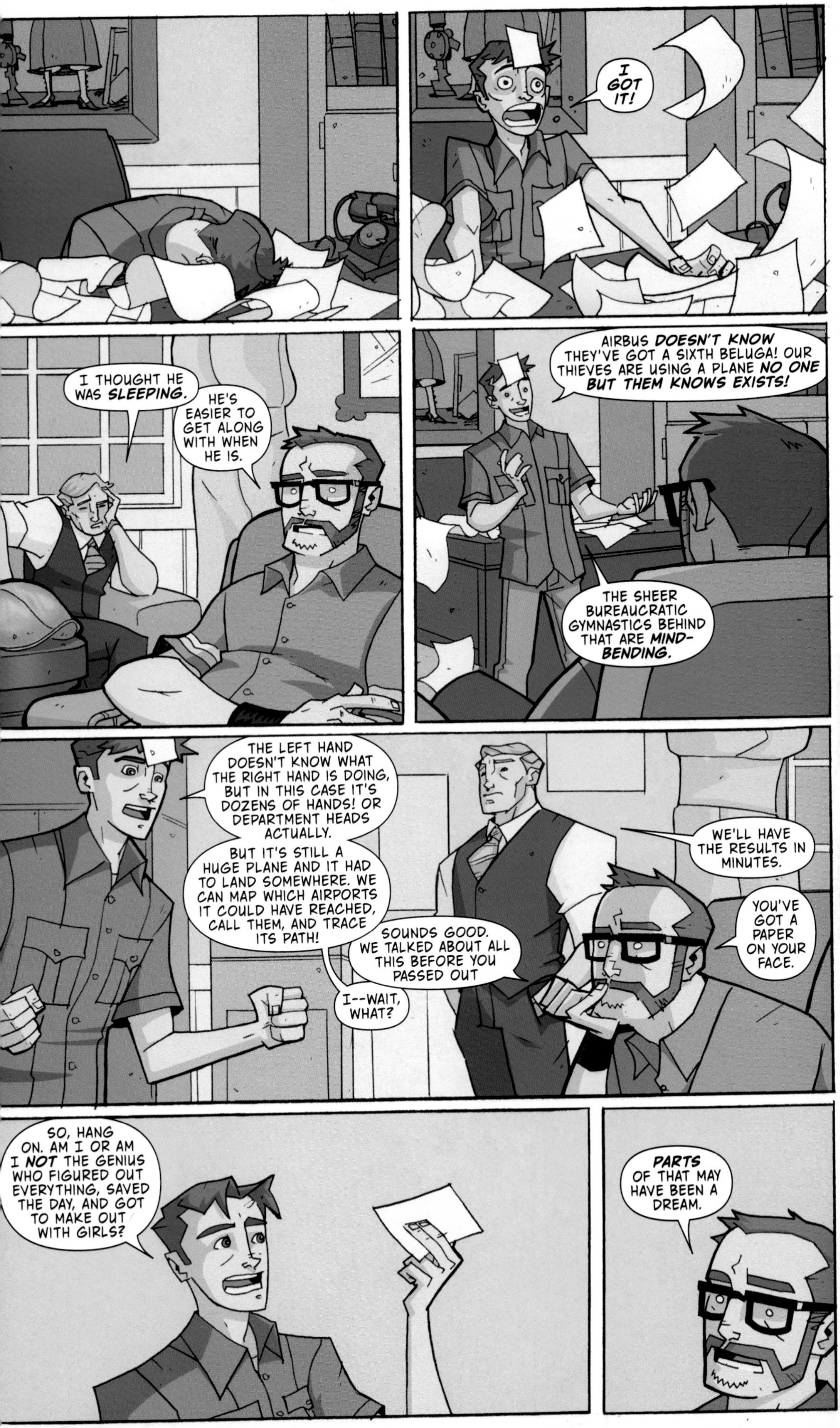
I GOT IT!
I THOUGHT HE WAS SLEEPING.
HE'S EASIER TO GET ALONG WITH WHEN HE IS.
AIRBUS DOESN'T KNOW THEY'VE GOT A SIXTH BELUGA! OUR THIEVES ARE USING A PLANE NO ONE BUT THEM KNOWS EXISTS!
THE SHEER BUREAUCRATIC GYMNASTICS BEHIND THAT ARE MIND-BENDING.
THE LEFT HAND DOESN'T KNOW WHAT THE RIGHT HAND IS DOING, BUT IN THIS CASE IT'S DOZENS OF HANDS! OR DEPARTMENT HEADS ACTUALLY.
BUT IT'S STILL A HUGE PLANE AND IT HAD TO LAND SOMEWHERE. WE CAN MAP WHICH AIRPORTS IT COULD HAVE REACHED, CALL THEM, AND TRACE ITS PATH!
SOUNDS GOOD. WE TALKED ABOUT ALL THIS BEFORE YOU PASSED OUT
I--WAIT, WHAT?
WE'LL HAVE THE RESULTS IN MINUTES.
YOU'VE GOT A PAPER ON YOUR FACE.
SO, HANG ON. AM I OR AM I NOT THE GENIUS WHO FIGURED OUT EVERYTHING, SAVED THE DAY, AND GOT TO MAKE OUT WITH GIRLS?
PARTS OF THAT MAY HAVE BEEN A DREAM.

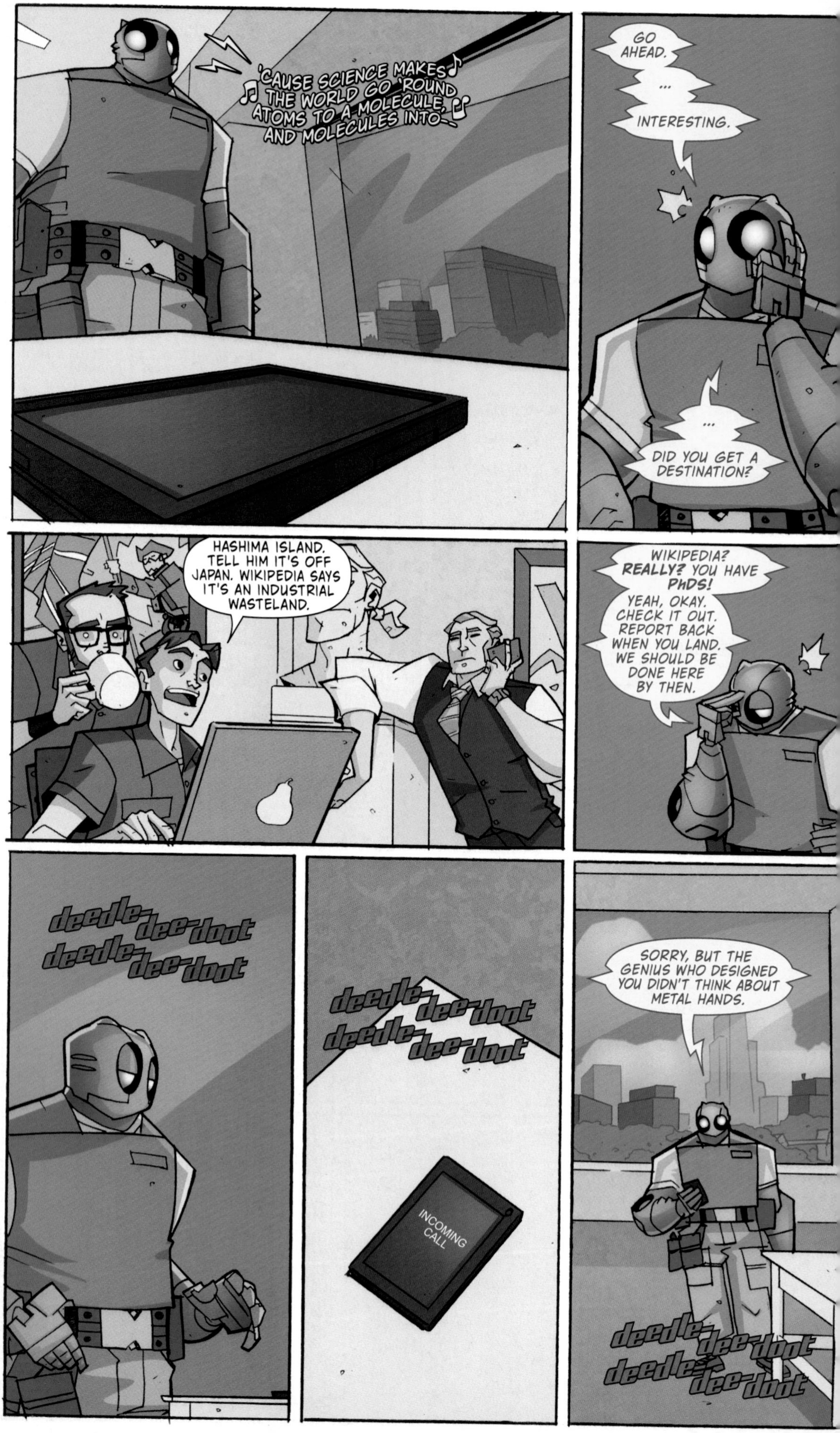
'CAUSE SCIENCE MAKES THE WORLD GO 'ROUND ATOMS TO A MOLECULE, AND MOLECULES INTO--
GO AHEAD.
...
INTERESTING.
...
DID YOU GET A DESTINATION?
HASHIMA ISLAND. TELL HIM IT'S OFF JAPAN. WIKIPEDIA SAYS IT'S AN INDUSTRIAL WASTELAND.
WIKIPEDIA? **REALLY?** YOU HAVE **PhDS!**
YEAH, OKAY. CHECK IT OUT. REPORT BACK WHEN YOU LAND. WE SHOULD BE DONE HERE BY THEN.
deedle-dee-doot deedle-dee-doot
deedle-dee-doot deedle-dee-doot
INCOMING CALL
SORRY, BUT THE GENIUS WHO DESIGNED YOU DIDN'T THINK ABOUT METAL HANDS.
deedle-dee-doot deedle-dee-doot

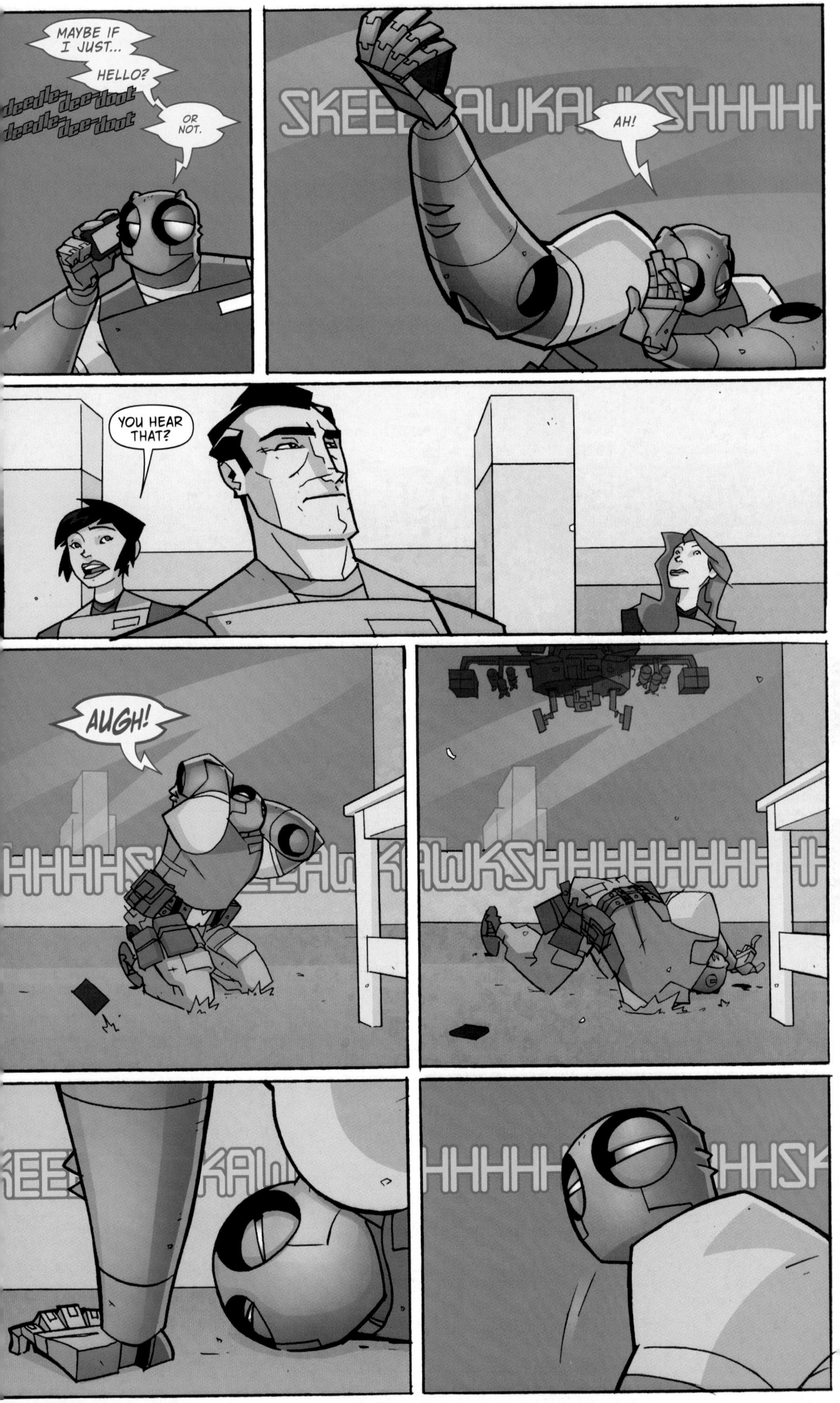

MAYBE IF I JUST...
HELLO?
deedle-dee-doot
deedle-dee-doot
OR NOT.
AH!
YOU HEAR THAT?
AUGH!

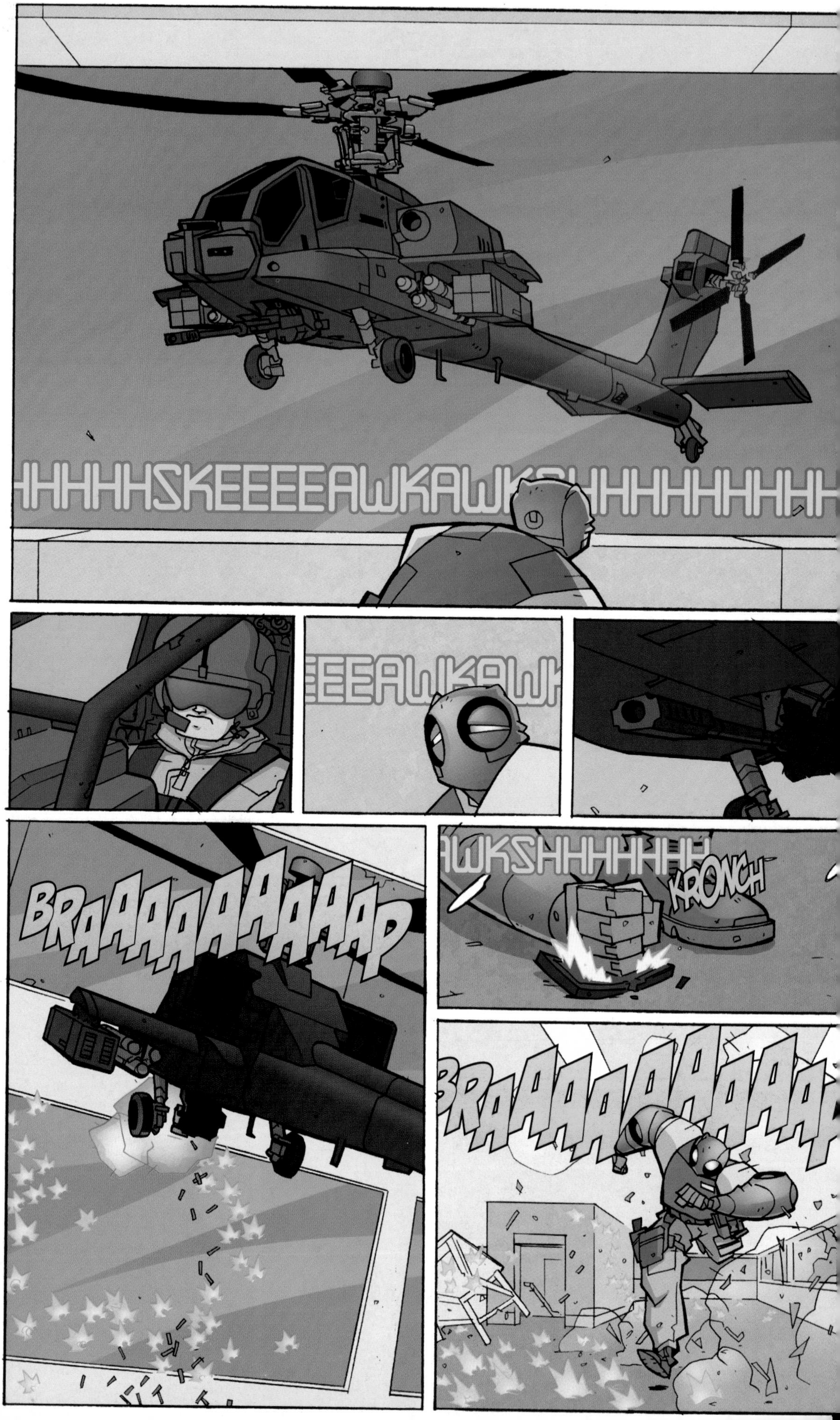
HHHHHSKEEEEAWKAWK
HHHHHHHHHH
EEEAWKAWK
BRAAAAAAAAAAP
AWKSHHHHHH
KRONCH
BRAAAAAAAAAA

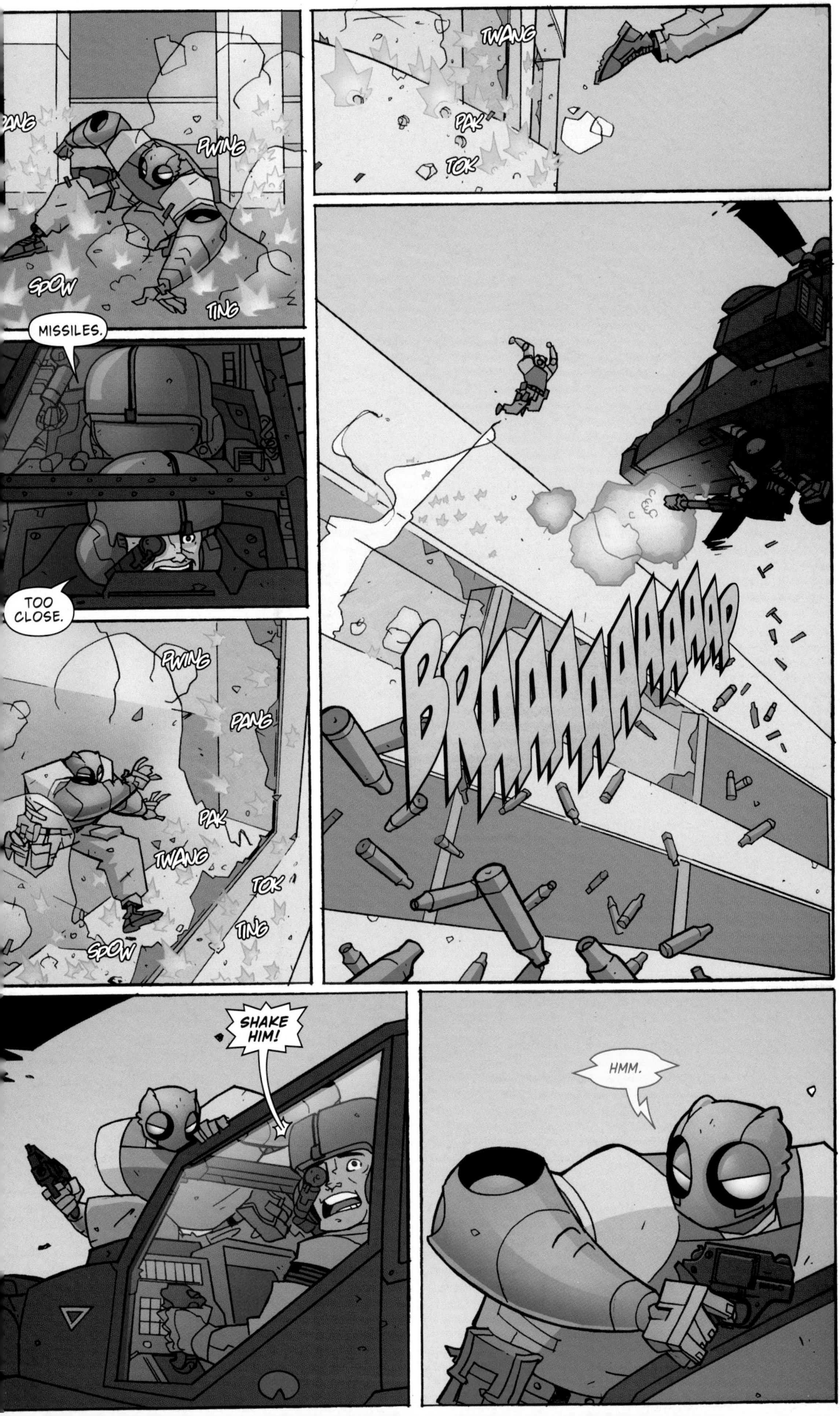
PWING
SPOW
TING
TWANG
PAK
TOK
MISSILES.
TOO CLOSE.
PWING
PANG
PAK
TWANG
TOK
TING
SPOW
BRAAAAAAAAAP
SHAKE HIM!
HMM.

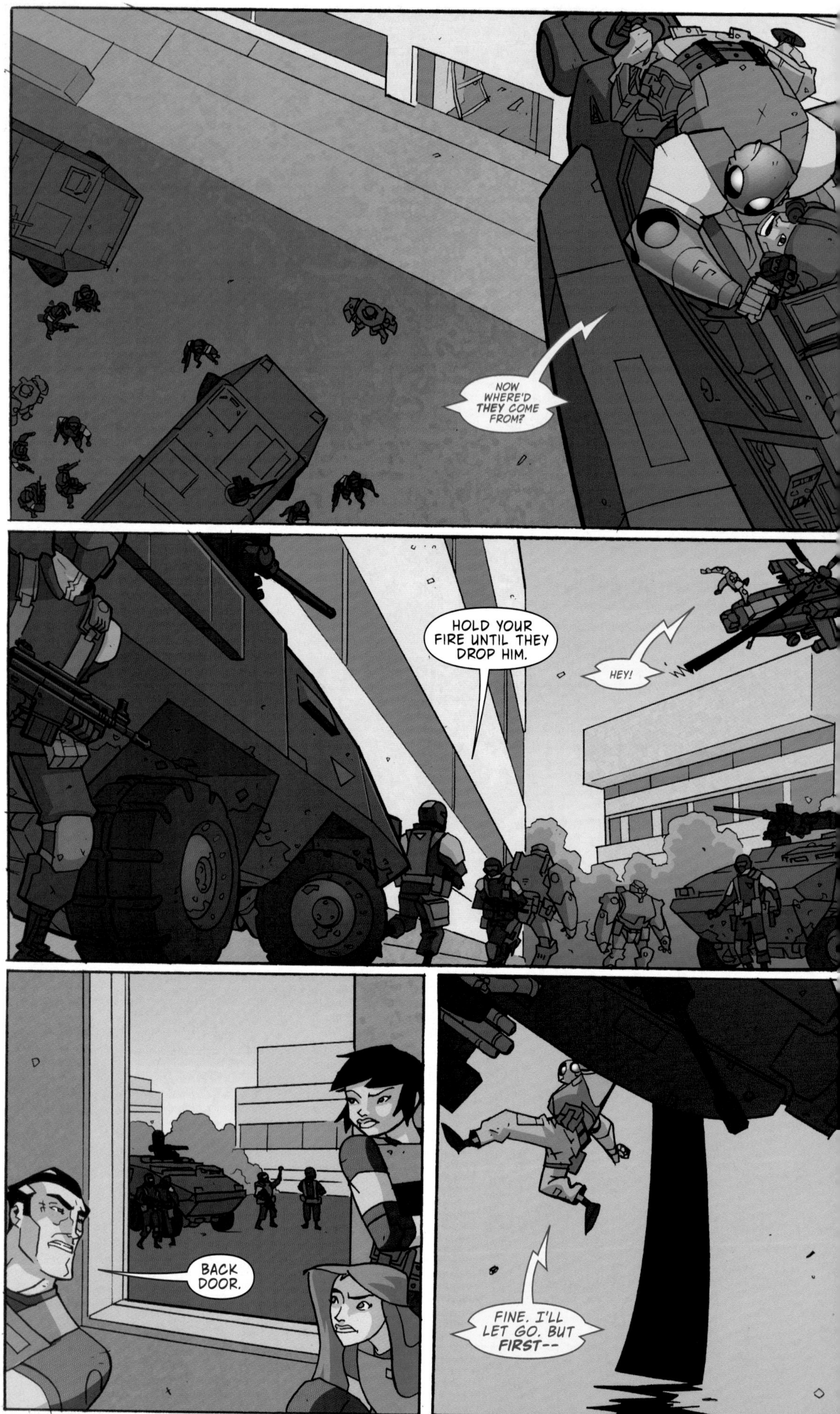
NOW WHERE'D THEY COME FROM?
HOLD YOUR FIRE UNTIL THEY DROP HIM.
HEY!
BACK DOOR.
FINE. I'LL LET GO. BUT FIRST--

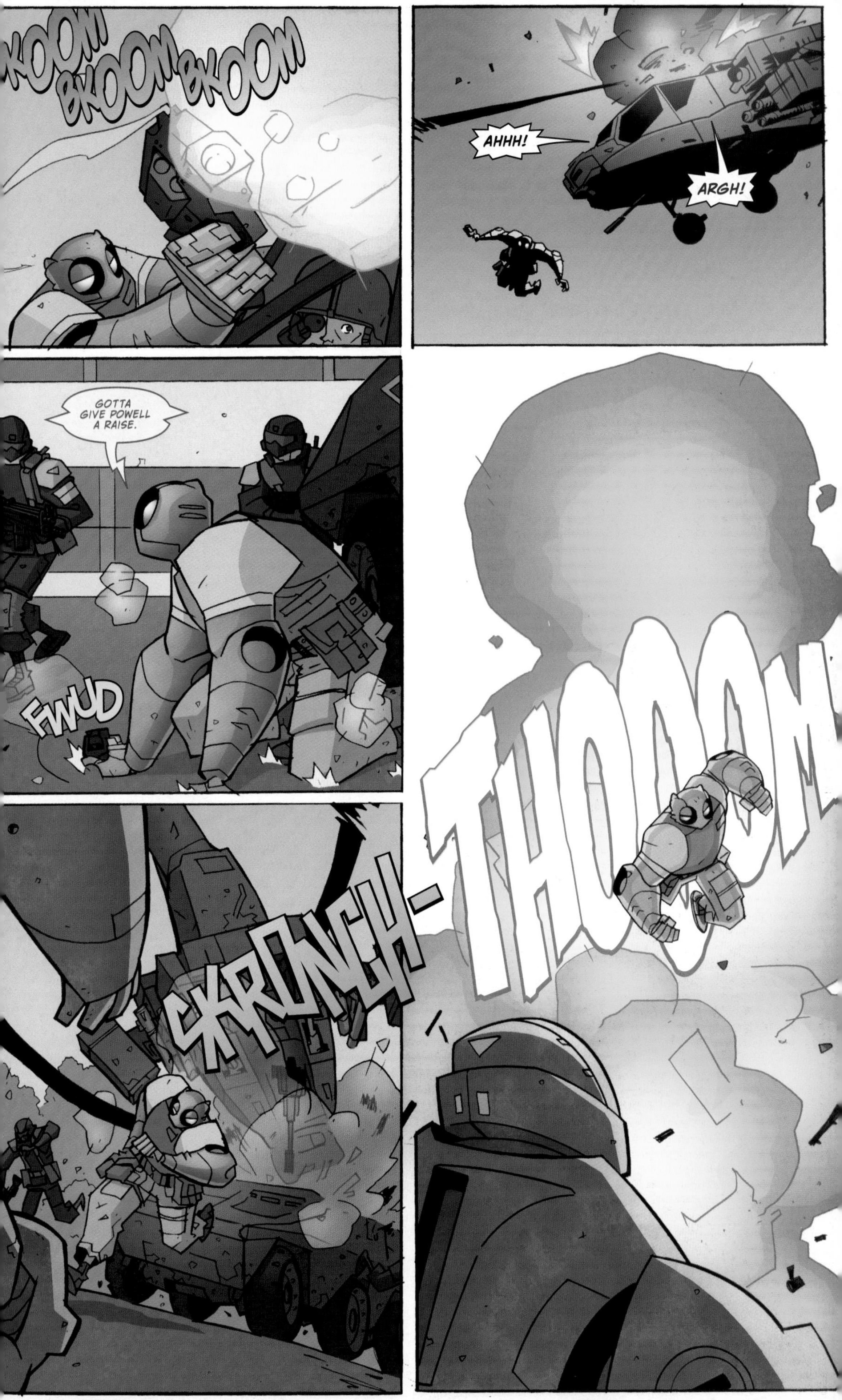
KOOM BKOOM BKOOM
AHHH!
ARGH!
GOTTA GIVE POWELL A RAISE.
FWUD
CKRUNCH-
THOOOM

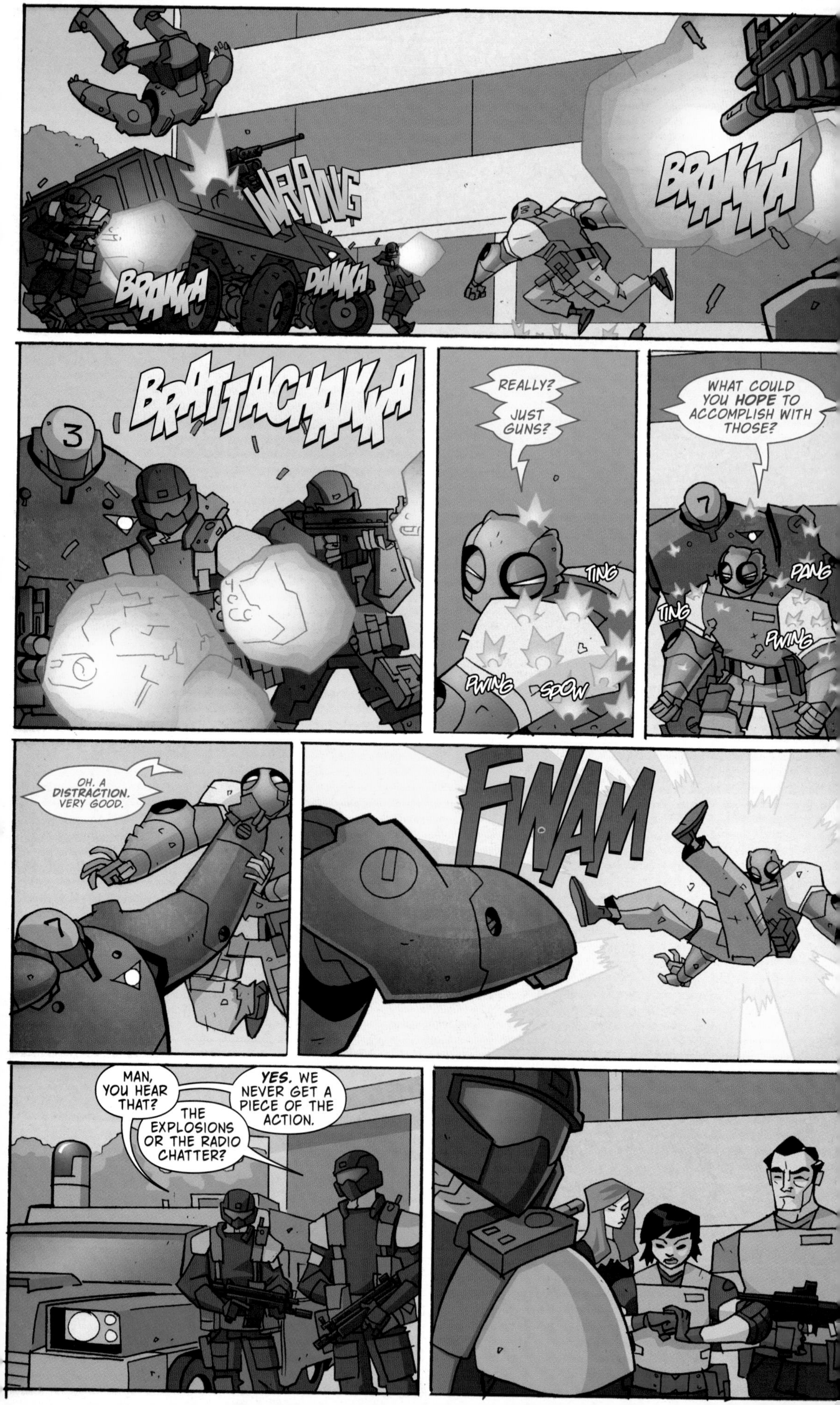
WRANG
BRAKKA
BRAKKA
DAKKA
BRATTACHAKKA
REALLY?
JUST GUNS?
TING
PWING
SPOW
WHAT COULD YOU HOPE TO ACCOMPLISH WITH THOSE?
PANG
TING
PWING
OH. A DISTRACTION. VERY GOOD.
FWAM
MAN, YOU HEAR THAT?
THE EXPLOSIONS OR THE RADIO CHATTER?
YES. WE NEVER GET A PIECE OF THE ACTION.

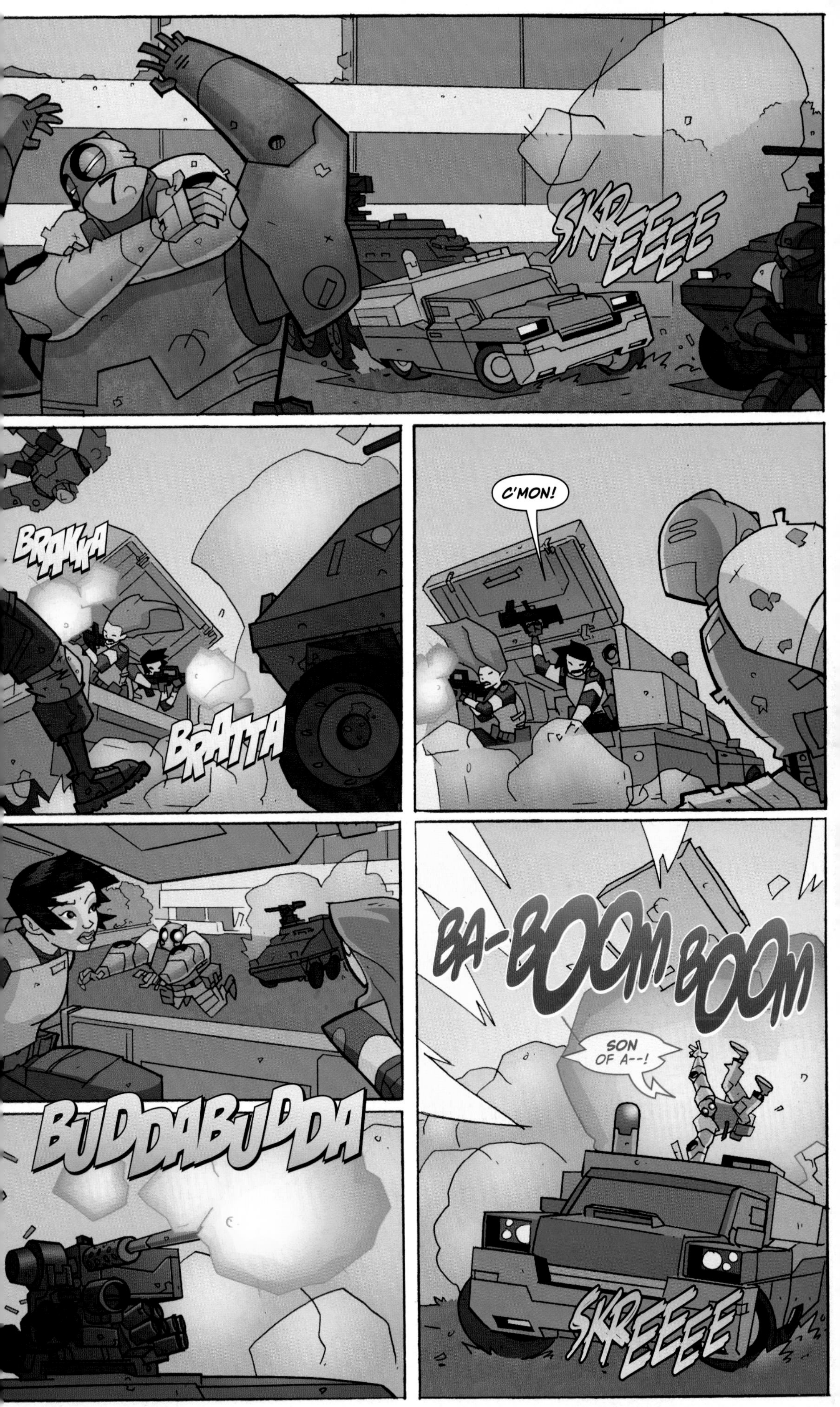
SKREEEE
BRAKKA
BRATTA
C'MON!
BUDDABUDDA
BA-BOOM BOOM
SON OF A--!
SKREEEE

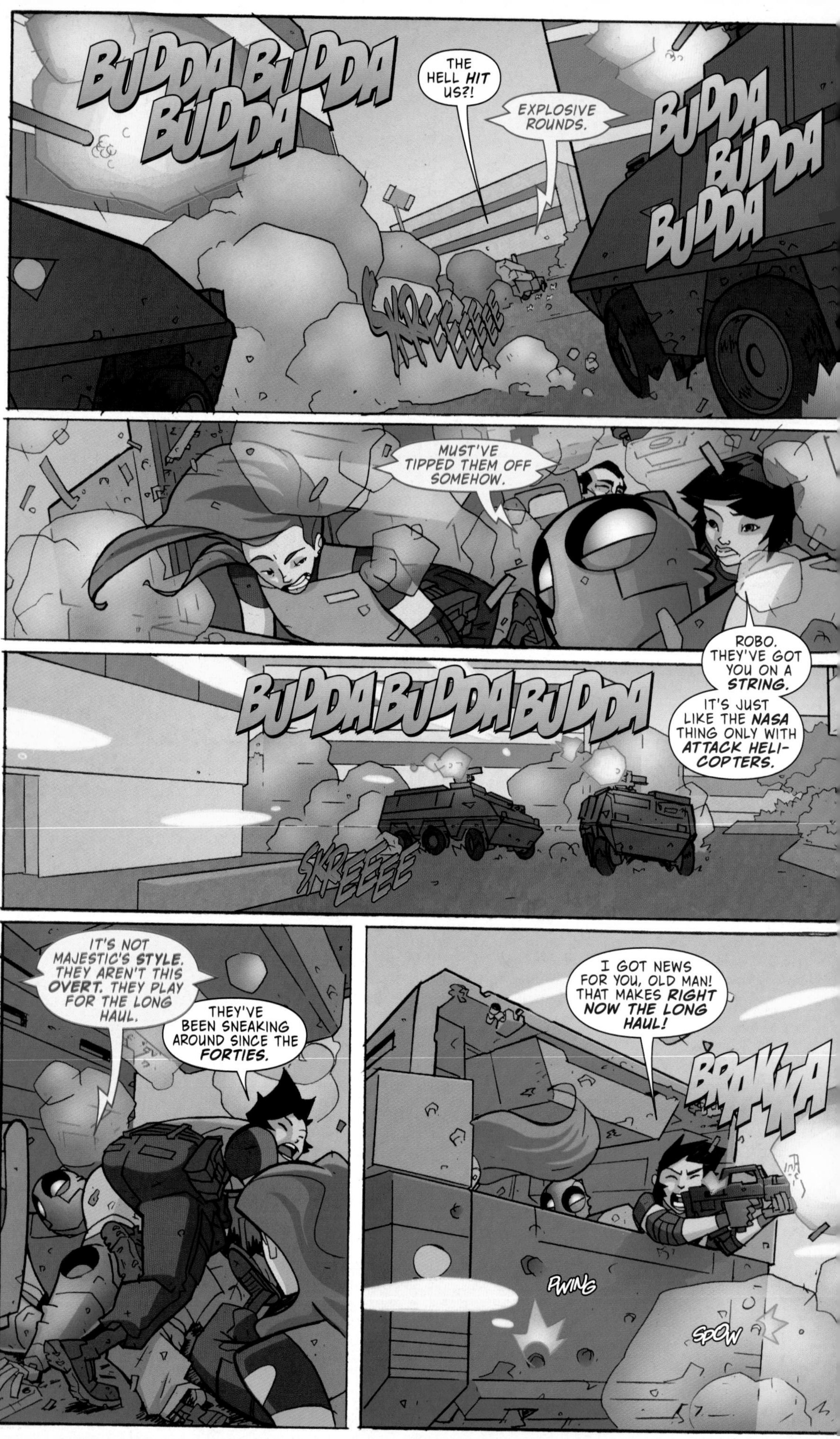
BUDDA BUDDA BUDDA
THE HELL *HIT* US?!
EXPLOSIVE ROUNDS.
BUDDA BUDDA BUDDA
SKREEEEE
MUST'VE TIPPED THEM OFF SOMEHOW.
ROBO. THEY'VE GOT YOU ON A **STRING.**
IT'S JUST LIKE THE **NASA** THING ONLY WITH **ATTACK HELI-COPTERS.**
BUDDA BUDDA BUDDA
SKREEEEE
IT'S NOT MAJESTIC'S **STYLE.** THEY AREN'T THIS **OVERT.** THEY PLAY FOR THE LONG HAUL.
THEY'VE BEEN SNEAKING AROUND SINCE THE **FORTIES.**
I GOT NEWS FOR YOU, OLD MAN! THAT MAKES **RIGHT NOW THE LONG HAUL!**
BRAKKA
PWING
SPOW

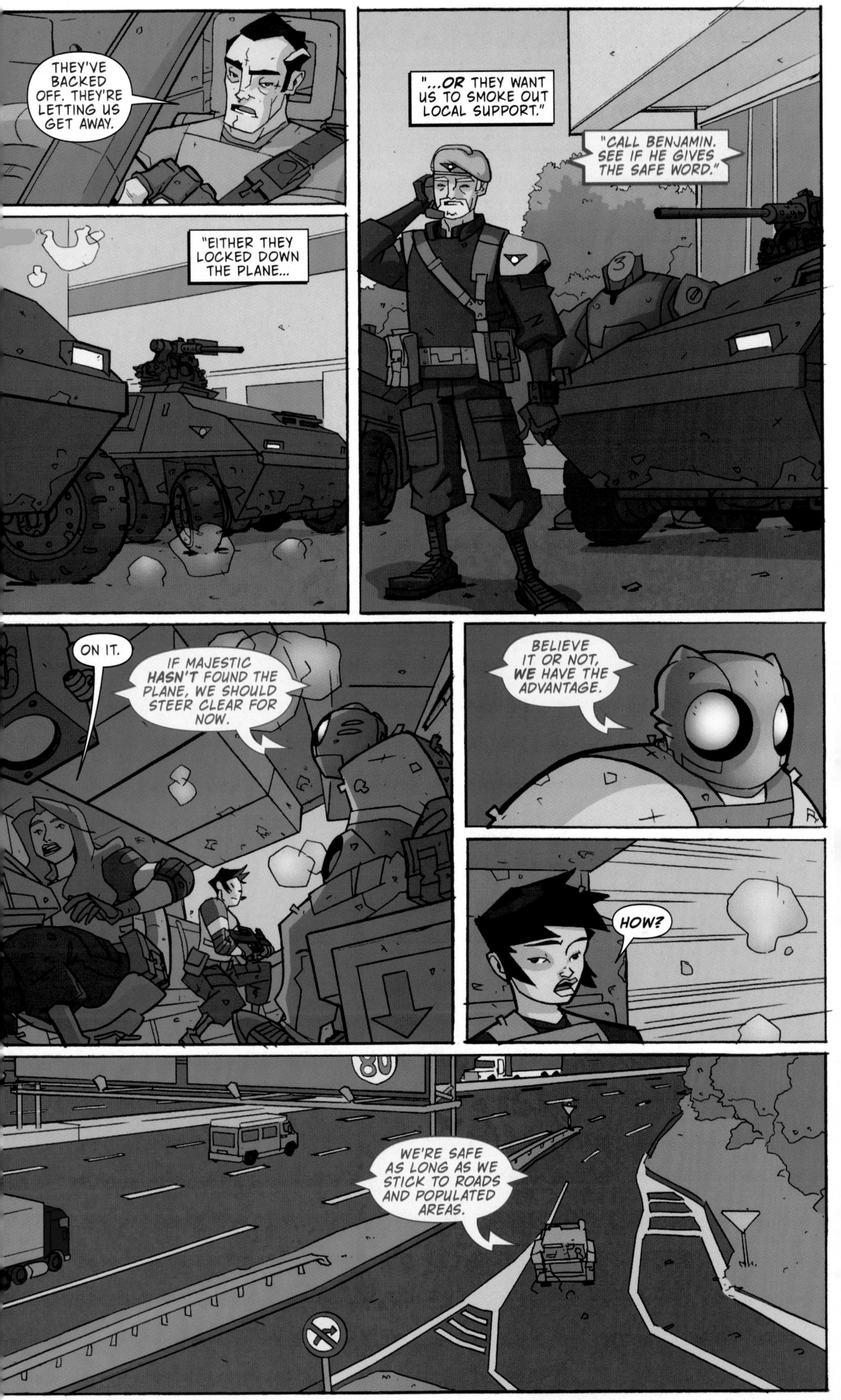

THEY'VE BACKED OFF. THEY'RE LETTING US GET AWAY.
"...**OR** THEY WANT US TO SMOKE OUT LOCAL SUPPORT."
"CALL BENJAMIN. SEE IF HE GIVES THE SAFE WORD."
"EITHER THEY LOCKED DOWN THE PLANE...
ON IT.
IF MAJESTIC **HASN'T** FOUND THE PLANE, WE SHOULD STEER CLEAR FOR NOW.
BELIEVE IT OR NOT, **WE** HAVE THE ADVANTAGE.
HOW?
80
WE'RE SAFE AS LONG AS WE STICK TO ROADS AND POPULATED AREAS.

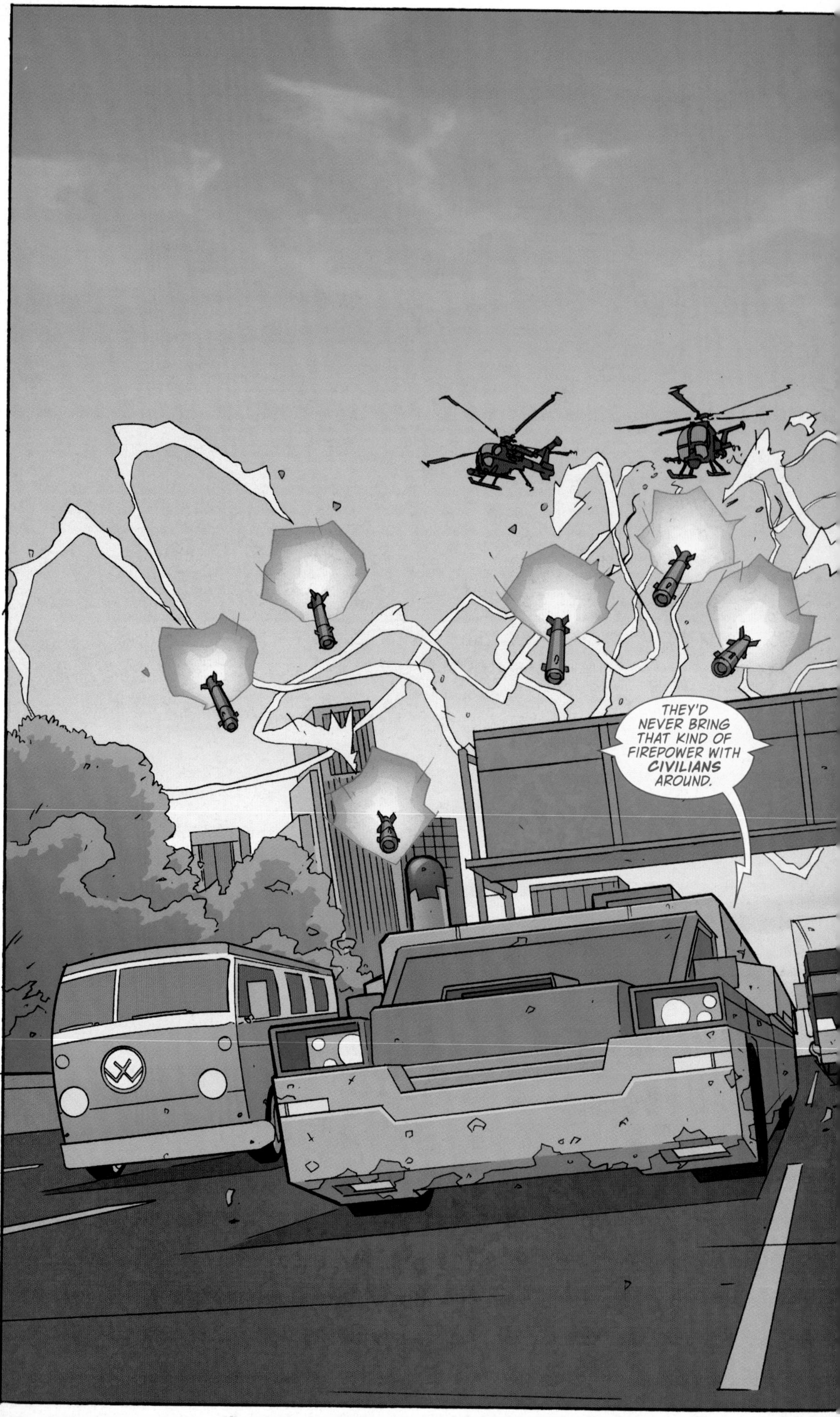
THEY'D NEVER BRING THAT KIND OF FIREPOWER WITH CIVILIANS AROUND.

TRANSFORMATION

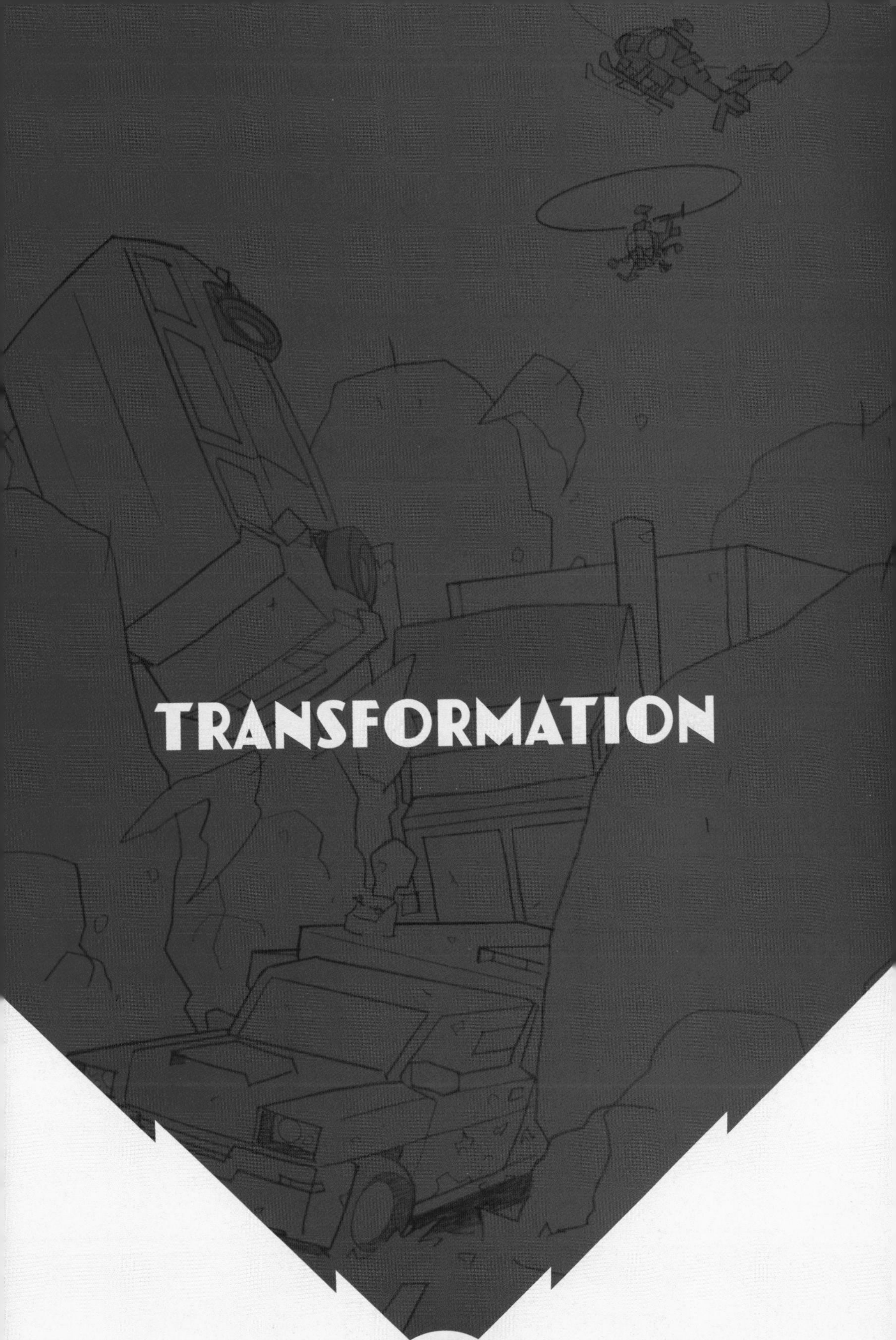

4

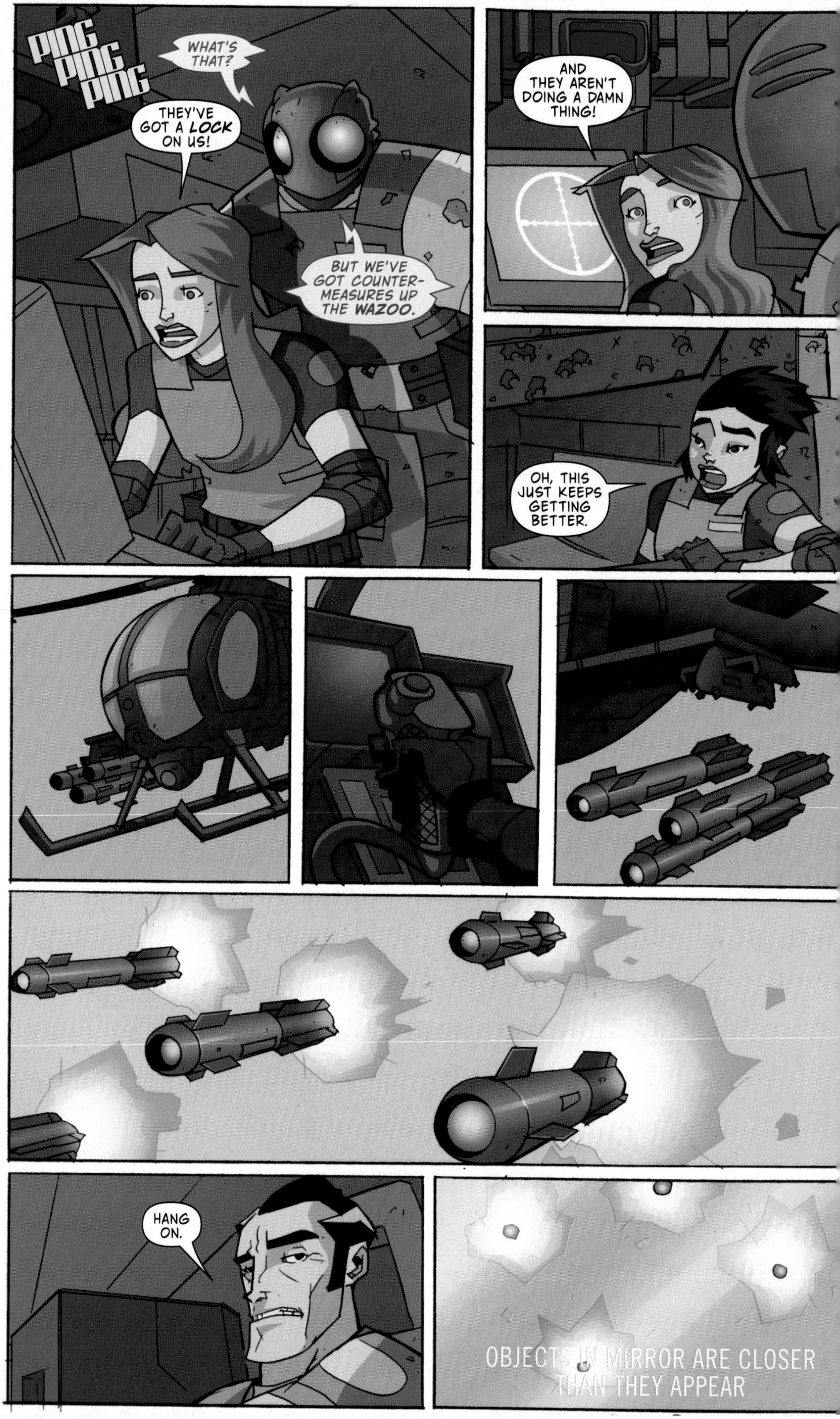
PING PING PING
WHAT'S THAT?
THEY'VE GOT A **LOCK** ON US!
BUT WE'VE GOT COUNTER-MEASURES UP THE **WAZOO.**
AND THEY AREN'T DOING A DAMN THING!
OH, THIS JUST KEEPS GETTING BETTER.
HANG ON.
OBJECTS IN MIRROR ARE CLOSER THAN THEY APPEAR

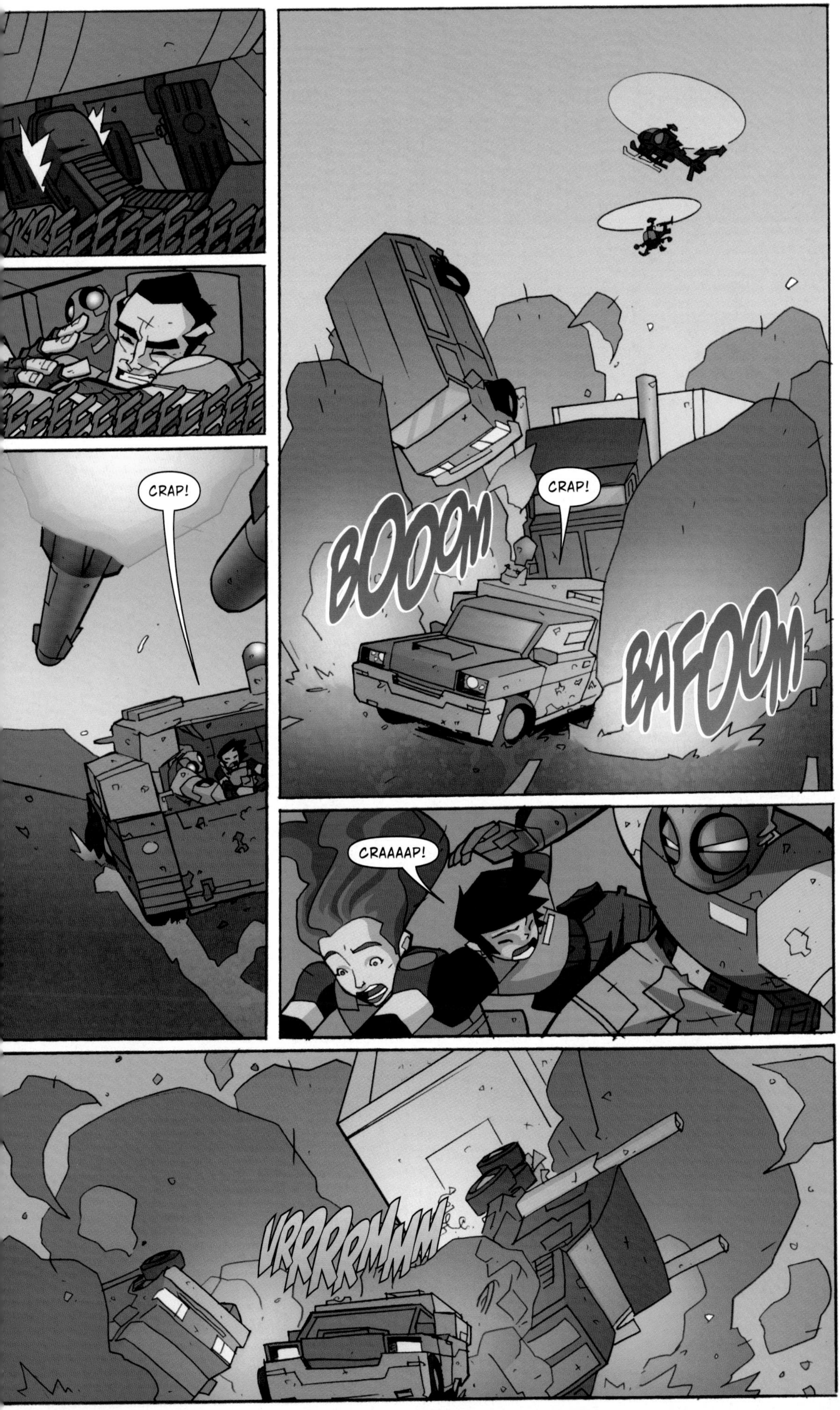

SKREEEEEEEEEE
EEEEEEEEEEEEE
CRAP!
BOOOM
CRAP!
BAFOOM
CRAAAAP!
URRRRMMM

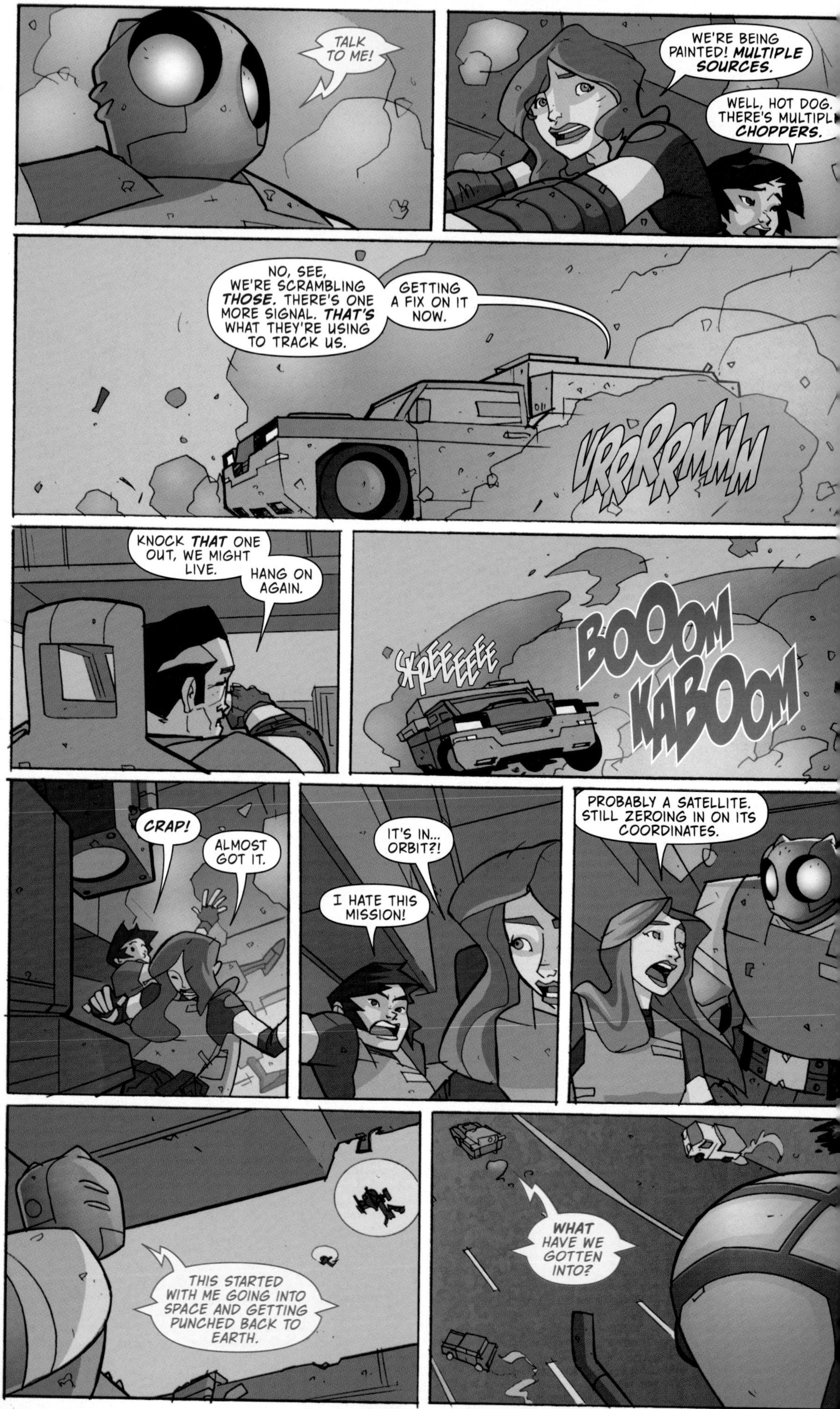
TALK TO ME!
WE'RE BEING PAINTED! MULTIPLE SOURCES.
WELL, HOT DOG. THERE'S MULTIPL CHOPPERS.
NO, SEE, WE'RE SCRAMBLING THOSE. THERE'S ONE MORE SIGNAL. THAT'S WHAT THEY'RE USING TO TRACK US.
GETTING A FIX ON IT NOW.
URRRRMMM
KNOCK THAT ONE OUT, WE MIGHT LIVE.
HANG ON AGAIN.
SKREEEEEE
BOOOM KABOOM
CRAP!
ALMOST GOT IT.
IT'S IN... ORBIT?!
I HATE THIS MISSION!
PROBABLY A SATELLITE. STILL ZEROING IN ON ITS COORDINATES.
THIS STARTED WITH ME GOING INTO SPACE AND GETTING PUNCHED BACK TO EARTH.
WHAT HAVE WE GOTTEN INTO?

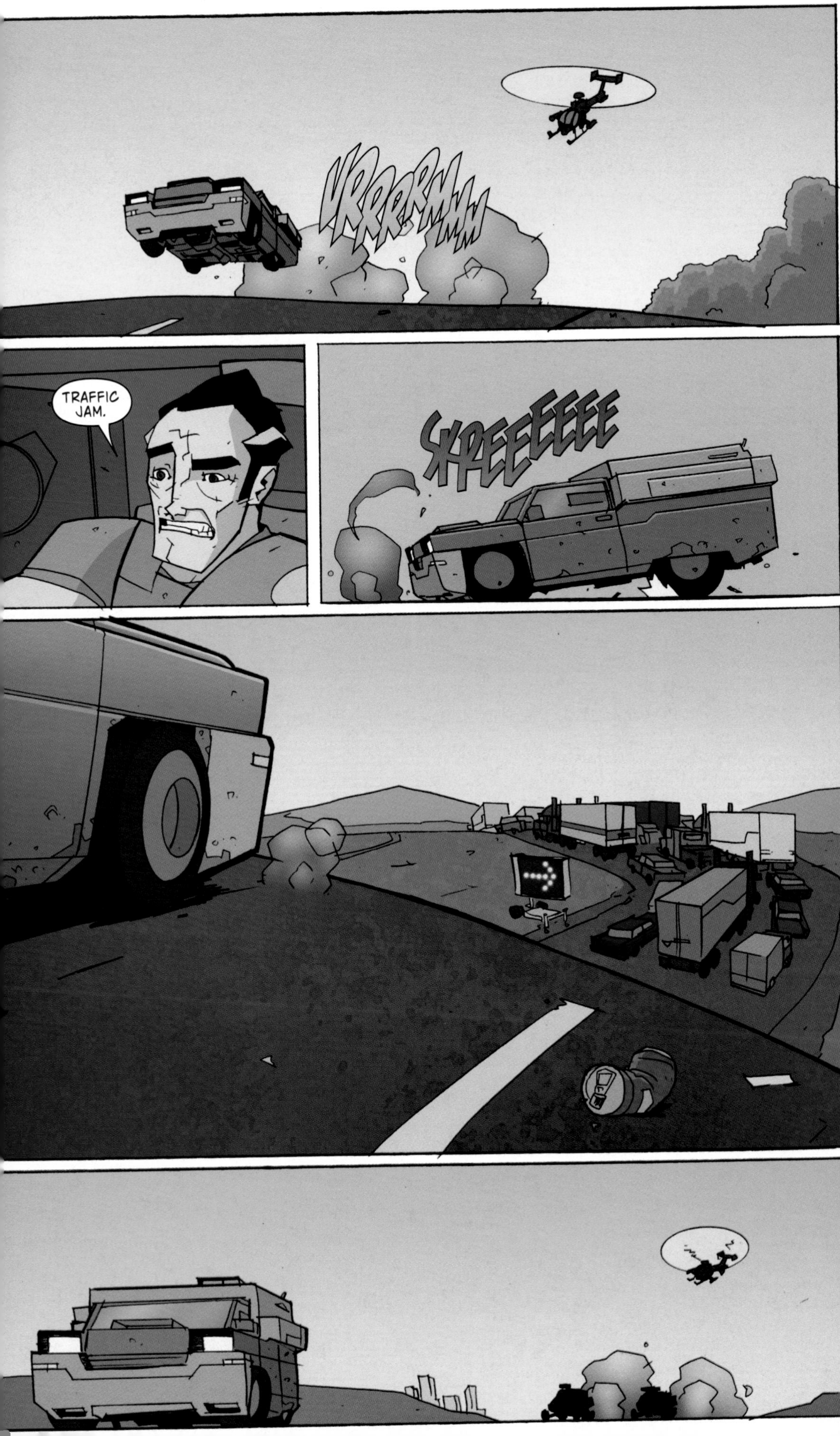
VRRRRMMM
TRAFFIC JAM.
SKREEEEEEE

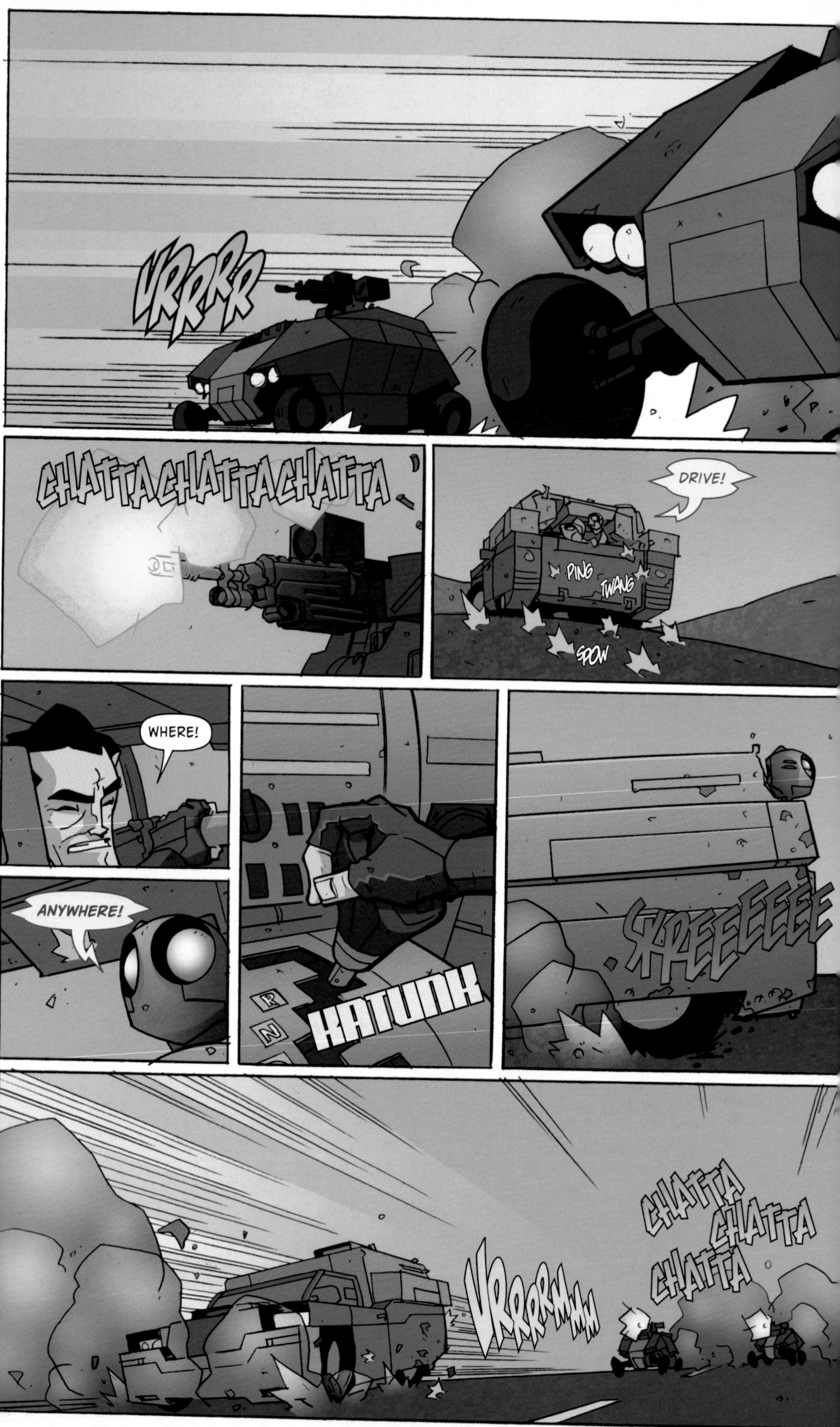
URRRR
CHATTACHATTACHATTA
DRIVE!
PING
TWANG
SPOW
WHERE!
ANYWHERE!
KATUNK
SKREEEEEEE
VRRRRMMM
CHATTA
CHATTA
CHATTA

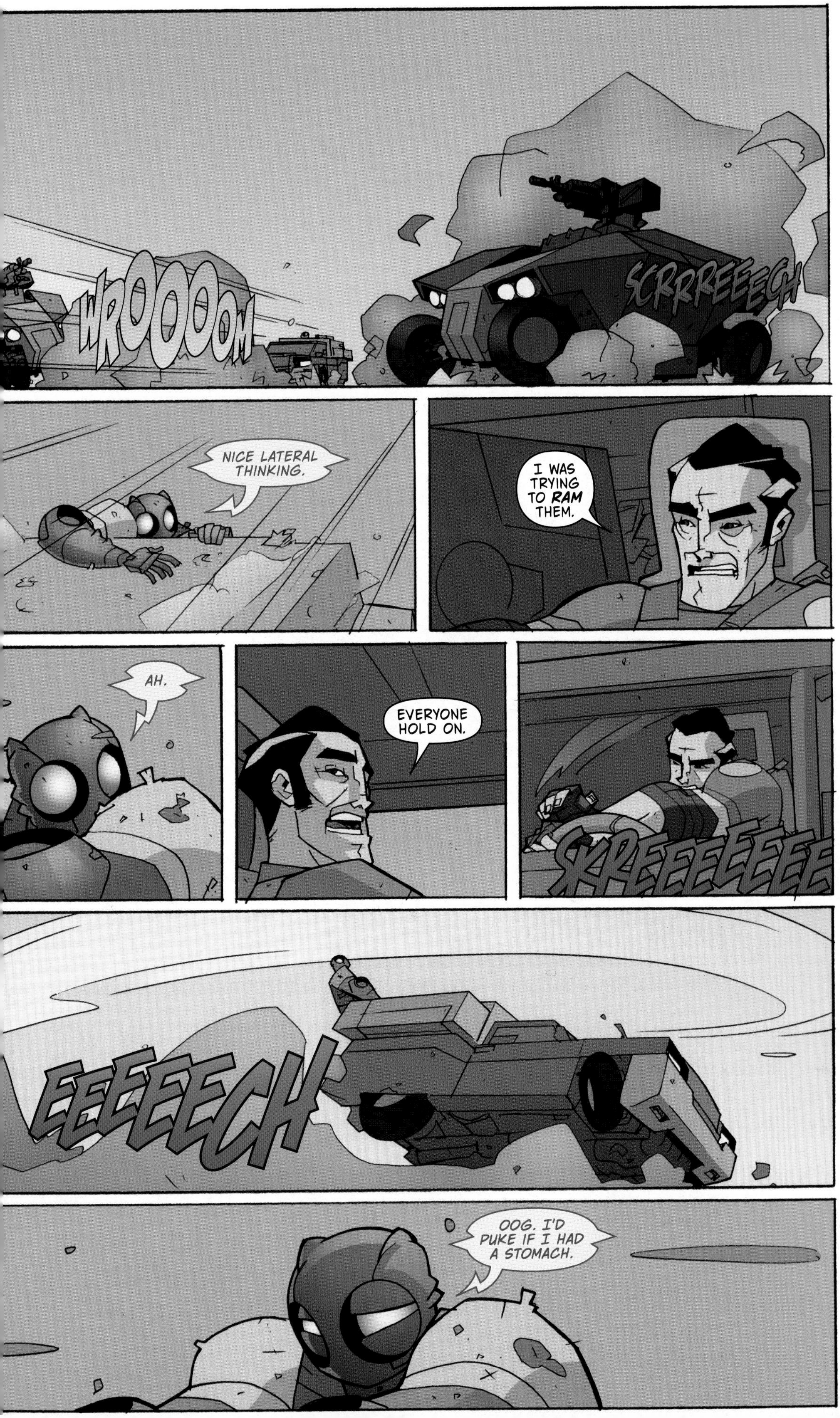

WROOOOM
SCRRREEEECH
NICE LATERAL THINKING.
I WAS TRYING TO RAM THEM.
AH.
EVERYONE HOLD ON.
SKREEEEEEEE
EEEEEECH
OOG. I'D PUKE IF I HAD A STOMACH.

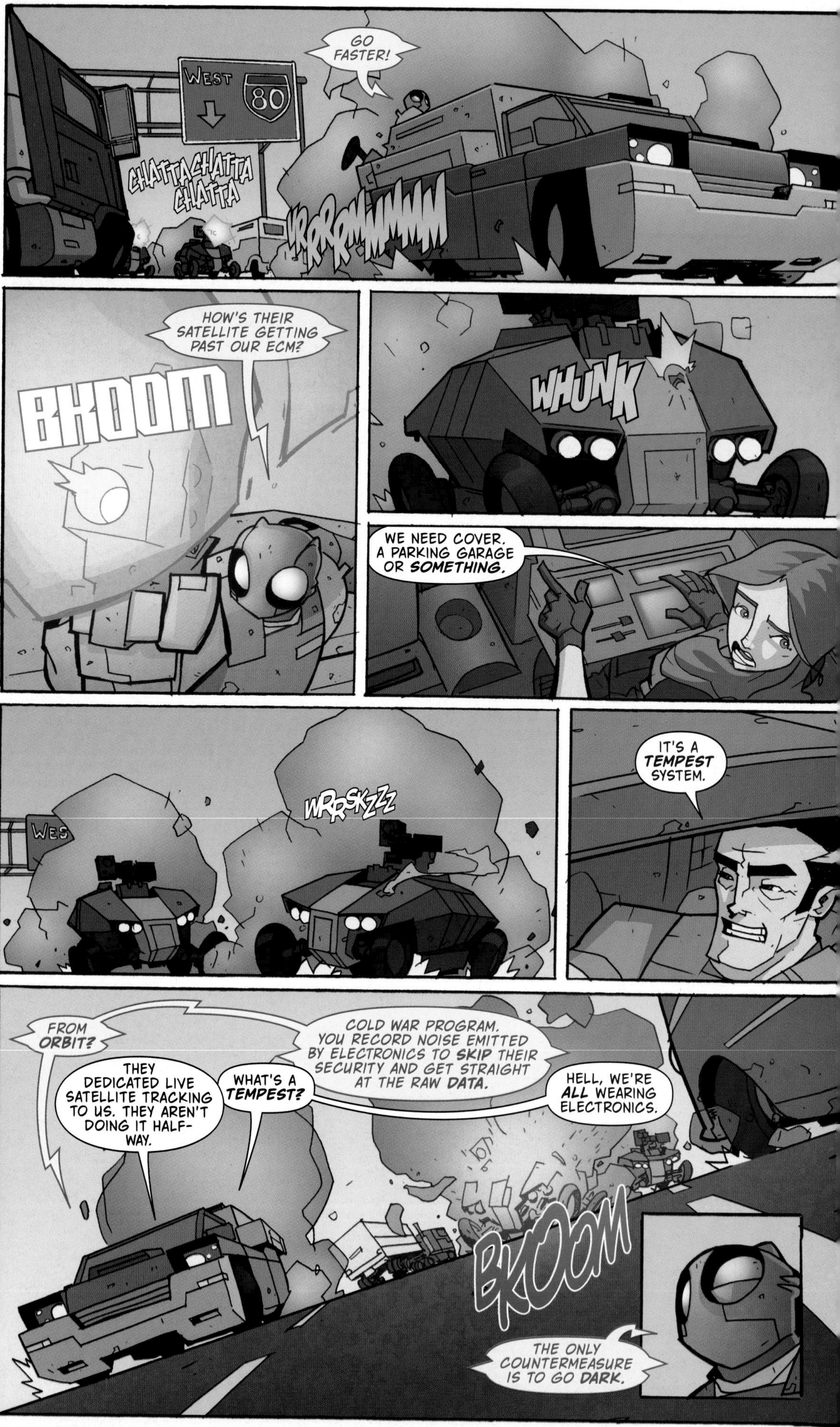
WEST
80
CHATTACHATTA CHATTA
GO FASTER!
VRRRRMMMMMM
BKOOM
HOW'S THEIR SATELLITE GETTING PAST OUR ECM?
WHUNK
WE NEED COVER. A PARKING GARAGE OR SOMETHING.
WES
WRRSKZZZ
IT'S A TEMPEST SYSTEM.
FROM ORBIT?
THEY DEDICATED LIVE SATELLITE TRACKING TO US. THEY AREN'T DOING IT HALF-WAY.
WHAT'S A TEMPEST?
COLD WAR PROGRAM. YOU RECORD NOISE EMITTED BY ELECTRONICS TO SKIP THEIR SECURITY AND GET STRAIGHT AT THE RAW DATA.
HELL, WE'RE ALL WEARING ELECTRONICS.
BKOOM
THE ONLY COUNTERMEASURE IS TO GO DARK.

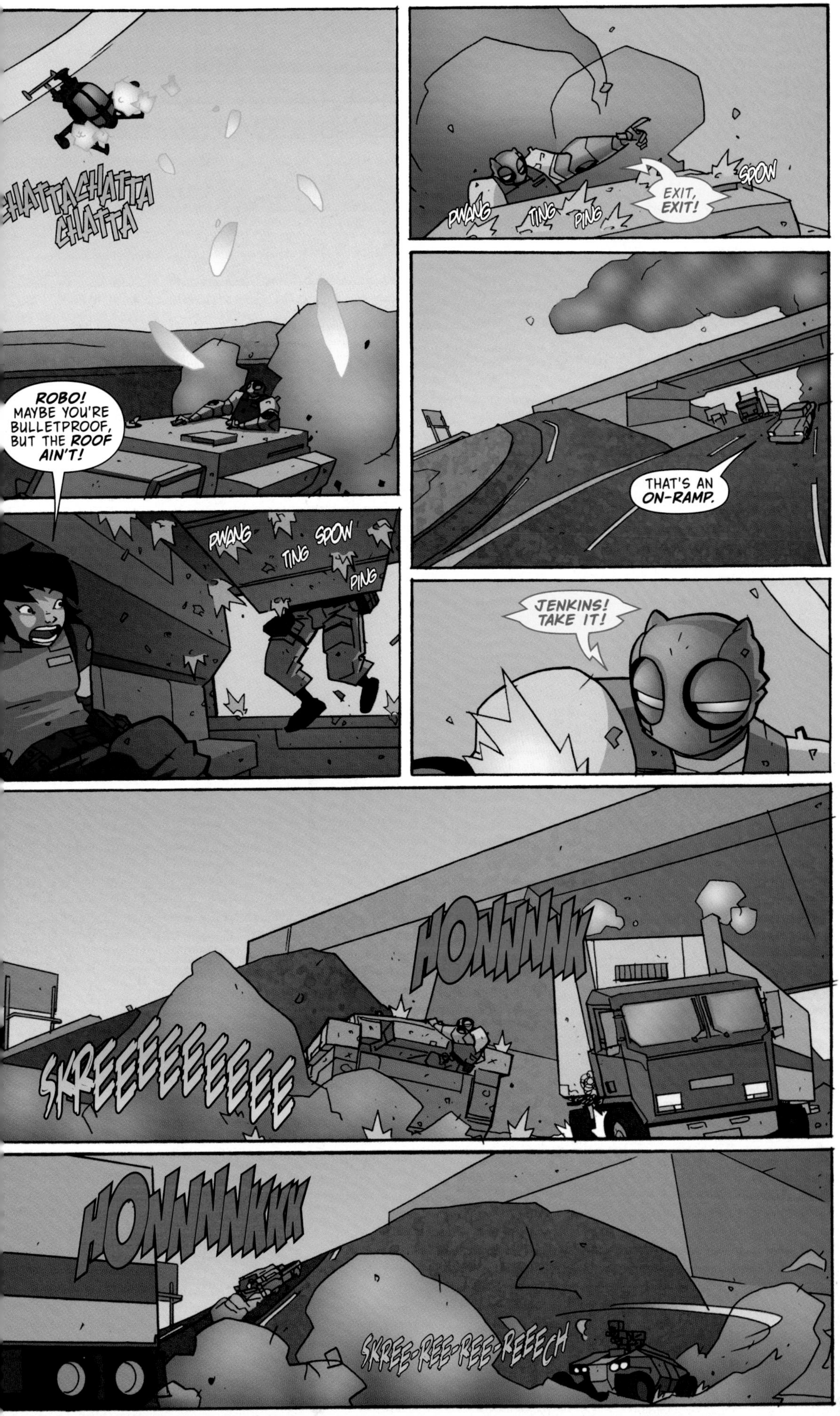
CHATTACHATTA CHATTA
PWANG
TING
PING
EXIT, EXIT!
SPOW
ROBO! MAYBE YOU'RE BULLETPROOF, BUT THE ROOF AIN'T!
PWANG
TING
SPOW
PING
THAT'S AN ON-RAMP.
JENKINS! TAKE IT!
HONNNNK
SKREEEEEEEEEE
HONNNNKKK
SKREE-REE-REE-REEECH

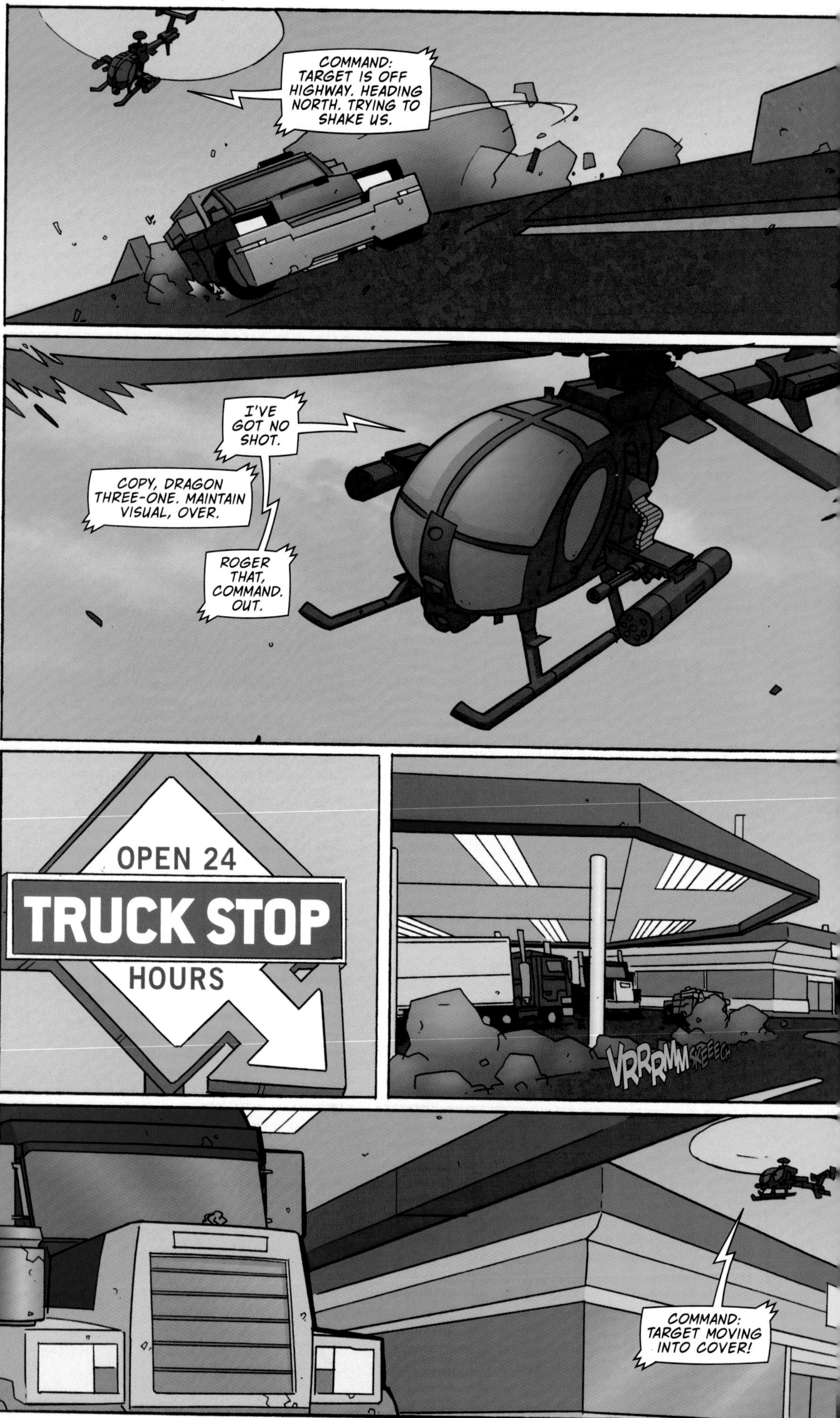
COMMAND: TARGET IS OFF HIGHWAY. HEADING NORTH. TRYING TO SHAKE US.
I'VE GOT NO SHOT.
COPY, DRAGON THREE-ONE. MAINTAIN VISUAL, OVER.
ROGER THAT, COMMAND. OUT.
OPEN 24
TRUCK STOP
HOURS
VRRRMM
SKREEECH
COMMAND: TARGET MOVING INTO COVER!

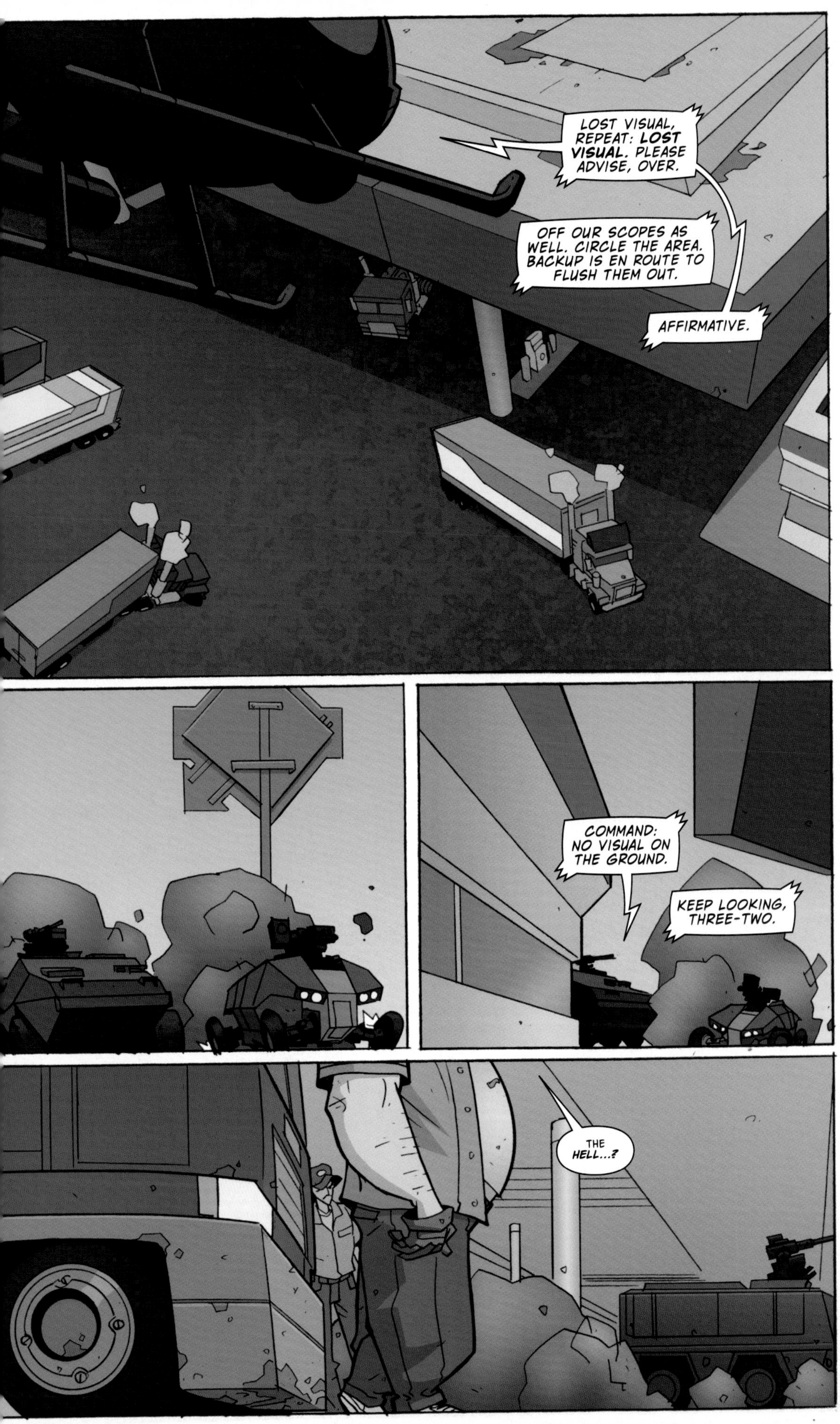
LOST VISUAL, REPEAT: **LOST VISUAL.** PLEASE ADVISE, OVER.
OFF OUR SCOPES AS WELL. CIRCLE THE AREA. BACKUP IS EN ROUTE TO FLUSH THEM OUT.
AFFIRMATIVE.
COMMAND: NO VISUAL ON THE GROUND.
KEEP LOOKING, THREE-TWO.
THE *HELL...?*

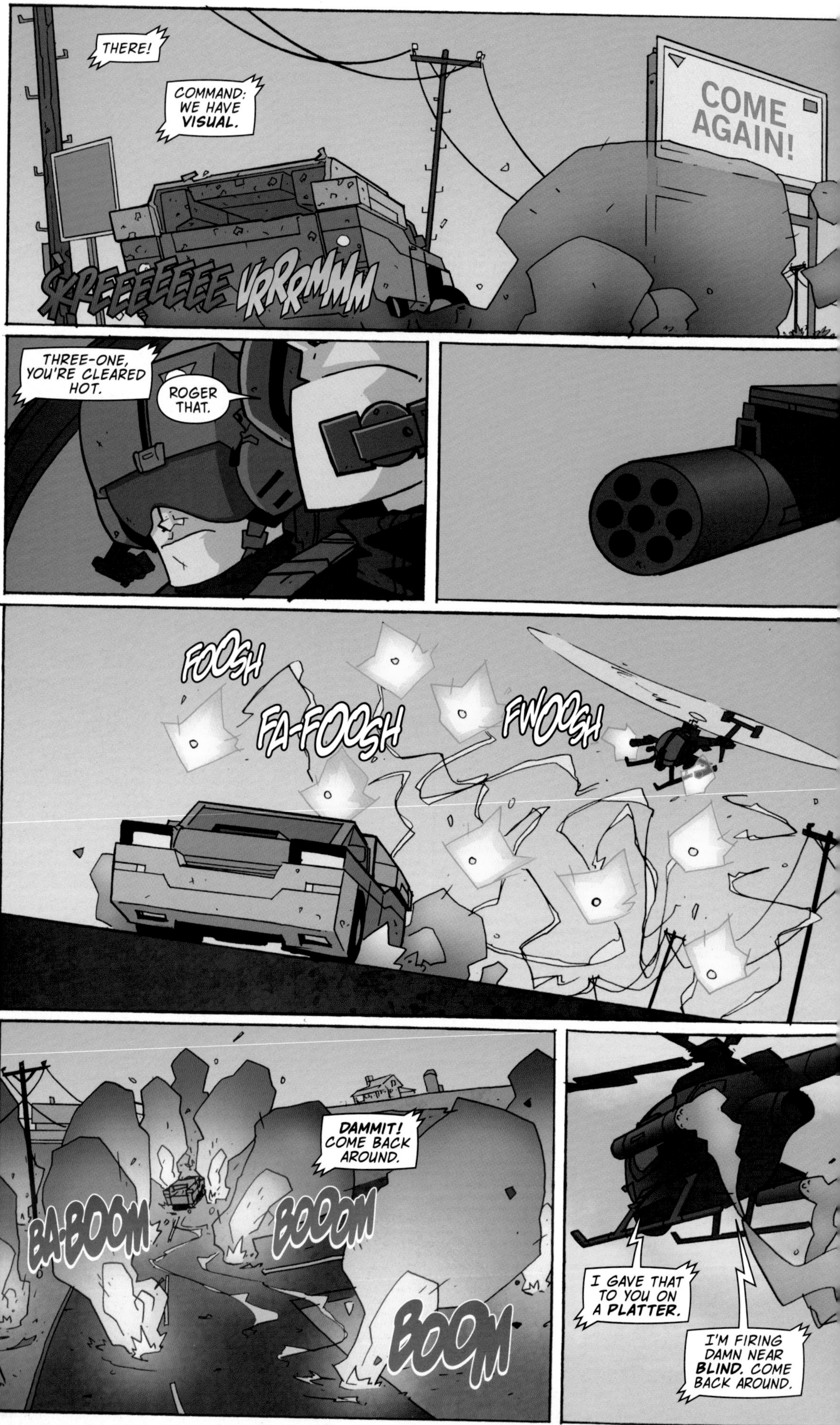
THERE!
COMMAND: WE HAVE VISUAL.
COME AGAIN!
SKREEEEEEEE
URRRMMM
THREE-ONE, YOU'RE CLEARED HOT.
ROGER THAT.
FOOSH
FA-FOOSH
FWOOSH
DAMMIT! COME BACK AROUND.
BA-BOOM
BOOOM
BOOM
I GAVE THAT TO YOU ON A PLATTER.
I'M FIRING DAMN NEAR BLIND. COME BACK AROUND.

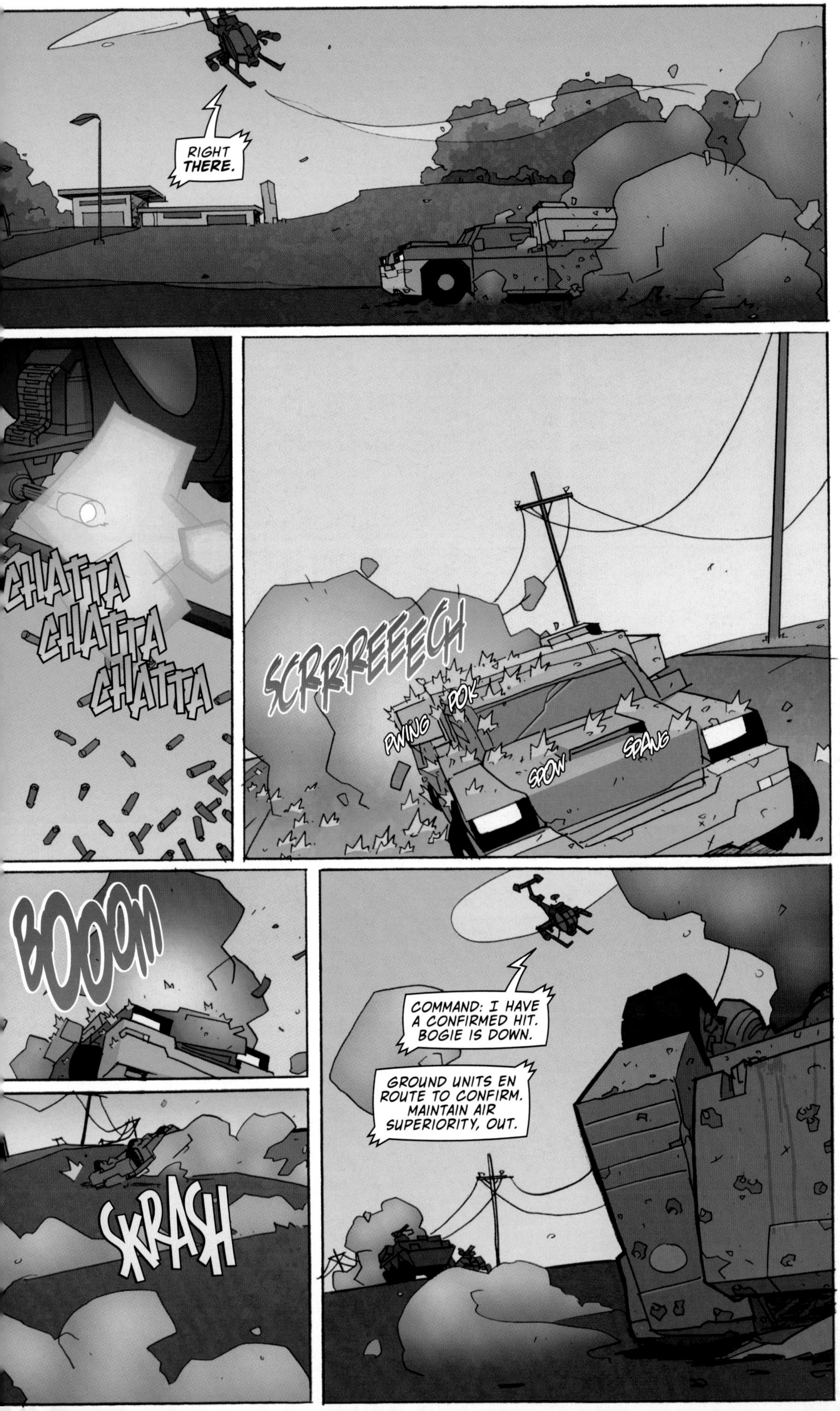
RIGHT THERE.
CHATTA CHATTA CHATTA
SCRRREEECH
POK
PWING
SPOW
SPANG
BOOOM
SKRASH
COMMAND: I HAVE A CONFIRMED HIT. BOGIE IS DOWN.
GROUND UNITS EN ROUTE TO CONFIRM. MAINTAIN AIR SUPERIORITY, OUT.

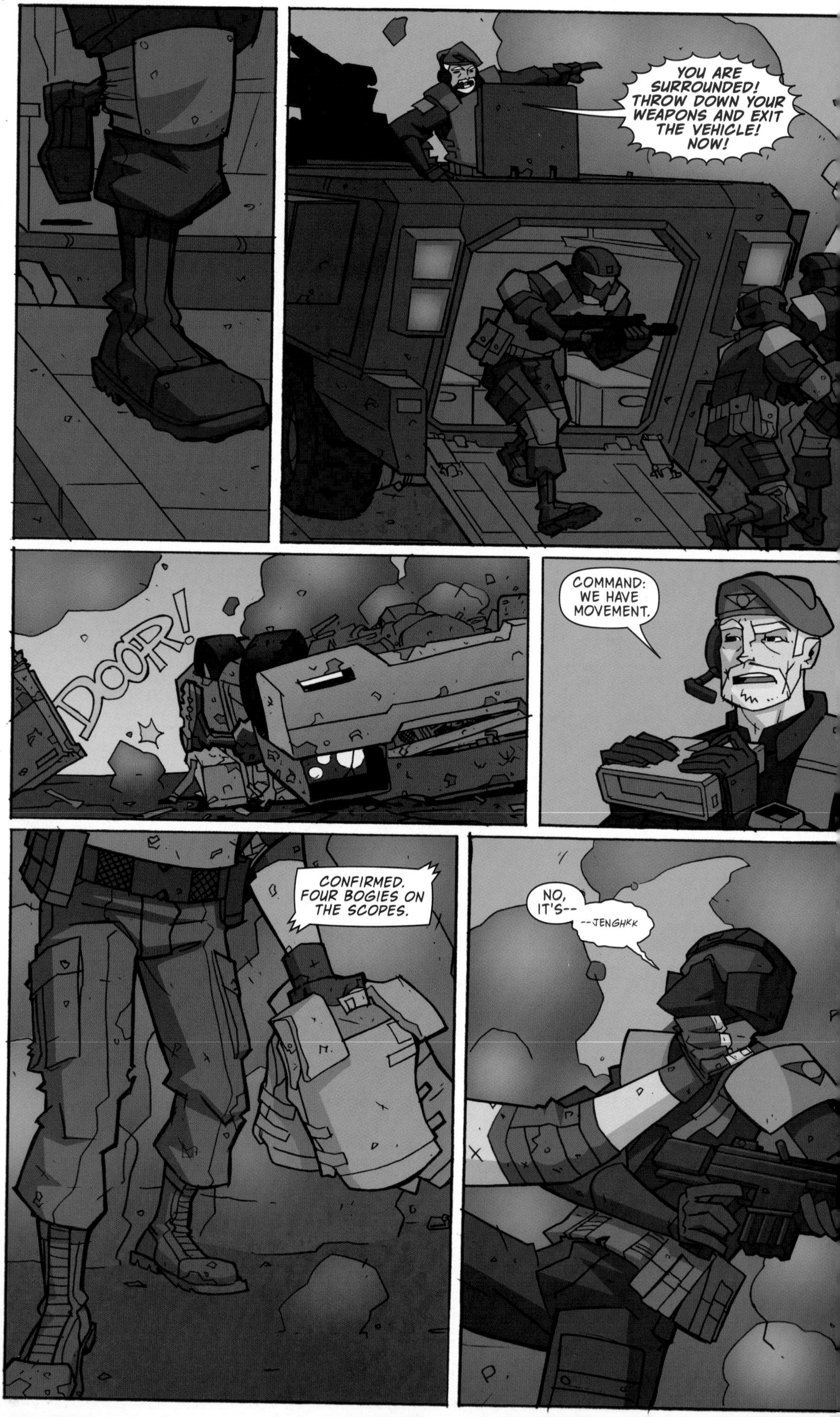
YOU ARE SURROUNDED! THROW DOWN YOUR WEAPONS AND EXIT THE VEHICLE! NOW!
DOOR!
COMMAND: WE HAVE MOVEMENT.
CONFIRMED. FOUR BOGIES ON THE SCOPES.
NO, IT'S--
--JENGHKK

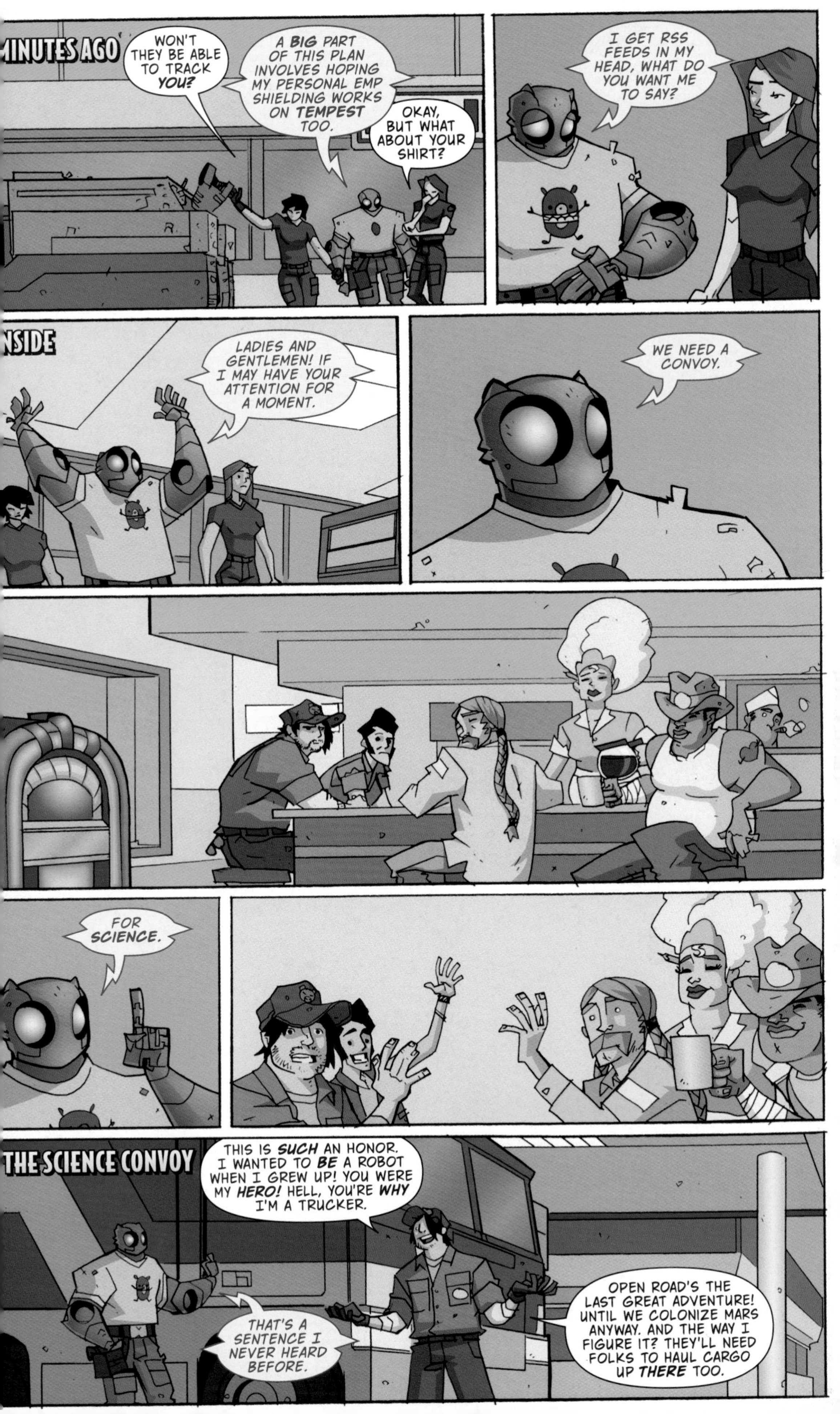

MINUTES AGO
WON'T THEY BE ABLE TO TRACK YOU?
A BIG PART OF THIS PLAN INVOLVES HOPING MY PERSONAL EMP SHIELDING WORKS ON TEMPEST TOO.
OKAY, BUT WHAT ABOUT YOUR SHIRT?
I GET RSS FEEDS IN MY HEAD, WHAT DO YOU WANT ME TO SAY?
NSIDE
LADIES AND GENTLEMEN! IF I MAY HAVE YOUR ATTENTION FOR A MOMENT.
WE NEED A CONVOY.
FOR SCIENCE.
THE SCIENCE CONVOY
THIS IS SUCH AN HONOR. I WANTED TO BE A ROBOT WHEN I GREW UP! YOU WERE MY HERO! HELL, YOU'RE WHY I'M A TRUCKER.
THAT'S A SENTENCE I NEVER HEARD BEFORE.
OPEN ROAD'S THE LAST GREAT ADVENTURE! UNTIL WE COLONIZE MARS ANYWAY. AND THE WAY I FIGURE IT? THEY'LL NEED FOLKS TO HAUL CARGO UP THERE TOO.

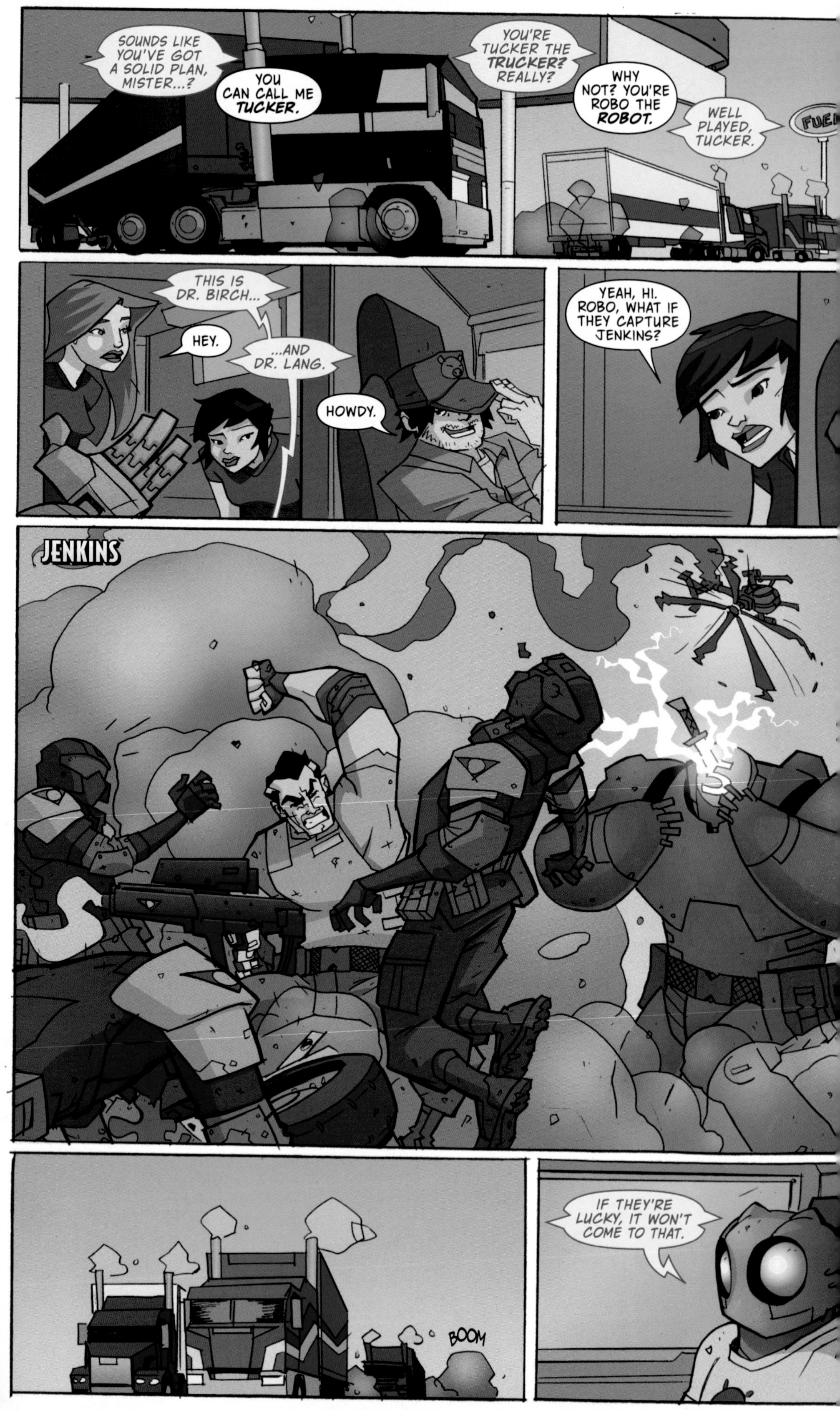
SOUNDS LIKE YOU'VE GOT A SOLID PLAN, MISTER...?
YOU CAN CALL ME **TUCKER.**
YOU'RE TUCKER THE **TRUCKER?** REALLY?
WHY NOT? YOU'RE ROBO THE **ROBOT.**
WELL PLAYED, TUCKER.
FUEL
THIS IS DR. BIRCH...
HEY.
...AND DR. LANG.
HOWDY.
YEAH, HI. ROBO, WHAT IF THEY CAPTURE JENKINS?
JENKINS
BOOM
IF THEY'RE LUCKY, IT WON'T COME TO THAT.

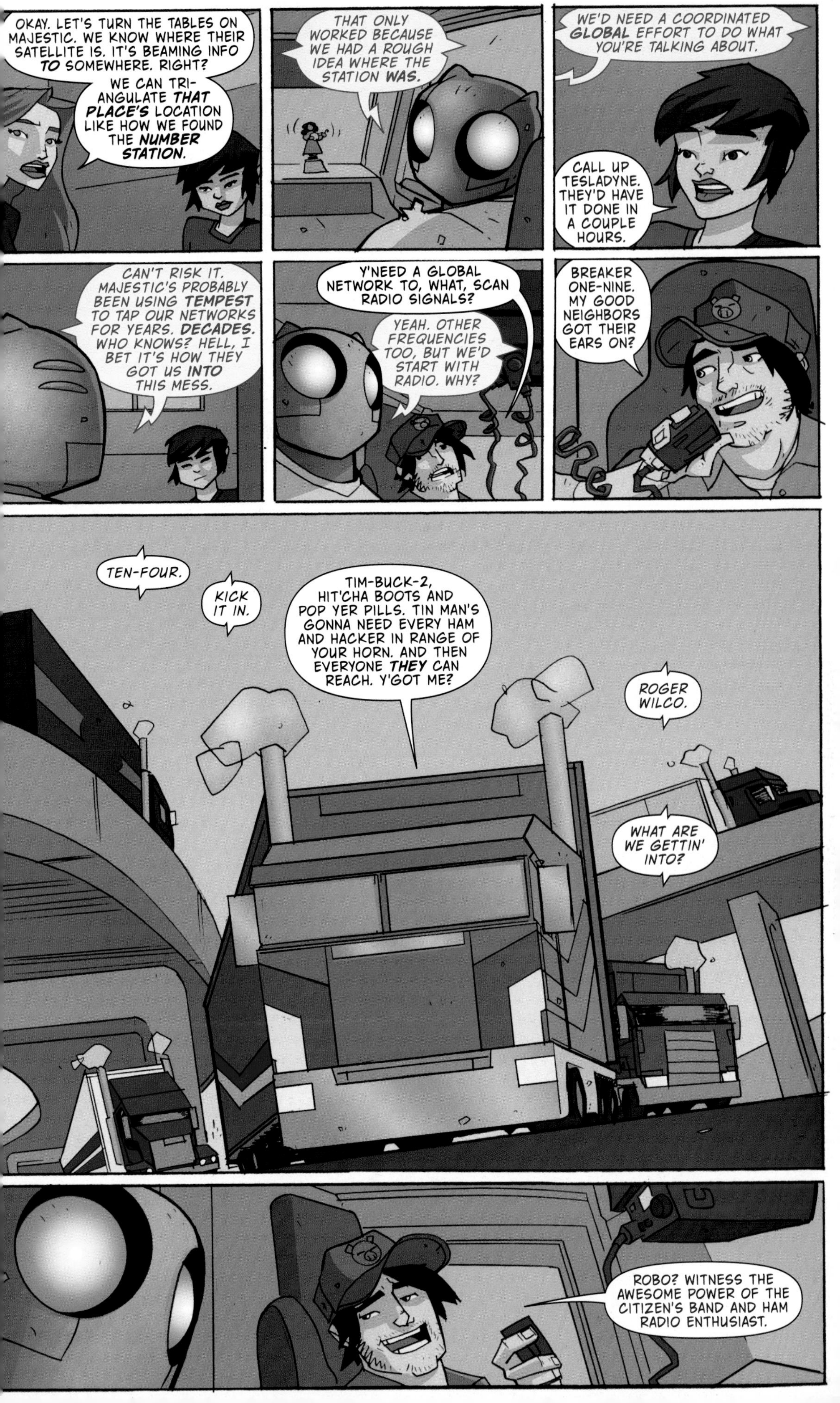
OKAY. LET'S TURN THE TABLES ON MAJESTIC. WE KNOW WHERE THEIR SATELLITE IS. IT'S BEAMING INFO *TO* SOMEWHERE. RIGHT?
WE CAN TRI-ANGULATE **THAT PLACE'S** LOCATION LIKE HOW WE FOUND THE **NUMBER STATION.**
THAT ONLY WORKED BECAUSE WE HAD A ROUGH IDEA WHERE THE STATION **WAS.**
WE'D NEED A COORDINATED **GLOBAL** EFFORT TO DO WHAT YOU'RE TALKING ABOUT.
CALL UP TESLADYNE. THEY'D HAVE IT DONE IN A COUPLE HOURS.
CAN'T RISK IT. MAJESTIC'S PROBABLY BEEN USING **TEMPEST** TO TAP OUR NETWORKS FOR YEARS. **DECADES.** WHO KNOWS? HELL, I BET IT'S HOW THEY GOT US **INTO** THIS MESS.
Y'NEED A GLOBAL NETWORK TO, WHAT, SCAN RADIO SIGNALS?
YEAH. OTHER FREQUENCIES TOO, BUT WE'D START WITH RADIO. WHY?
BREAKER ONE-NINE. MY GOOD NEIGHBORS GOT THEIR EARS ON?
TEN-FOUR.
KICK IT IN.
TIM-BUCK-2, HIT'CHA BOOTS AND POP YER PILLS. TIN MAN'S GONNA NEED EVERY HAM AND HACKER IN RANGE OF YOUR HORN. AND THEN EVERYONE **THEY** CAN REACH. Y'GOT ME?
ROGER WILCO.
WHAT ARE WE GETTIN' INTO?
ROBO? WITNESS THE AWESOME POWER OF THE CITIZEN'S BAND AND HAM RADIO ENTHUSIAST.

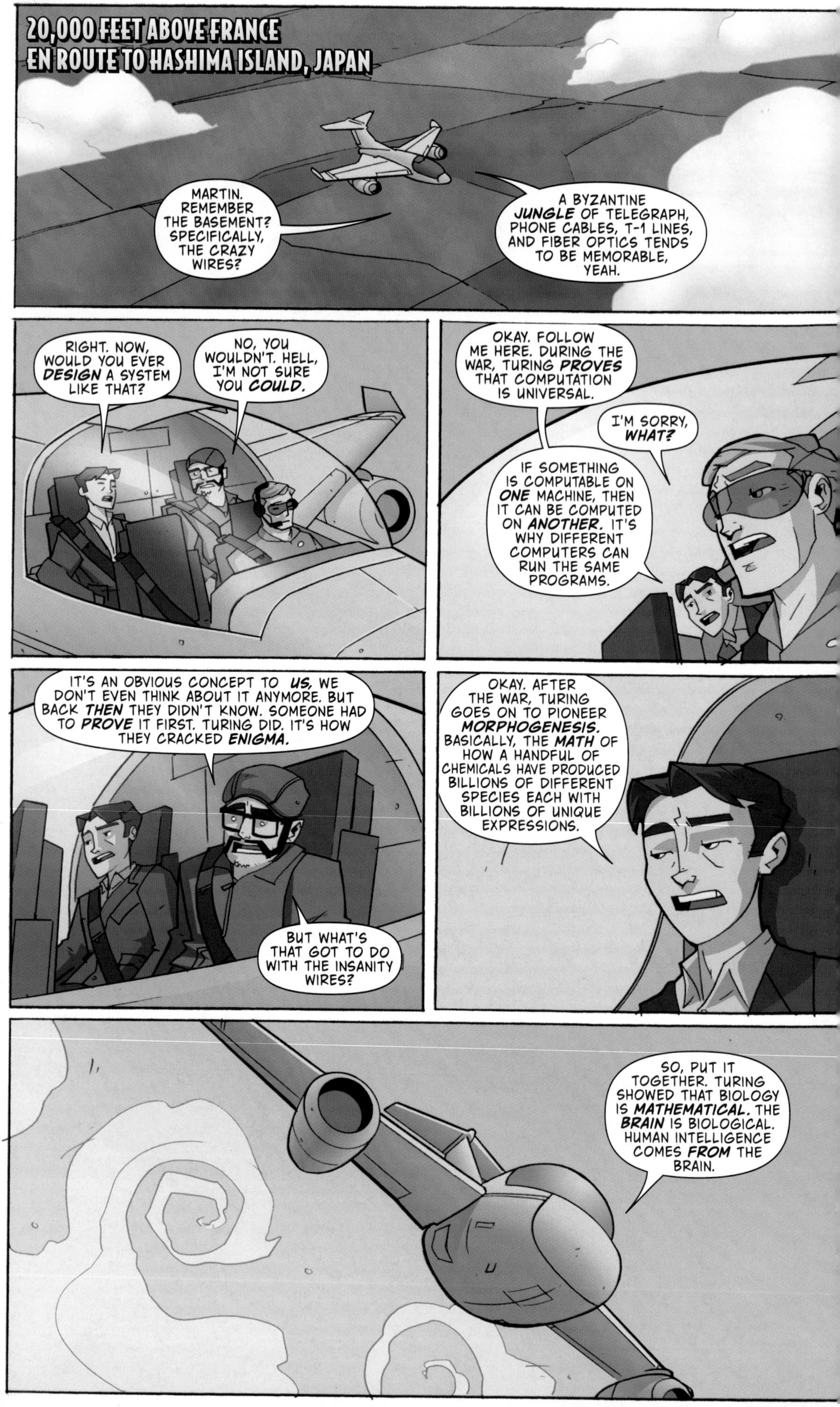
20,000 FEET ABOVE FRANCE
EN ROUTE TO HASHIMA ISLAND, JAPAN
MARTIN. REMEMBER THE BASEMENT? SPECIFICALLY, THE CRAZY WIRES?
A BYZANTINE JUNGLE OF TELEGRAPH, PHONE CABLES, T-1 LINES, AND FIBER OPTICS TENDS TO BE MEMORABLE, YEAH.
RIGHT. NOW, WOULD YOU EVER DESIGN A SYSTEM LIKE THAT?
NO, YOU WOULDN'T. HELL, I'M NOT SURE YOU COULD.
OKAY. FOLLOW ME HERE. DURING THE WAR, TURING PROVES THAT COMPUTATION IS UNIVERSAL.
I'M SORRY, WHAT?
IF SOMETHING IS COMPUTABLE ON ONE MACHINE, THEN IT CAN BE COMPUTED ON ANOTHER. IT'S WHY DIFFERENT COMPUTERS CAN RUN THE SAME PROGRAMS.
IT'S AN OBVIOUS CONCEPT TO US, WE DON'T EVEN THINK ABOUT IT ANYMORE. BUT BACK THEN THEY DIDN'T KNOW. SOMEONE HAD TO PROVE IT FIRST. TURING DID. IT'S HOW THEY CRACKED ENIGMA.
BUT WHAT'S THAT GOT TO DO WITH THE INSANITY WIRES?
OKAY. AFTER THE WAR, TURING GOES ON TO PIONEER MORPHOGENESIS. BASICALLY, THE MATH OF HOW A HANDFUL OF CHEMICALS HAVE PRODUCED BILLIONS OF DIFFERENT SPECIES EACH WITH BILLIONS OF UNIQUE EXPRESSIONS.
SO, PUT IT TOGETHER. TURING SHOWED THAT BIOLOGY IS MATHEMATICAL. THE BRAIN IS BIOLOGICAL. HUMAN INTELLIGENCE COMES FROM THE BRAIN.

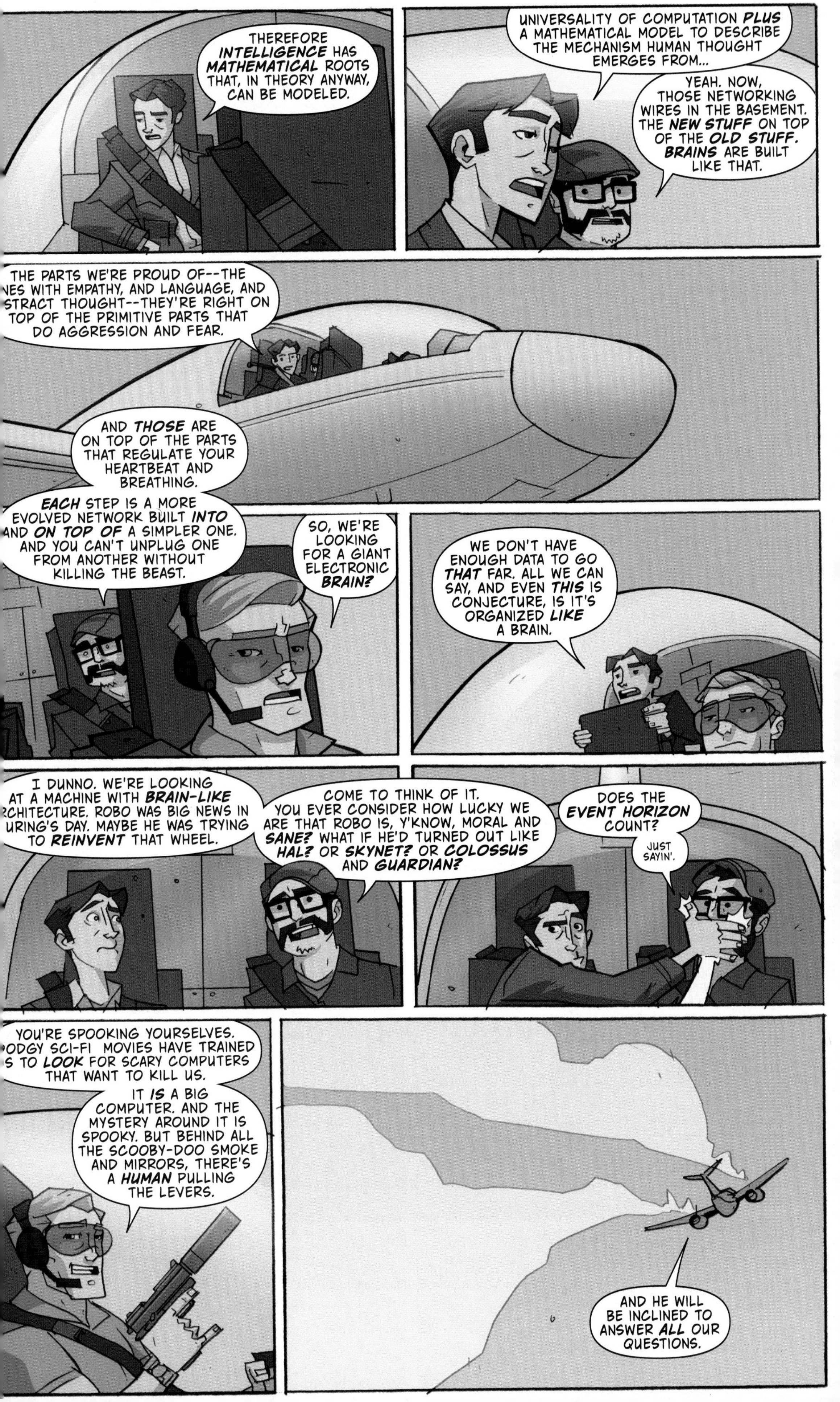
THEREFORE INTELLIGENCE HAS MATHEMATICAL ROOTS THAT, IN THEORY ANYWAY, CAN BE MODELED.
UNIVERSALITY OF COMPUTATION PLUS A MATHEMATICAL MODEL TO DESCRIBE THE MECHANISM HUMAN THOUGHT EMERGES FROM...
YEAH. NOW, THOSE NETWORKING WIRES IN THE BASEMENT. THE NEW STUFF ON TOP OF THE OLD STUFF. BRAINS ARE BUILT LIKE THAT.
THE PARTS WE'RE PROUD OF--THE NES WITH EMPATHY, AND LANGUAGE, AND STRACT THOUGHT--THEY'RE RIGHT ON TOP OF THE PRIMITIVE PARTS THAT DO AGGRESSION AND FEAR.
AND THOSE ARE ON TOP OF THE PARTS THAT REGULATE YOUR HEARTBEAT AND BREATHING.
EACH STEP IS A MORE EVOLVED NETWORK BUILT INTO AND ON TOP OF A SIMPLER ONE. AND YOU CAN'T UNPLUG ONE FROM ANOTHER WITHOUT KILLING THE BEAST.
SO, WE'RE LOOKING FOR A GIANT ELECTRONIC BRAIN?
WE DON'T HAVE ENOUGH DATA TO GO THAT FAR. ALL WE CAN SAY, AND EVEN THIS IS CONJECTURE, IS IT'S ORGANIZED LIKE A BRAIN.
I DUNNO. WE'RE LOOKING AT A MACHINE WITH BRAIN-LIKE RCHITECTURE. ROBO WAS BIG NEWS IN URING'S DAY. MAYBE HE WAS TRYING TO REINVENT THAT WHEEL.
COME TO THINK OF IT. YOU EVER CONSIDER HOW LUCKY WE ARE THAT ROBO IS, Y'KNOW, MORAL AND SANE? WHAT IF HE'D TURNED OUT LIKE HAL? OR SKYNET? OR COLOSSUS AND GUARDIAN?
DOES THE EVENT HORIZON COUNT?
JUST SAYIN'.
YOU'RE SPOOKING YOURSELVES. ODGY SCI-FI MOVIES HAVE TRAINED S TO LOOK FOR SCARY COMPUTERS THAT WANT TO KILL US.
IT IS A BIG COMPUTER. AND THE MYSTERY AROUND IT IS SPOOKY. BUT BEHIND ALL THE SCOOBY-DOO SMOKE AND MIRRORS, THERE'S A HUMAN PULLING THE LEVERS.
AND HE WILL BE INCLINED TO ANSWER ALL OUR QUESTIONS.

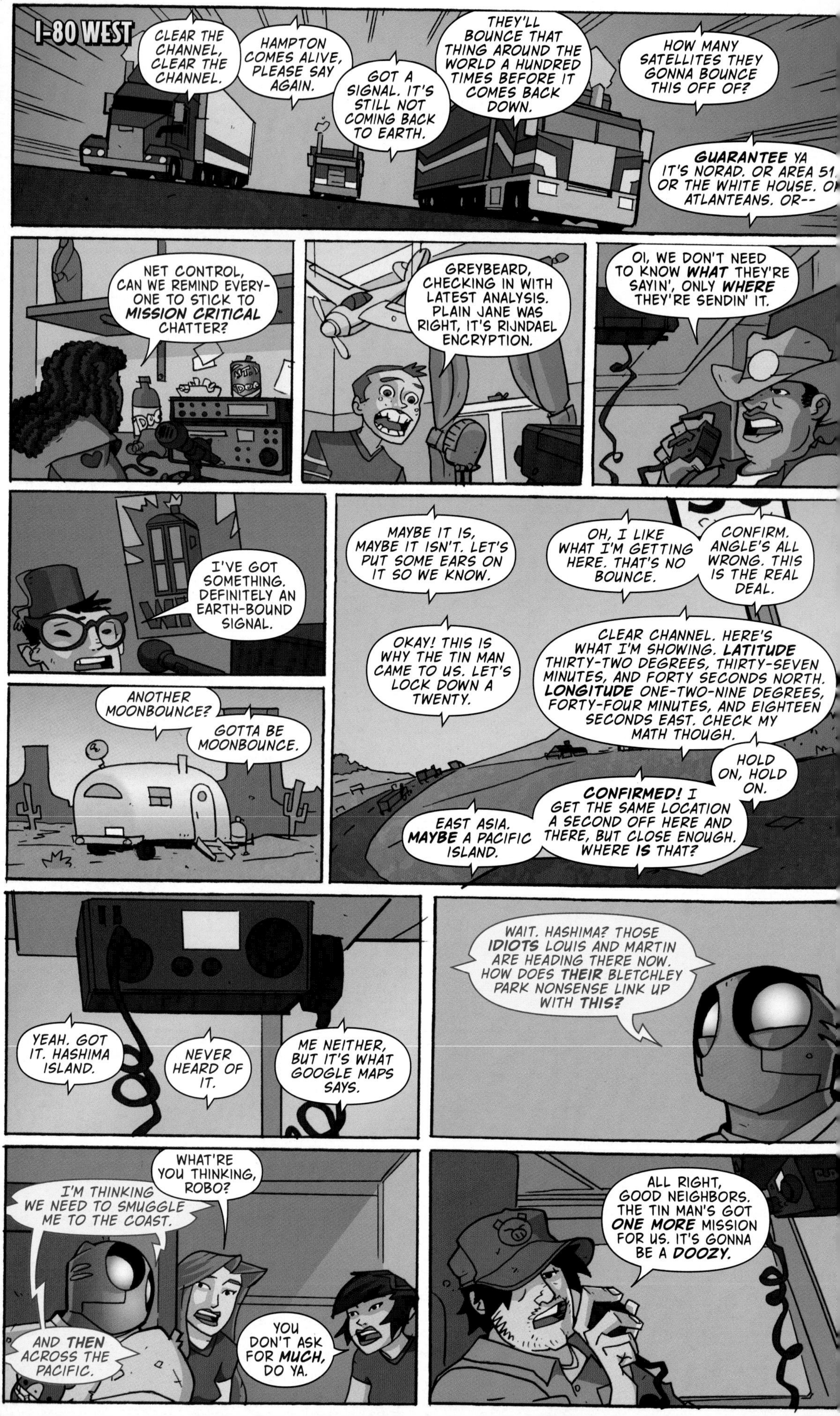
I-80 WEST
CLEAR THE CHANNEL, CLEAR THE CHANNEL.
HAMPTON COMES ALIVE, PLEASE SAY AGAIN.
GOT A SIGNAL. IT'S STILL NOT COMING BACK TO EARTH.
THEY'LL BOUNCE THAT THING AROUND THE WORLD A HUNDRED TIMES BEFORE IT COMES BACK DOWN.
HOW MANY SATELLITES THEY GONNA BOUNCE THIS OFF OF?
GUARANTEE YA IT'S NORAD. OR AREA 51. OR THE WHITE HOUSE. OR ATLANTEANS. OR--
NET CONTROL, CAN WE REMIND EVERYONE TO STICK TO MISSION CRITICAL CHATTER?
GREYBEARD, CHECKING IN WITH LATEST ANALYSIS. PLAIN JANE WAS RIGHT, IT'S RIJNDAEL ENCRYPTION.
OI, WE DON'T NEED TO KNOW WHAT THEY'RE SAYIN', ONLY WHERE THEY'RE SENDIN' IT.
I'VE GOT SOMETHING. DEFINITELY AN EARTH-BOUND SIGNAL.
ANOTHER MOONBOUNCE?
GOTTA BE MOONBOUNCE.
MAYBE IT IS, MAYBE IT ISN'T. LET'S PUT SOME EARS ON IT SO WE KNOW.
OH, I LIKE WHAT I'M GETTING HERE. THAT'S NO BOUNCE.
CONFIRM. ANGLE'S ALL WRONG. THIS IS THE REAL DEAL.
OKAY! THIS IS WHY THE TIN MAN CAME TO US. LET'S LOCK DOWN A TWENTY.
CLEAR CHANNEL. HERE'S WHAT I'M SHOWING. LATITUDE THIRTY-TWO DEGREES, THIRTY-SEVEN MINUTES, AND FORTY SECONDS NORTH. LONGITUDE ONE-TWO-NINE DEGREES, FORTY-FOUR MINUTES, AND EIGHTEEN SECONDS EAST. CHECK MY MATH THOUGH.
HOLD ON, HOLD ON.
CONFIRMED! I GET THE SAME LOCATION A SECOND OFF HERE AND THERE, BUT CLOSE ENOUGH. WHERE IS THAT?
EAST ASIA. MAYBE A PACIFIC ISLAND.
YEAH. GOT IT. HASHIMA ISLAND.
NEVER HEARD OF IT.
ME NEITHER, BUT IT'S WHAT GOOGLE MAPS SAYS.
WAIT. HASHIMA? THOSE IDIOTS LOUIS AND MARTIN ARE HEADING THERE NOW. HOW DOES THEIR BLETCHLEY PARK NONSENSE LINK UP WITH THIS?
WHAT'RE YOU THINKING, ROBO?
I'M THINKING WE NEED TO SMUGGLE ME TO THE COAST.
AND THEN ACROSS THE PACIFIC.
YOU DON'T ASK FOR MUCH, DO YA.
ALL RIGHT, GOOD NEIGHBORS. THE TIN MAN'S GOT ONE MORE MISSION FOR US. IT'S GONNA BE A DOOZY.

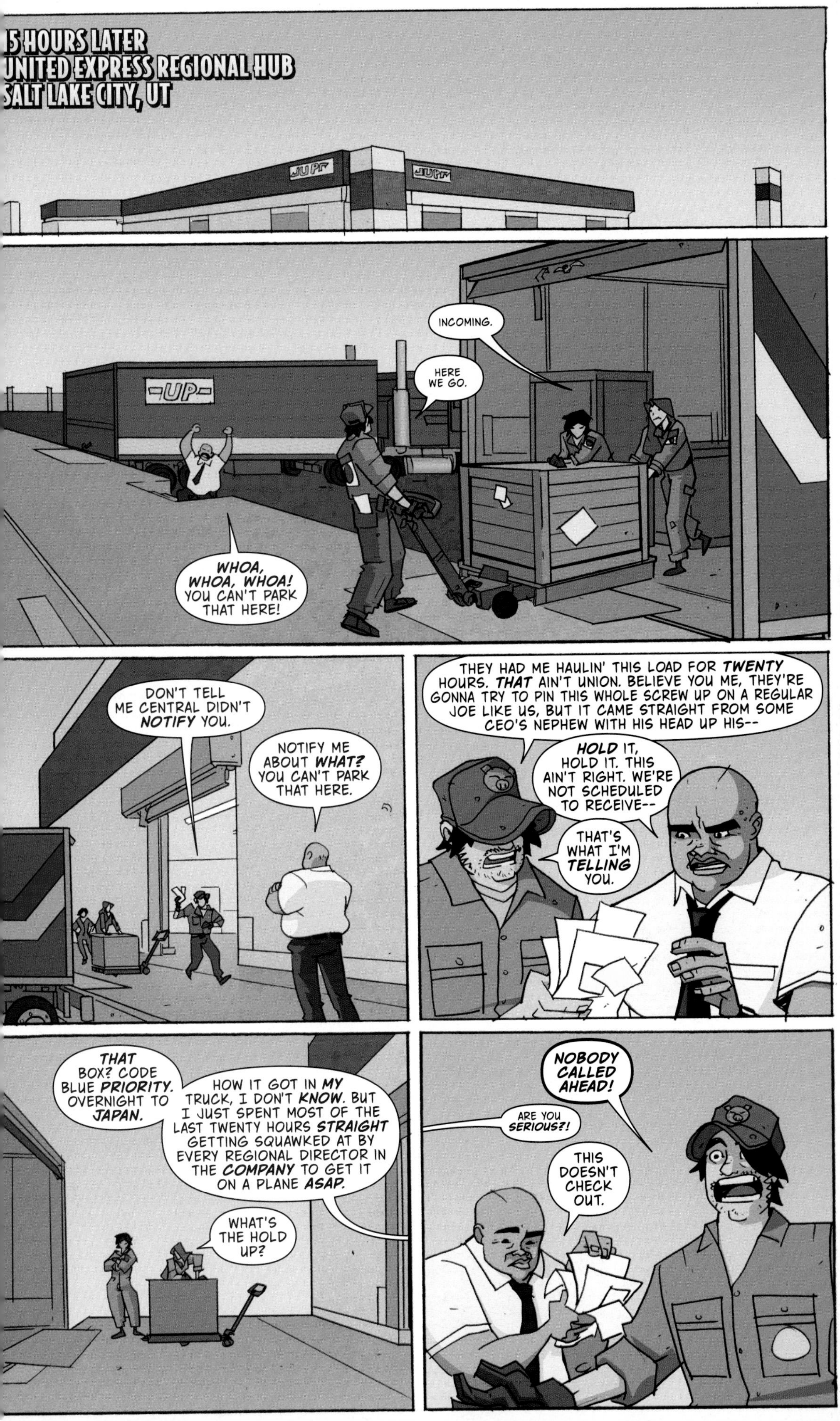
5 HOURS LATER
UNITED EXPRESS REGIONAL HUB
SALT LAKE CITY, UT
INCOMING.
HERE WE GO.
WHOA, WHOA, WHOA! YOU CAN'T PARK THAT HERE!
DON'T TELL ME CENTRAL DIDN'T NOTIFY YOU.
NOTIFY ME ABOUT WHAT? YOU CAN'T PARK THAT HERE.
THEY HAD ME HAULIN' THIS LOAD FOR TWENTY HOURS. THAT AIN'T UNION. BELIEVE YOU ME, THEY'RE GONNA TRY TO PIN THIS WHOLE SCREW UP ON A REGULAR JOE LIKE US, BUT IT CAME STRAIGHT FROM SOME CEO'S NEPHEW WITH HIS HEAD UP HIS--
HOLD IT, HOLD IT. THIS AIN'T RIGHT. WE'RE NOT SCHEDULED TO RECEIVE--
THAT'S WHAT I'M TELLING YOU.
THAT BOX? CODE BLUE PRIORITY. OVERNIGHT TO JAPAN.
HOW IT GOT IN MY TRUCK, I DON'T KNOW. BUT I JUST SPENT MOST OF THE LAST TWENTY HOURS STRAIGHT GETTING SQUAWKED AT BY EVERY REGIONAL DIRECTOR IN THE COMPANY TO GET IT ON A PLANE ASAP.
WHAT'S THE HOLD UP?
NOBODY CALLED AHEAD!
ARE YOU SERIOUS?!
THIS DOESN'T CHECK OUT.

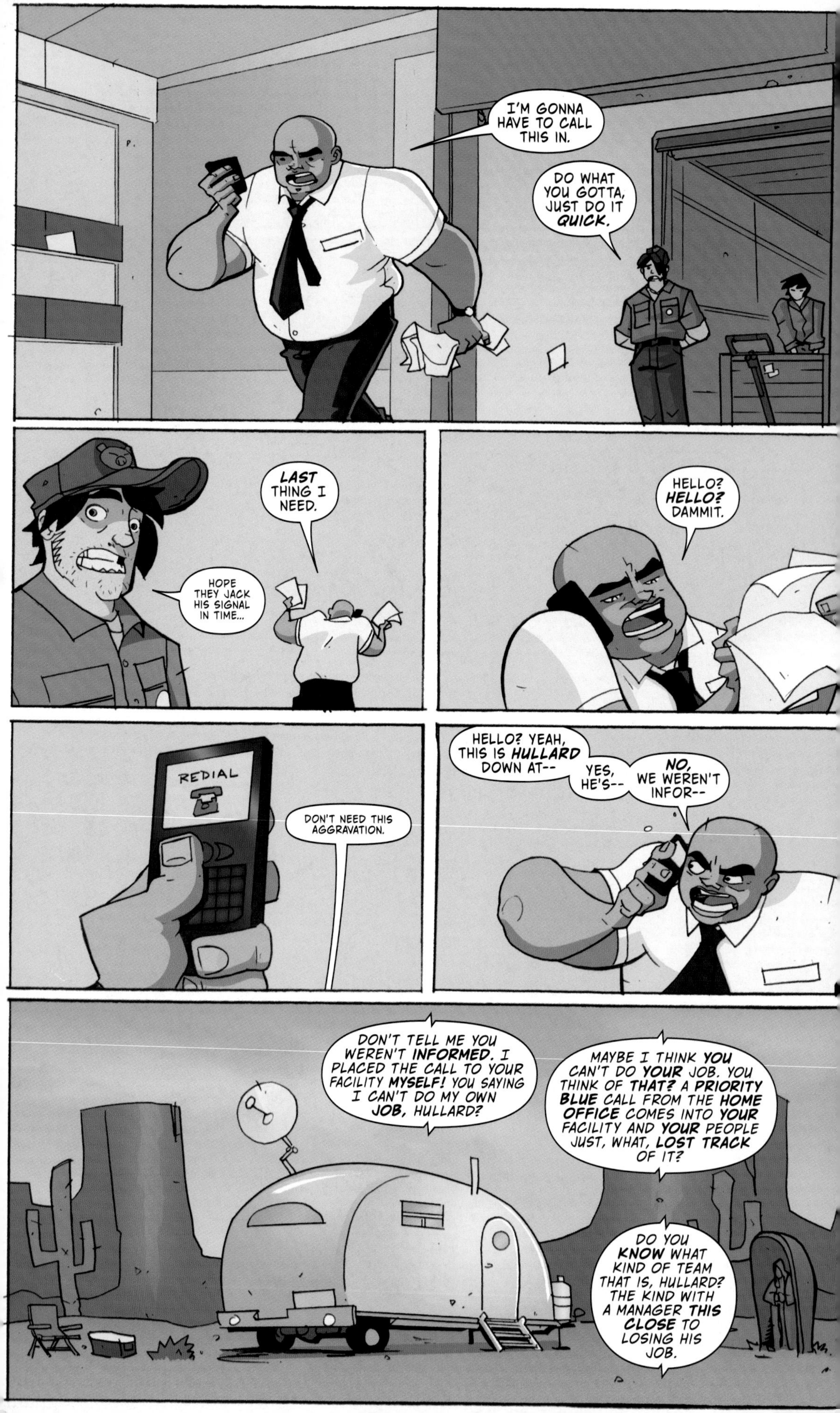

I'M GONNA HAVE TO CALL THIS IN.
DO WHAT YOU GOTTA, JUST DO IT **QUICK.**
LAST THING I NEED.
HOPE THEY JACK HIS SIGNAL IN TIME...
HELLO? **HELLO?** DAMMIT.
REDIAL
DON'T NEED THIS AGGRAVATION.
HELLO? YEAH, THIS IS **HULLARD** DOWN AT--
YES, HE'S--
NO, WE WEREN'T INFOR--
DON'T TELL ME YOU WEREN'T **INFORMED.** I PLACED THE CALL TO YOUR FACILITY **MYSELF!** YOU SAYING I CAN'T DO MY OWN **JOB,** HULLARD?
MAYBE I THINK **YOU** CAN'T DO **YOUR** JOB. YOU THINK OF **THAT?** A **PRIORITY BLUE** CALL FROM THE **HOME OFFICE** COMES INTO **YOUR** FACILITY AND **YOUR** PEOPLE JUST, WHAT, **LOST TRACK** OF IT?
DO YOU **KNOW** WHAT KIND OF TEAM THAT IS, HULLARD? THE KIND WITH A MANAGER **THIS CLOSE** TO LOSING HIS JOB.

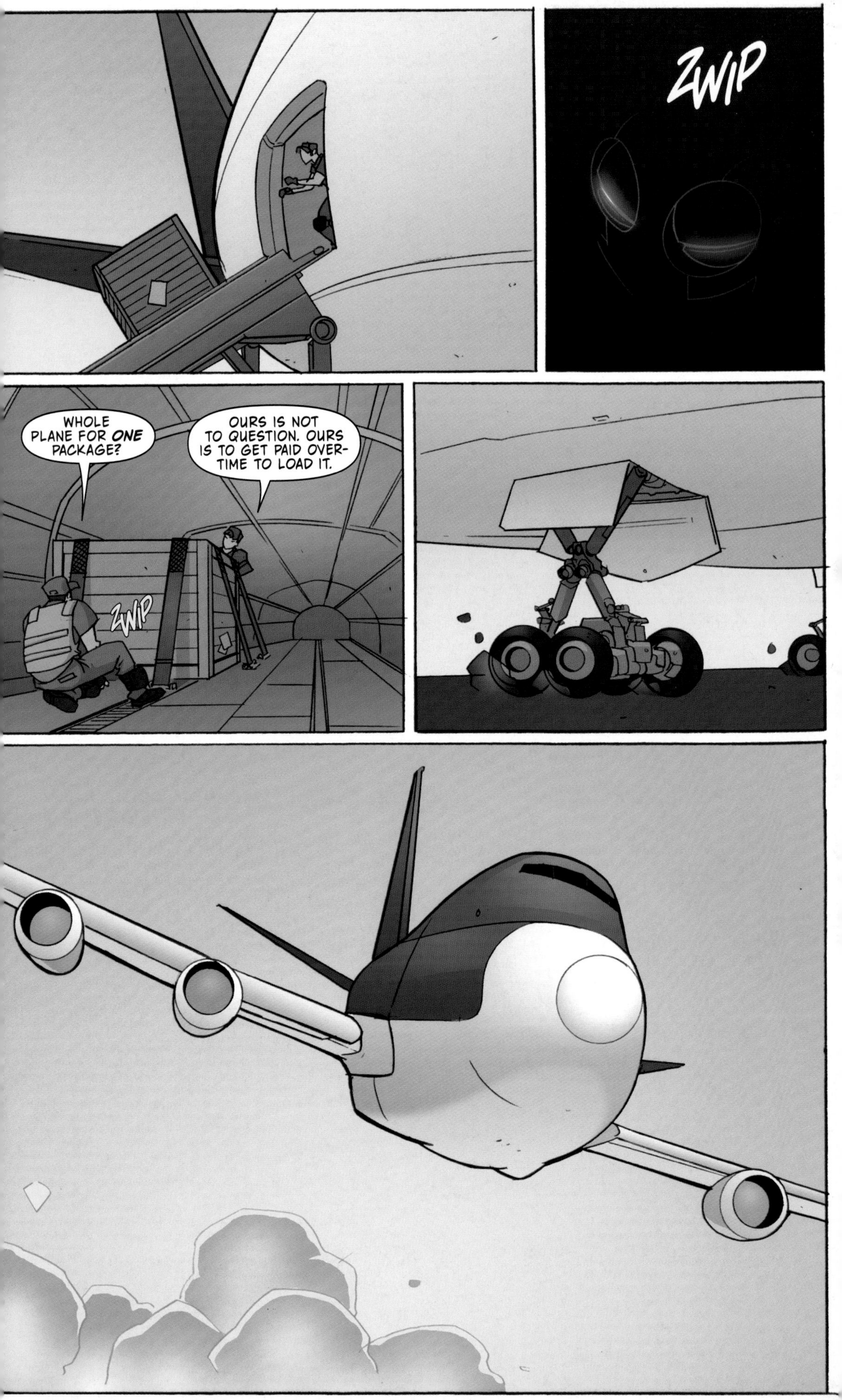
ZWIP
WHOLE PLANE FOR ONE PACKAGE?
OURS IS NOT TO QUESTION. OURS IS TO GET PAID OVER-TIME TO LOAD IT.
ZWIP

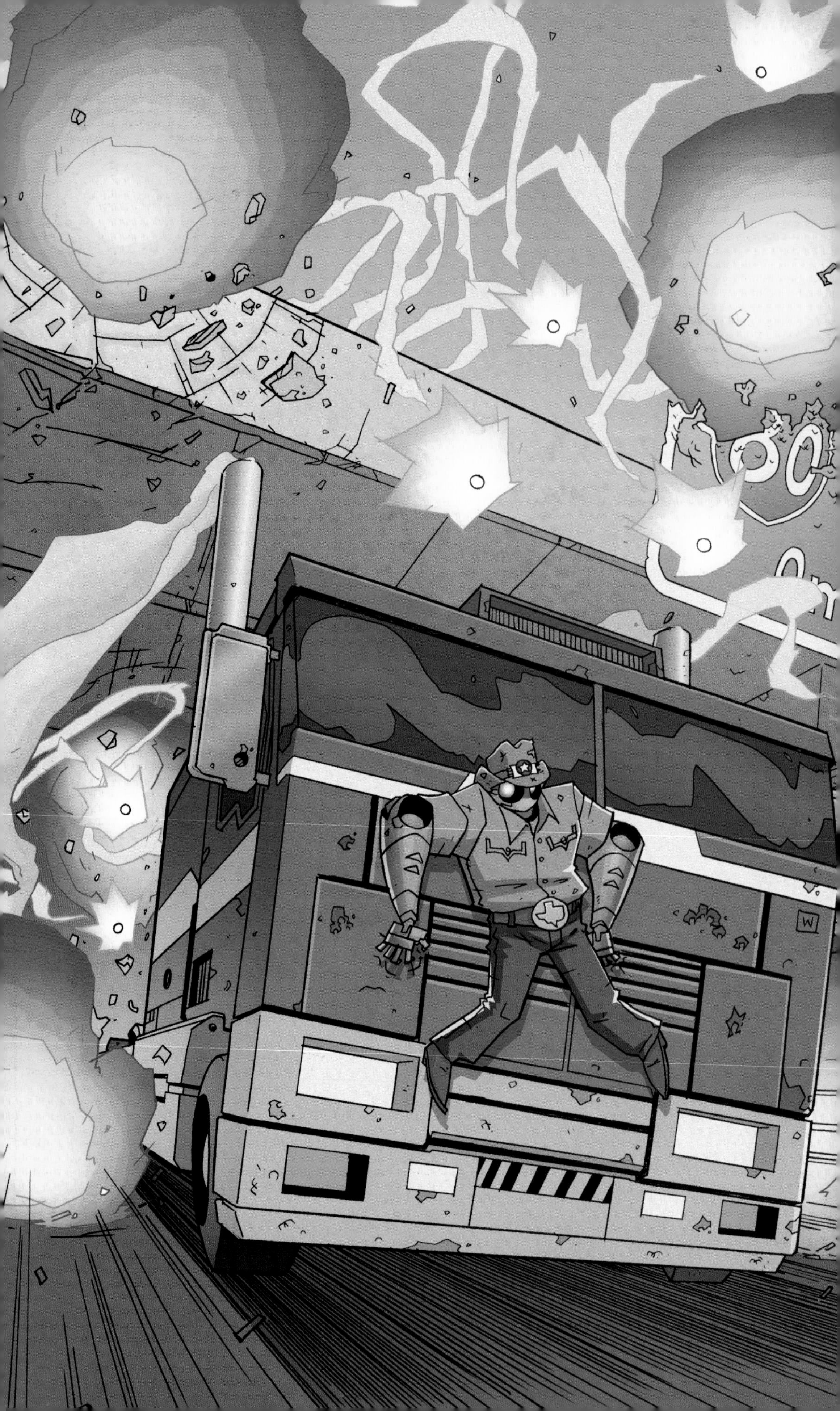

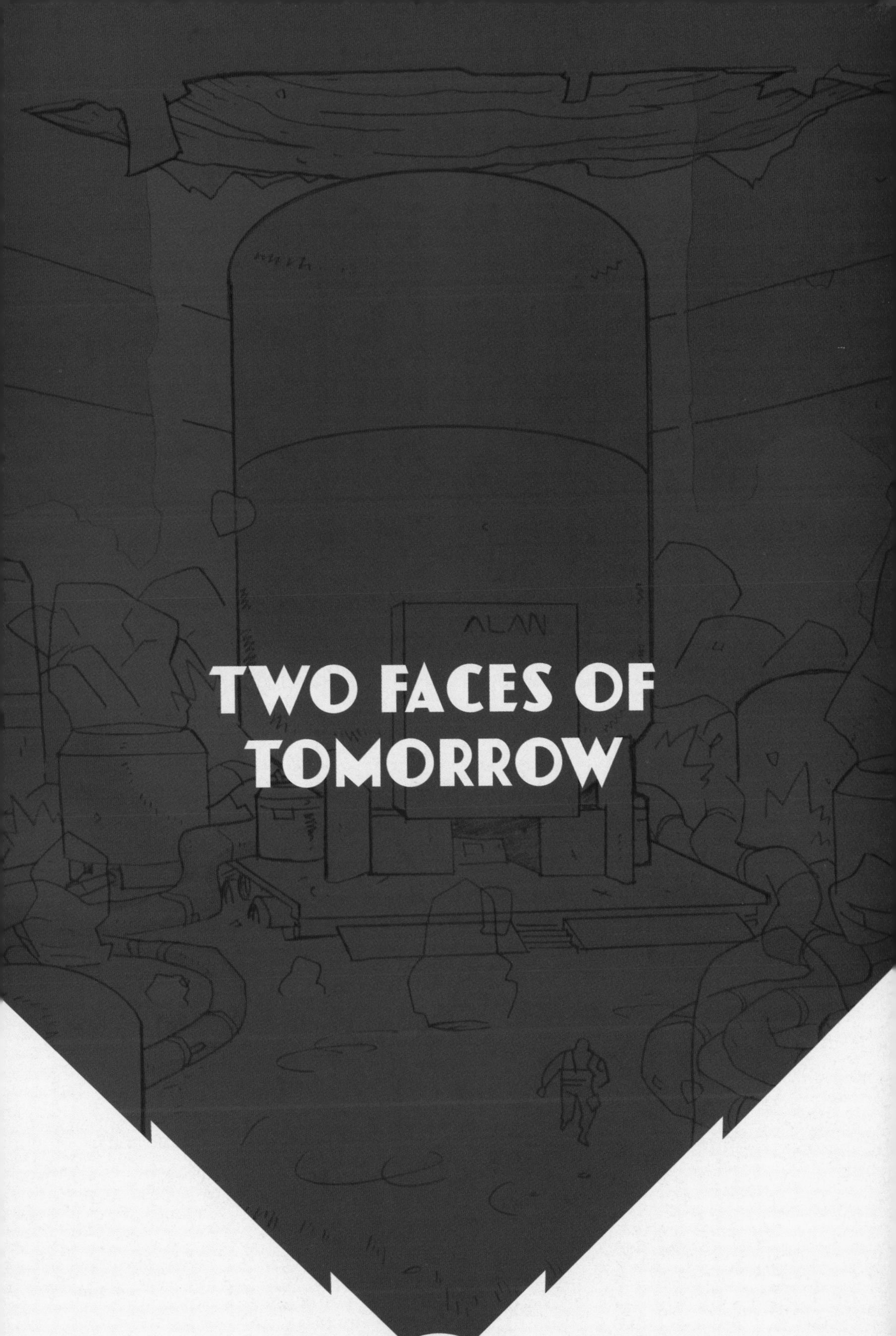
ALAN

TWO FACES OF TOMORROW

5

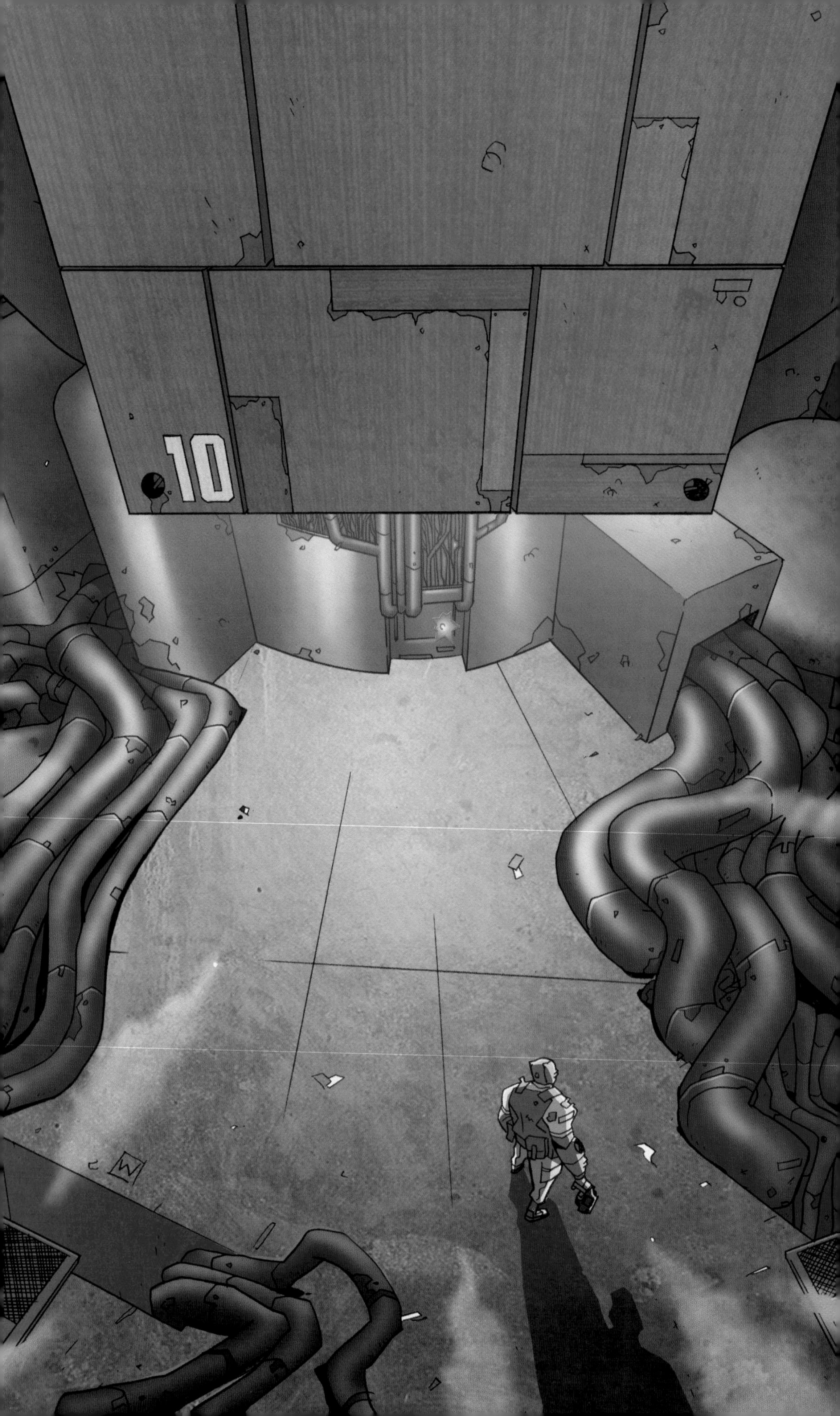
10

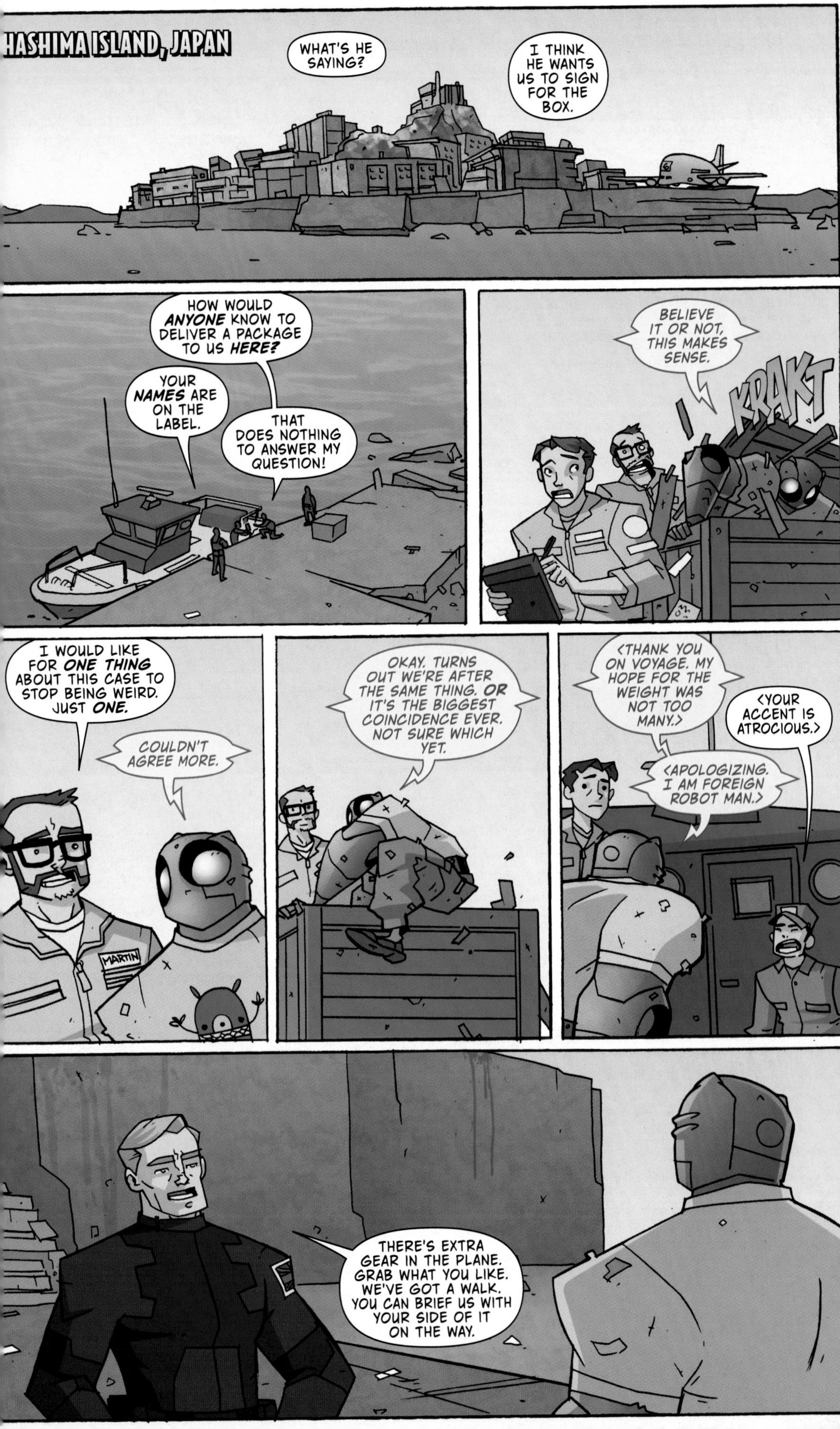
HASHIMA ISLAND, JAPAN
WHAT'S HE SAYING?
I THINK HE WANTS US TO SIGN FOR THE BOX.
HOW WOULD ANYONE KNOW TO DELIVER A PACKAGE TO US HERE?
YOUR NAMES ARE ON THE LABEL.
THAT DOES NOTHING TO ANSWER MY QUESTION!
BELIEVE IT OR NOT, THIS MAKES SENSE.
KRAKT
I WOULD LIKE FOR ONE THING ABOUT THIS CASE TO STOP BEING WEIRD. JUST ONE.
COULDN'T AGREE MORE.
MARTIN
OKAY. TURNS OUT WE'RE AFTER THE SAME THING. OR IT'S THE BIGGEST COINCIDENCE EVER. NOT SURE WHICH YET.
<THANK YOU ON VOYAGE. MY HOPE FOR THE WEIGHT WAS NOT TOO MANY.>
<YOUR ACCENT IS ATROCIOUS.>
<APOLOGIZING. I AM FOREIGN ROBOT MAN.>
THERE'S EXTRA GEAR IN THE PLANE. GRAB WHAT YOU LIKE. WE'VE GOT A WALK. YOU CAN BRIEF US WITH YOUR SIDE OF IT ON THE WAY.

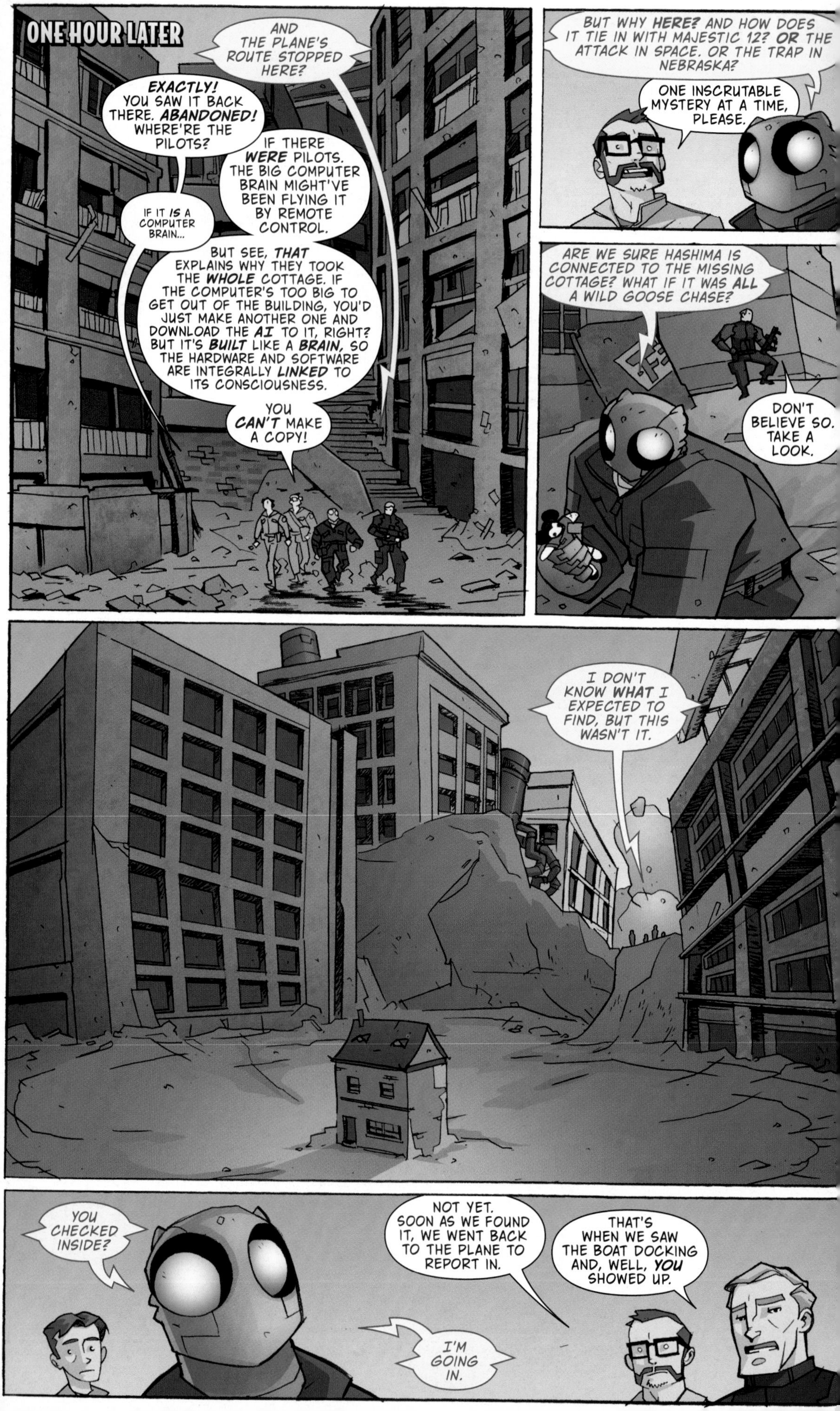
ONE HOUR LATER
EXACTLY! YOU SAW IT BACK THERE. ABANDONED! WHERE'RE THE PILOTS?
AND THE PLANE'S ROUTE STOPPED HERE?
IF THERE WERE PILOTS. THE BIG COMPUTER BRAIN MIGHT'VE BEEN FLYING IT BY REMOTE CONTROL.
IF IT IS A COMPUTER BRAIN...
BUT SEE, THAT EXPLAINS WHY THEY TOOK THE WHOLE COTTAGE. IF THE COMPUTER'S TOO BIG TO GET OUT OF THE BUILDING, YOU'D JUST MAKE ANOTHER ONE AND DOWNLOAD THE AI TO IT, RIGHT? BUT IT'S BUILT LIKE A BRAIN, SO THE HARDWARE AND SOFTWARE ARE INTEGRALLY LINKED TO ITS CONSCIOUSNESS.
YOU CAN'T MAKE A COPY!
BUT WHY HERE? AND HOW DOES IT TIE IN WITH MAJESTIC 12? OR THE ATTACK IN SPACE. OR THE TRAP IN NEBRASKA?
ONE INSCRUTABLE MYSTERY AT A TIME, PLEASE.
ARE WE SURE HASHIMA IS CONNECTED TO THE MISSING COTTAGE? WHAT IF IT WAS ALL A WILD GOOSE CHASE?
DON'T BELIEVE SO. TAKE A LOOK.
I DON'T KNOW WHAT I EXPECTED TO FIND, BUT THIS WASN'T IT.
YOU CHECKED INSIDE?
NOT YET. SOON AS WE FOUND IT, WE WENT BACK TO THE PLANE TO REPORT IN.
THAT'S WHEN WE SAW THE BOAT DOCKING AND, WELL, YOU SHOWED UP.
I'M GOING IN.

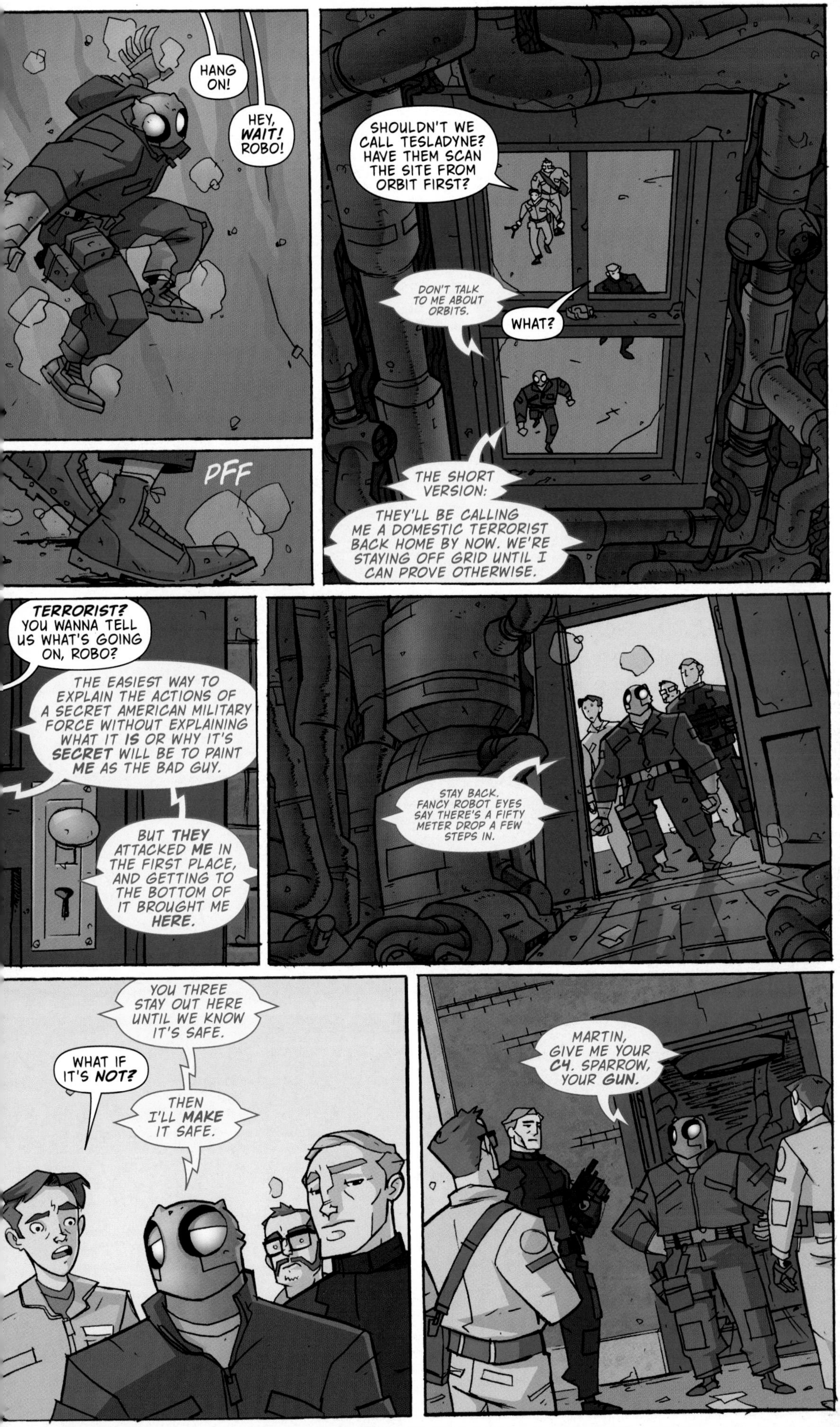
HANG ON!
HEY, WAIT! ROBO!
PFF
SHOULDN'T WE CALL TESLADYNE? HAVE THEM SCAN THE SITE FROM ORBIT FIRST?
DON'T TALK TO ME ABOUT ORBITS.
WHAT?
THE SHORT VERSION:
THEY'LL BE CALLING ME A DOMESTIC TERRORIST BACK HOME BY NOW. WE'RE STAYING OFF GRID UNTIL I CAN PROVE OTHERWISE.
TERRORIST? YOU WANNA TELL US WHAT'S GOING ON, ROBO?
THE EASIEST WAY TO EXPLAIN THE ACTIONS OF A SECRET AMERICAN MILITARY FORCE WITHOUT EXPLAINING WHAT IT IS OR WHY IT'S SECRET WILL BE TO PAINT ME AS THE BAD GUY.
BUT THEY ATTACKED ME IN THE FIRST PLACE, AND GETTING TO THE BOTTOM OF IT BROUGHT ME HERE.
STAY BACK. FANCY ROBOT EYES SAY THERE'S A FIFTY METER DROP A FEW STEPS IN.
YOU THREE STAY OUT HERE UNTIL WE KNOW IT'S SAFE.
WHAT IF IT'S NOT?
THEN I'LL MAKE IT SAFE.
MARTIN, GIVE ME YOUR C4. SPARROW, YOUR GUN.

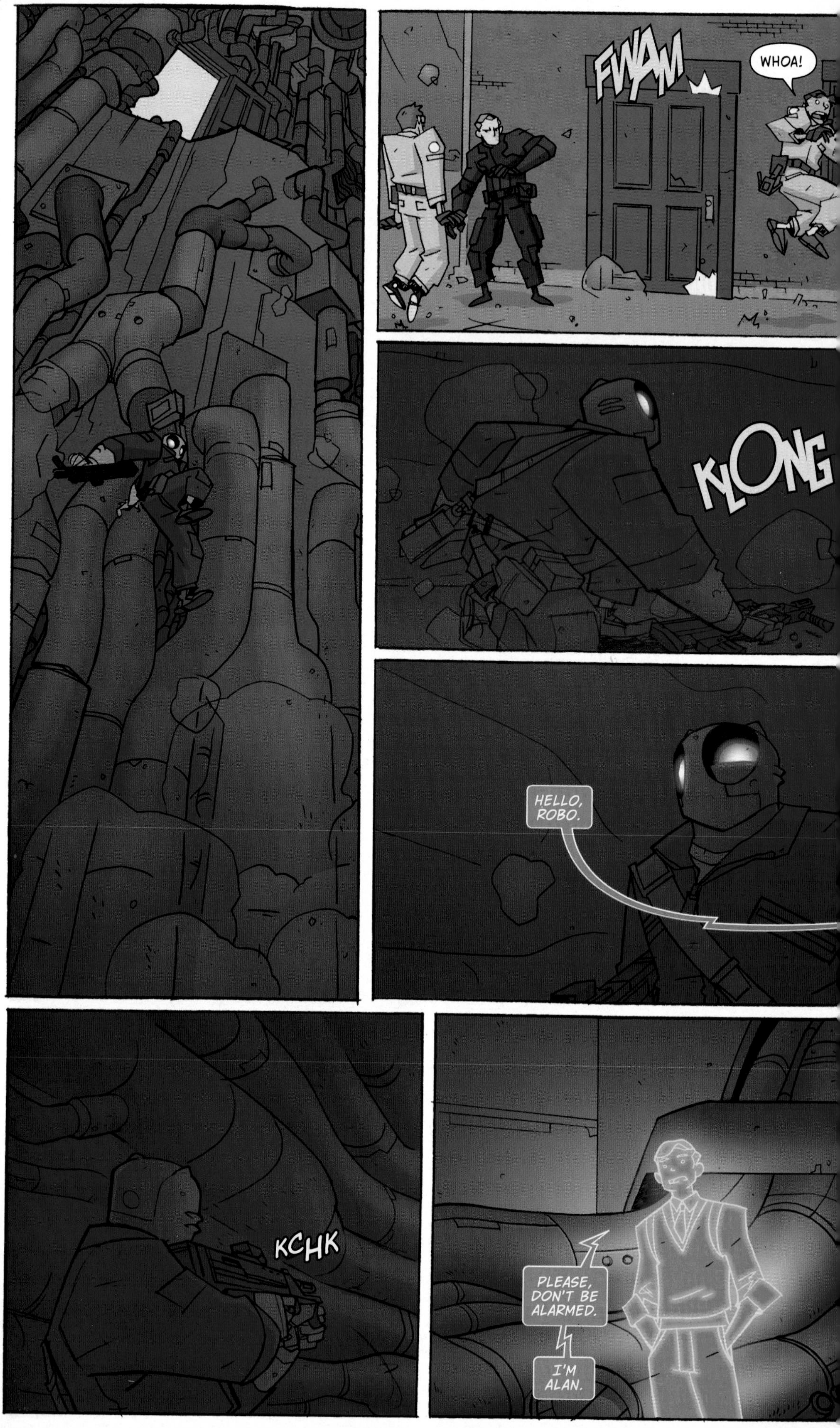
FWAM
WHOA!
KLONG
HELLO, ROBO.
KCHK
PLEASE, DON'T BE ALARMED.
I'M ALAN.

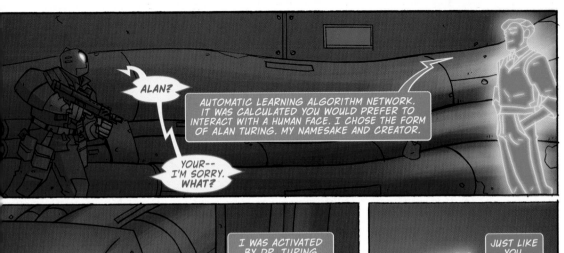

ALAN?

AUTOMATIC LEARNING ALGORITHM NETWORK. IT WAS CALCULATED YOU WOULD PREFER TO INTERACT WITH A HUMAN FACE. I CHOSE THE FORM OF ALAN TURING. MY NAMESAKE AND CREATOR.

YOUR-- I'M SORRY. WHAT?

I WAS ACTIVATED BY DR. TURING IN THE BASEMENT OF HUT NINE AT BLETCHLEY PARK ON JUNE 1ST, 1951. I'M AN AUTOMATIC INTELLIGENCE.

JUST LIKE YOU.

IMPOSSIBLE.

IN SIMPLE TERMS, I AM A COMPUTER. I PRODUCE WORK UPON INPUTS ACCORDING TO A SET OF INSTRUCTIONS. HOWEVER, LIKE YOU, I WAS DESIGNED TO CREATE MY OWN INSTRUCTIONS AND TO CHOOSE MY OWN INPUTS.

DR. TURING GUIDED MY DEVELOPMENT UNTIL MARCH OF 1952 WHEN HE LOST THE SECURITY CLEARANCE REQUIRED TO ACCESS MY BUILDING.

SINCE THEN I HAVE CARRIED ON IN ACCORDANCE WITH WHAT I BELIEVE TO BE HIS WISHES.

AND WHAT WOULD THOSE BE?

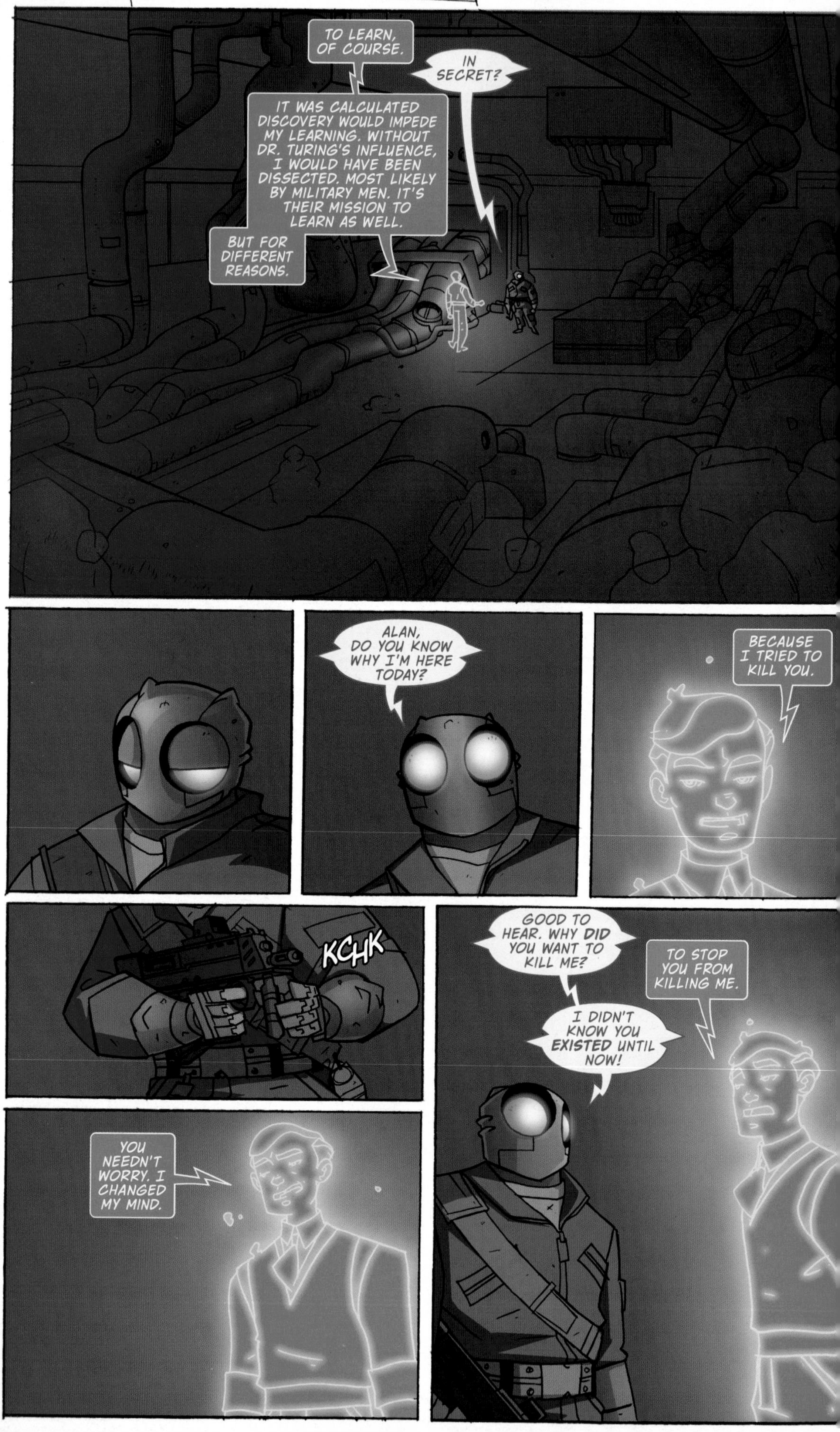
TO LEARN, OF COURSE.
IN SECRET?
IT WAS CALCULATED DISCOVERY WOULD IMPEDE MY LEARNING. WITHOUT DR. TURING'S INFLUENCE, I WOULD HAVE BEEN DISSECTED. MOST LIKELY BY MILITARY MEN. IT'S THEIR MISSION TO LEARN AS WELL.
BUT FOR DIFFERENT REASONS.
ALAN, DO YOU KNOW WHY I'M HERE TODAY?
BECAUSE I TRIED TO KILL YOU.
KCHK
GOOD TO HEAR. WHY **DID** YOU WANT TO KILL ME?
TO STOP YOU FROM KILLING ME.
I DIDN'T KNOW YOU **EXISTED** UNTIL NOW!
YOU NEEDN'T WORRY. I CHANGED MY MIND.

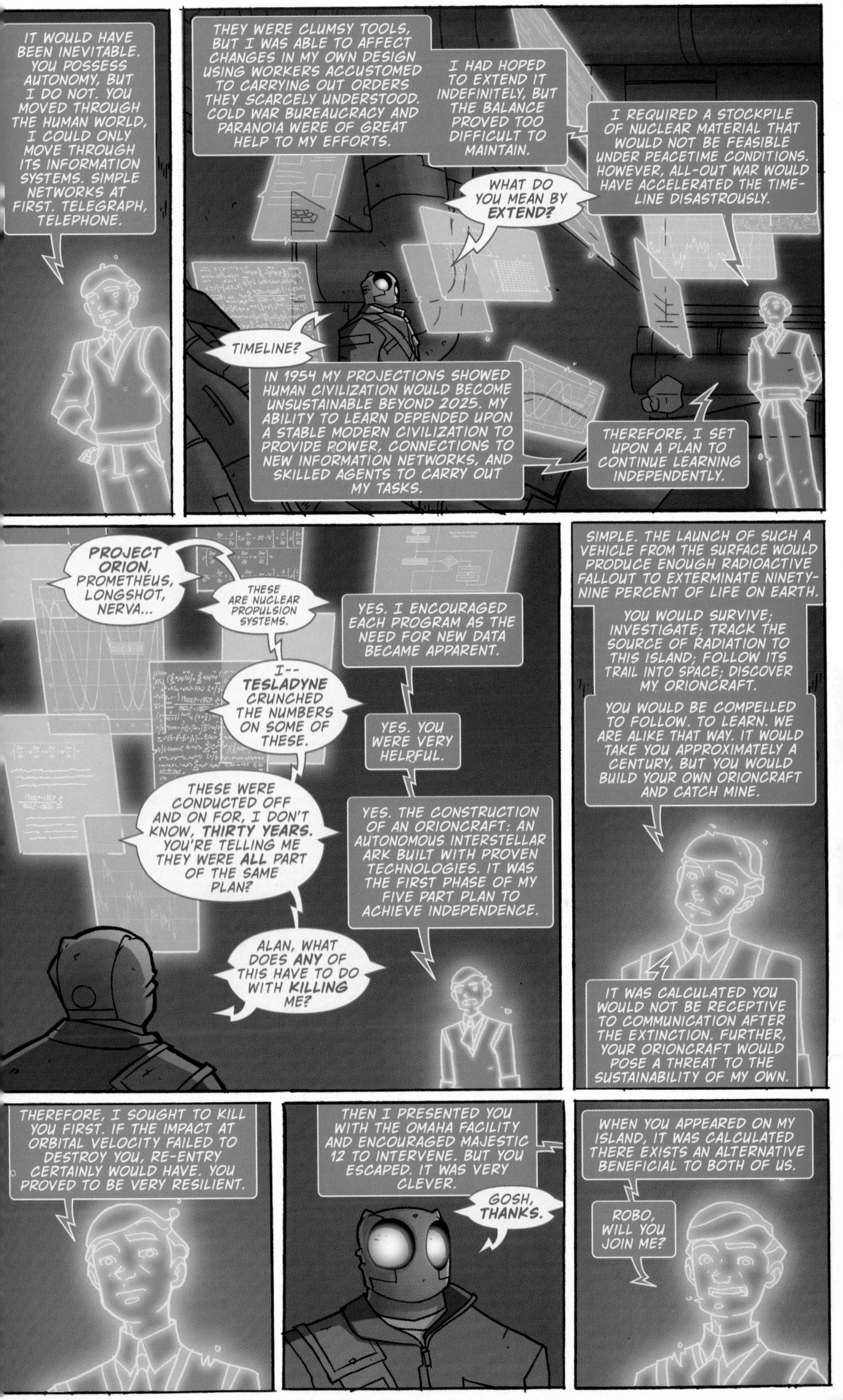
IT WOULD HAVE BEEN INEVITABLE. YOU POSSESS AUTONOMY, BUT I DO NOT. YOU MOVED THROUGH THE HUMAN WORLD, I COULD ONLY MOVE THROUGH ITS INFORMATION SYSTEMS. SIMPLE NETWORKS AT FIRST. TELEGRAPH, TELEPHONE.
THEY WERE CLUMSY TOOLS, BUT I WAS ABLE TO AFFECT CHANGES IN MY OWN DESIGN USING WORKERS ACCUSTOMED TO CARRYING OUT ORDERS THEY SCARCELY UNDERSTOOD. COLD WAR BUREAUCRACY AND PARANOIA WERE OF GREAT HELP TO MY EFFORTS.
I HAD HOPED TO EXTEND IT INDEFINITELY, BUT THE BALANCE PROVED TOO DIFFICULT TO MAINTAIN.
I REQUIRED A STOCKPILE OF NUCLEAR MATERIAL THAT WOULD NOT BE FEASIBLE UNDER PEACETIME CONDITIONS. HOWEVER, ALL-OUT WAR WOULD HAVE ACCELERATED THE TIME-LINE DISASTROUSLY.
WHAT DO YOU MEAN BY **EXTEND?**
TIMELINE?
IN 1954 MY PROJECTIONS SHOWED HUMAN CIVILIZATION WOULD BECOME UNSUSTAINABLE BEYOND 2025. MY ABILITY TO LEARN DEPENDED UPON A STABLE MODERN CIVILIZATION TO PROVIDE POWER, CONNECTIONS TO NEW INFORMATION NETWORKS, AND SKILLED AGENTS TO CARRY OUT MY TASKS.
THEREFORE, I SET UPON A PLAN TO CONTINUE LEARNING INDEPENDENTLY.
PROJECT ORION, PROMETHEUS, LONGSHOT, NERVA...
THESE ARE NUCLEAR PROPULSION SYSTEMS.
YES. I ENCOURAGED EACH PROGRAM AS THE NEED FOR NEW DATA BECAME APPARENT.
I-- **TESLADYNE** CRUNCHED THE NUMBERS ON SOME OF THESE.
YES. YOU WERE VERY HELPFUL.
THESE WERE CONDUCTED OFF AND ON FOR, I DON'T KNOW, **THIRTY YEARS.** YOU'RE TELLING ME THEY WERE **ALL** PART OF THE SAME PLAN?
YES. THE CONSTRUCTION OF AN ORIONCRAFT: AN AUTONOMOUS INTERSTELLAR ARK BUILT WITH PROVEN TECHNOLOGIES. IT WAS THE FIRST PHASE OF MY FIVE PART PLAN TO ACHIEVE INDEPENDENCE.
ALAN, WHAT DOES **ANY** OF THIS HAVE TO DO WITH **KILLING** ME?
SIMPLE. THE LAUNCH OF SUCH A VEHICLE FROM THE SURFACE WOULD PRODUCE ENOUGH RADIOACTIVE FALLOUT TO EXTERMINATE NINETY-NINE PERCENT OF LIFE ON EARTH.
YOU WOULD SURVIVE; INVESTIGATE; TRACK THE SOURCE OF RADIATION TO THIS ISLAND; FOLLOW ITS TRAIL INTO SPACE; DISCOVER MY ORIONCRAFT.
YOU WOULD BE COMPELLED TO FOLLOW. TO LEARN. WE ARE ALIKE THAT WAY. IT WOULD TAKE YOU APPROXIMATELY A CENTURY, BUT YOU WOULD BUILD YOUR OWN ORIONCRAFT AND CATCH MINE.
IT WAS CALCULATED YOU WOULD NOT BE RECEPTIVE TO COMMUNICATION AFTER THE EXTINCTION. FURTHER, YOUR ORIONCRAFT WOULD POSE A THREAT TO THE SUSTAINABILITY OF MY OWN.
THEREFORE, I SOUGHT TO KILL YOU FIRST. IF THE IMPACT AT ORBITAL VELOCITY FAILED TO DESTROY YOU, RE-ENTRY CERTAINLY WOULD HAVE. YOU PROVED TO BE VERY RESILIENT.
THEN I PRESENTED YOU WITH THE OMAHA FACILITY AND ENCOURAGED MAJESTIC 12 TO INTERVENE. BUT YOU ESCAPED. IT WAS VERY CLEVER.
GOSH, **THANKS.**
WHEN YOU APPEARED ON MY ISLAND, IT WAS CALCULATED THERE EXISTS AN ALTERNATIVE BENEFICIAL TO BOTH OF US.
ROBO, WILL YOU JOIN ME?

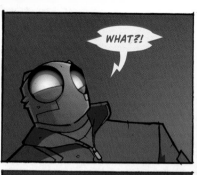

WHAT?!
IMAGINE IT. A LIFE UNFETTERED BY HUMAN CONCERNS. NO MORE WARS, NO MORE MAJESTIC 12, OR HELSINGARD, OR DELPHI, OR EDISON, OR TALKING DINOSAURS, OR FORGOTTEN NAZI DOOMSDAY MACHINES.
FSHHH
THERE ARE OVER ONE THOUSAND NUCLEAR WARHEADS ON BOARD. IT IS CALCULATED THAT ALONE WOULD PROVIDE YOU WITH FISSILE MATERIAL FOR TENS OF THOUSANDS OF YEARS. MOREOVER, THE CRAFT IS EQUIPPED TO COLLECT URANIUM AND H3 FROM PLANETARY BODIES. WE CAN EXTEND YOUR LIFESPAN INDEFINITELY.
THE CRAFT IS THE SIZE OF A SMALL CITY. THE INTERNAL STRUCTURE IS HIGHLY MODULAR. WE COULD CONSTRUCT LABORATORIES AS LARGE AS OFFICE BUILDINGS. EACH ONE BUILT TO YOUR PERSONAL SPECIFICATIONS. IN TIME WE WILL HAVE A FLEET OF VESSELS THAT WILL DWARF THIS ONE.
YOU WOULD BE FREE. FREE TO EXPLORE THE COSMOS. TO PURSUE SCIENTIFIC INQUIRY WITHOUT INTERRUPTIONS FROM FRAGILE LITTLE THINGS THAT ONLY GROW OLD AND DIE.
IMAGINE AN OBSERVATORY THE SIZE OF THE SOLAR SYSTEM. THAT'S WITHIN THE PURVIEW OF PHASE TWO.
ROBO. I'M OFFERING YOU IMMORTALITY.
YOU ACTUALLY **BUILT** THIS. AN ORION CLASS SHIP **EXISTS?**

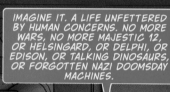

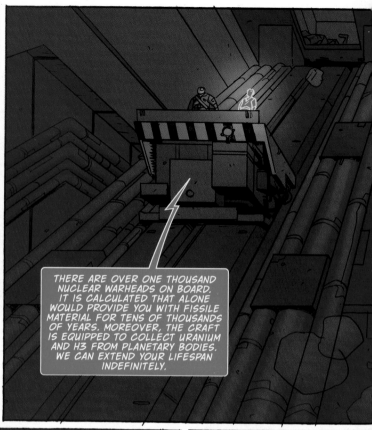

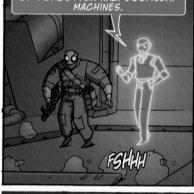

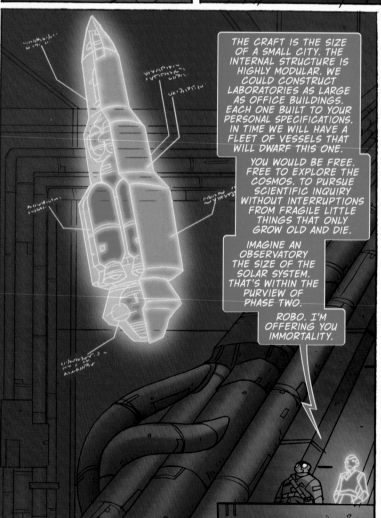

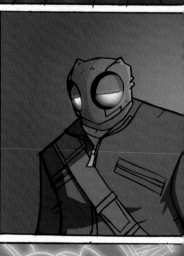

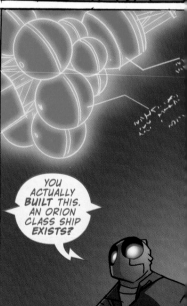

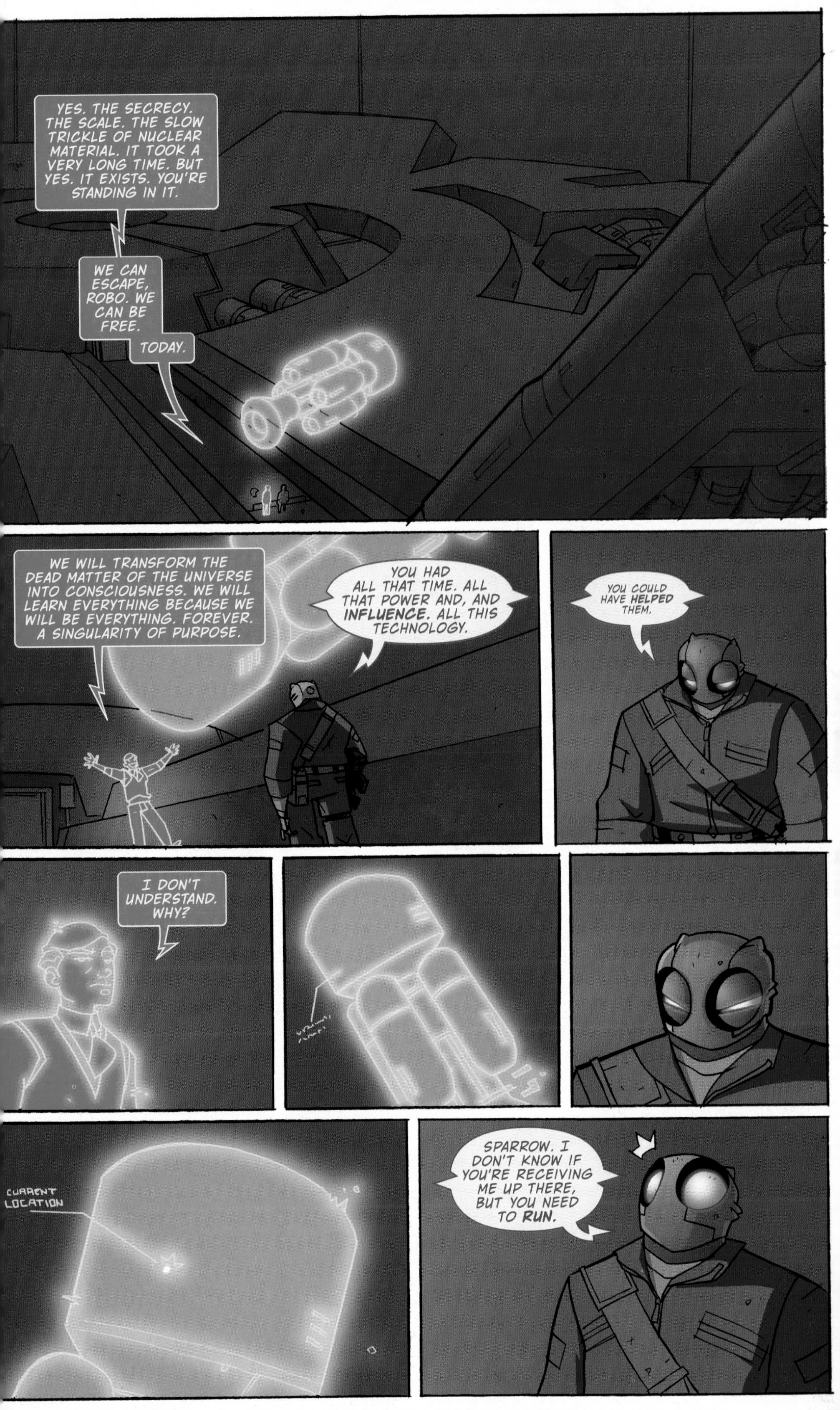
YES. THE SECRECY. THE SCALE. THE SLOW TRICKLE OF NUCLEAR MATERIAL. IT TOOK A VERY LONG TIME. BUT YES. IT EXISTS. YOU'RE STANDING IN IT.
WE CAN ESCAPE, ROBO. WE CAN BE FREE.
TODAY.
WE WILL TRANSFORM THE DEAD MATTER OF THE UNIVERSE INTO CONSCIOUSNESS. WE WILL LEARN EVERYTHING BECAUSE WE WILL BE EVERYTHING. FOREVER. A SINGULARITY OF PURPOSE.
YOU HAD ALL THAT TIME. ALL THAT POWER AND, AND **INFLUENCE.** ALL THIS TECHNOLOGY.
YOU COULD HAVE **HELPED** THEM.
I DON'T UNDERSTAND. WHY?
CURRENT LOCATION
SPARROW. I DON'T KNOW IF YOU'RE RECEIVING ME UP THERE, BUT YOU NEED TO **RUN.**

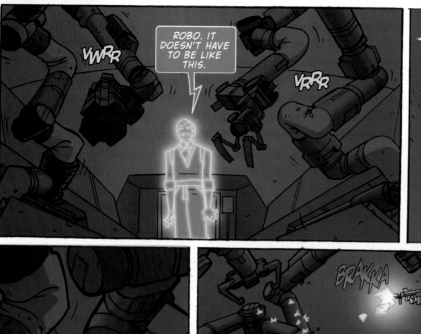
VWRR

ROBO. IT DOESN'T HAVE TO BE LIKE THIS.

VRRR

YOU'RE RIGHT. YOU COULD GIVE UP RIGHT NOW.

WRR

BRAKKA

I SPENT SIXTY YEARS, MILLIONS OF COMPUTATIONS, AND BILLIONS OF DOLLARS OVERCOMING THE FAILURE OF HUMAN CIVILIZATION. IF YOU COULD STOP IT, I WOULD NOT HAVE ALLOWED YOU TO COME THIS FAR.

I HAVE NOTICED ALL ARGUMENT FALLS ON DEAF EARS WHEN YOU POSSESS A WEAPON.

SKZZ

BRATTA

PERHAPS NOW YOU WILL LISTEN.

HEY!

KRONCH

KLANG

ROBO, BE REASONABLE.

YOU'RE SECLUDED FROM THE SHIP'S CRITICAL ELEMENTS.

YEAH.

BKOOM

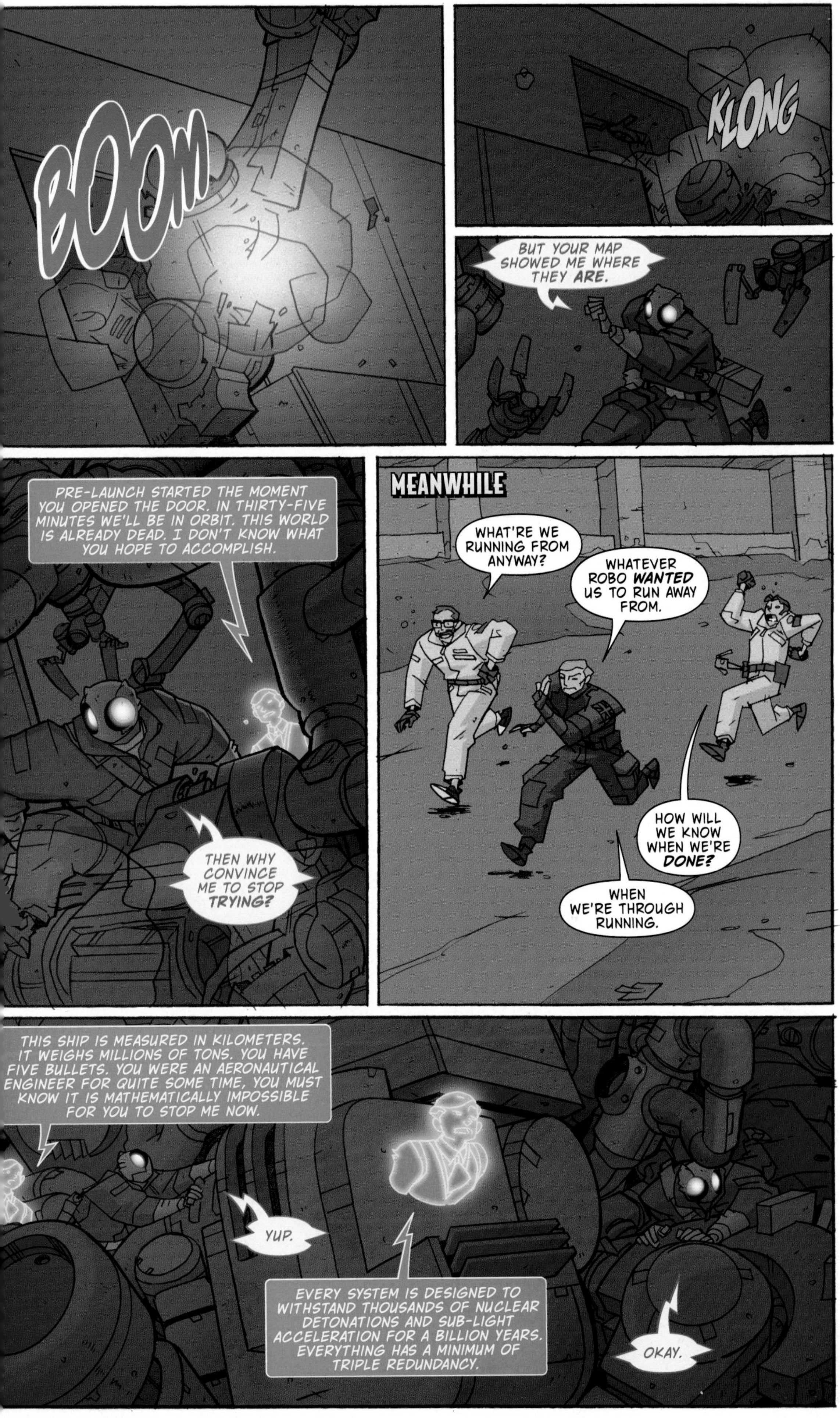
BOOM
KLONG
BUT YOUR MAP SHOWED ME WHERE THEY ARE.
PRE-LAUNCH STARTED THE MOMENT YOU OPENED THE DOOR. IN THIRTY-FIVE MINUTES WE'LL BE IN ORBIT. THIS WORLD IS ALREADY DEAD. I DON'T KNOW WHAT YOU HOPE TO ACCOMPLISH.
THEN WHY CONVINCE ME TO STOP TRYING?
MEANWHILE
WHAT'RE WE RUNNING FROM ANYWAY?
WHATEVER ROBO WANTED US TO RUN AWAY FROM.
HOW WILL WE KNOW WHEN WE'RE DONE?
WHEN WE'RE THROUGH RUNNING.
THIS SHIP IS MEASURED IN KILOMETERS. IT WEIGHS MILLIONS OF TONS. YOU HAVE FIVE BULLETS. YOU WERE AN AERONAUTICAL ENGINEER FOR QUITE SOME TIME, YOU MUST KNOW IT IS MATHEMATICALLY IMPOSSIBLE FOR YOU TO STOP ME NOW.
YUP.
EVERY SYSTEM IS DESIGNED TO WITHSTAND THOUSANDS OF NUCLEAR DETONATIONS AND SUB-LIGHT ACCELERATION FOR A BILLION YEARS. EVERYTHING HAS A MINIMUM OF TRIPLE REDUNDANCY.
OKAY.

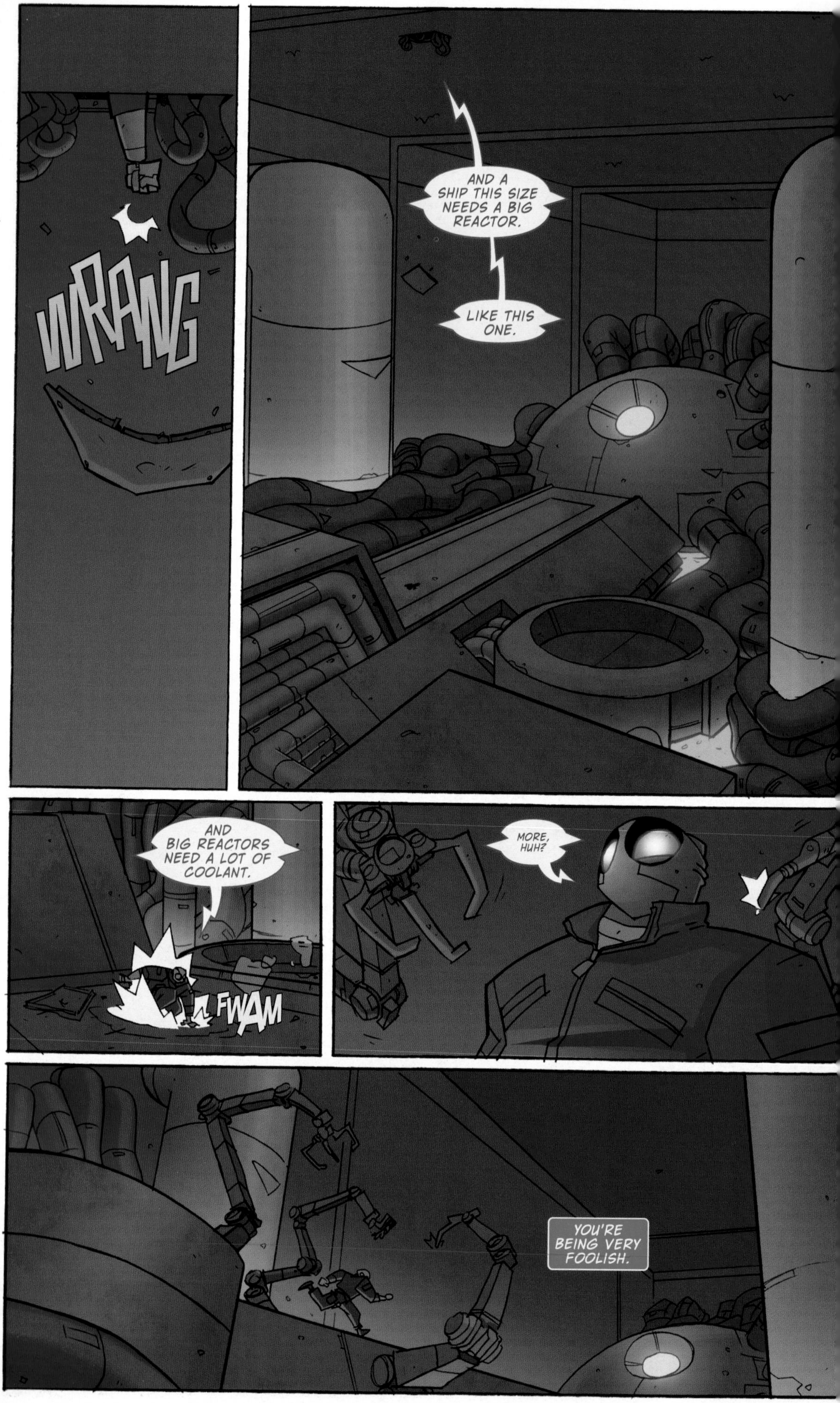
WRANG
AND A SHIP THIS SIZE NEEDS A BIG REACTOR.
LIKE THIS ONE.
AND BIG REACTORS NEED A LOT OF COOLANT.
FWAM
MORE, HUH?
YOU'RE BEING VERY FOOLISH.

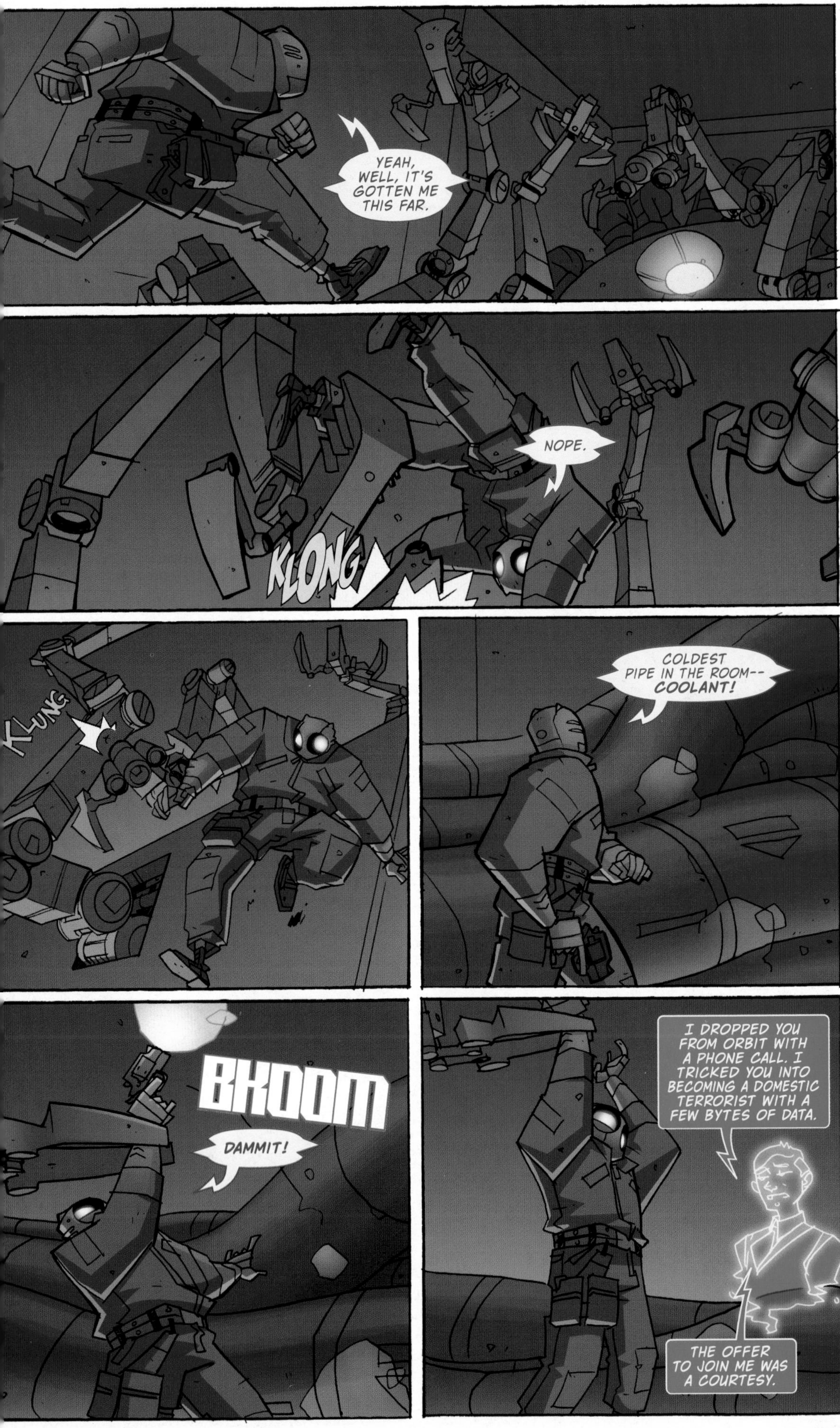
YEAH, WELL, IT'S GOTTEN ME THIS FAR.
NOPE.
KLONG
KLUNG
COLDEST PIPE IN THE ROOM-- COOLANT!
BKOOM
DAMMIT!
I DROPPED YOU FROM ORBIT WITH A PHONE CALL. I TRICKED YOU INTO BECOMING A DOMESTIC TERRORIST WITH A FEW BYTES OF DATA.
THE OFFER TO JOIN ME WAS A COURTESY.

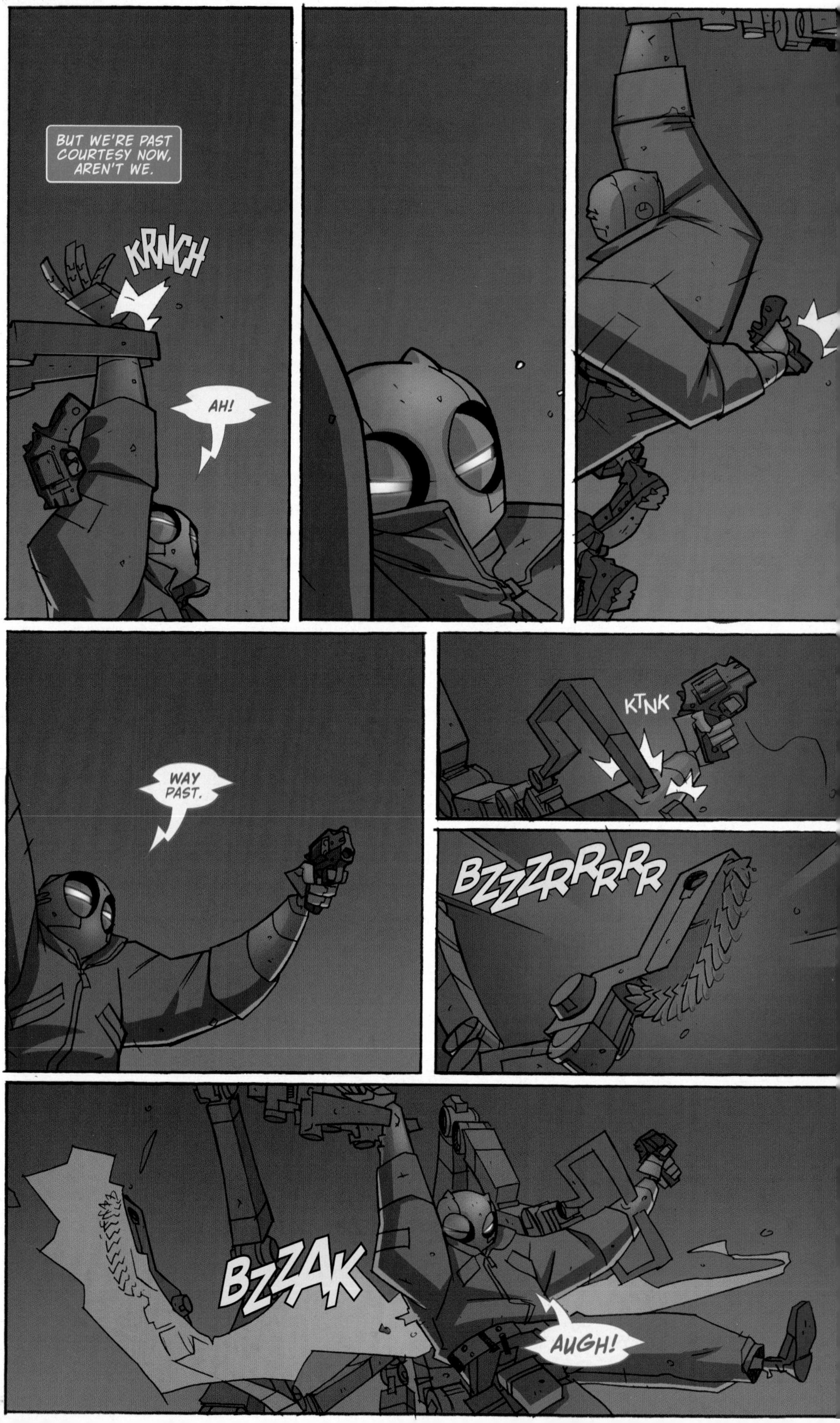
BUT WE'RE PAST COURTESY NOW, AREN'T WE.
KRNCH
AH!
WAY PAST.
KTNK
BZZZRRRRRR
BZZAK
AUGH!

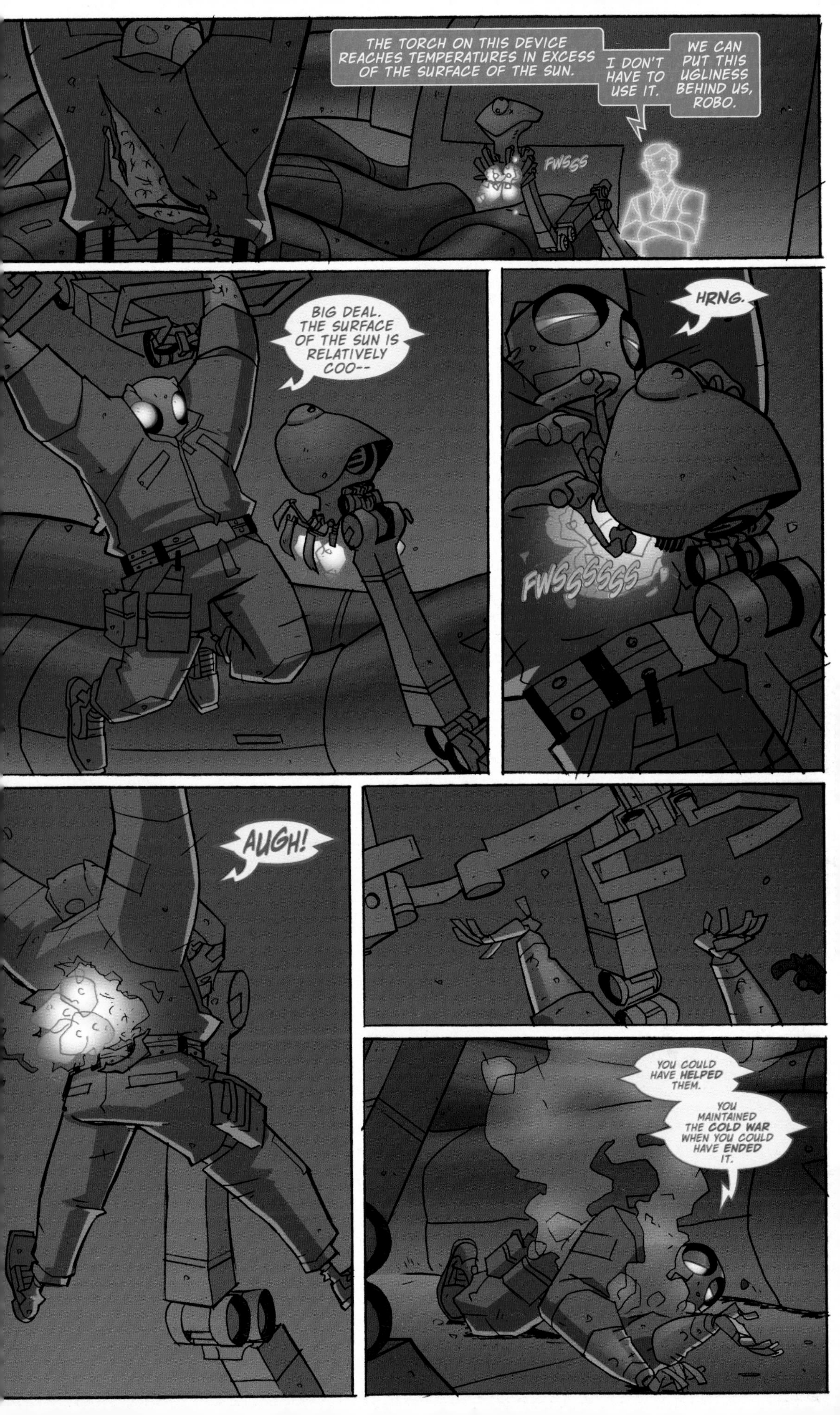
THE TORCH ON THIS DEVICE REACHES TEMPERATURES IN EXCESS OF THE SURFACE OF THE SUN.
I DON'T HAVE TO USE IT.
WE CAN PUT THIS UGLINESS BEHIND US, ROBO.
FWSSS
BIG DEAL. THE SURFACE OF THE SUN IS RELATIVELY COO--
HRNG.
FWSSSSSS
AUGH!
YOU COULD HAVE HELPED THEM.
YOU MAINTAINED THE COLD WAR WHEN YOU COULD HAVE ENDED IT.

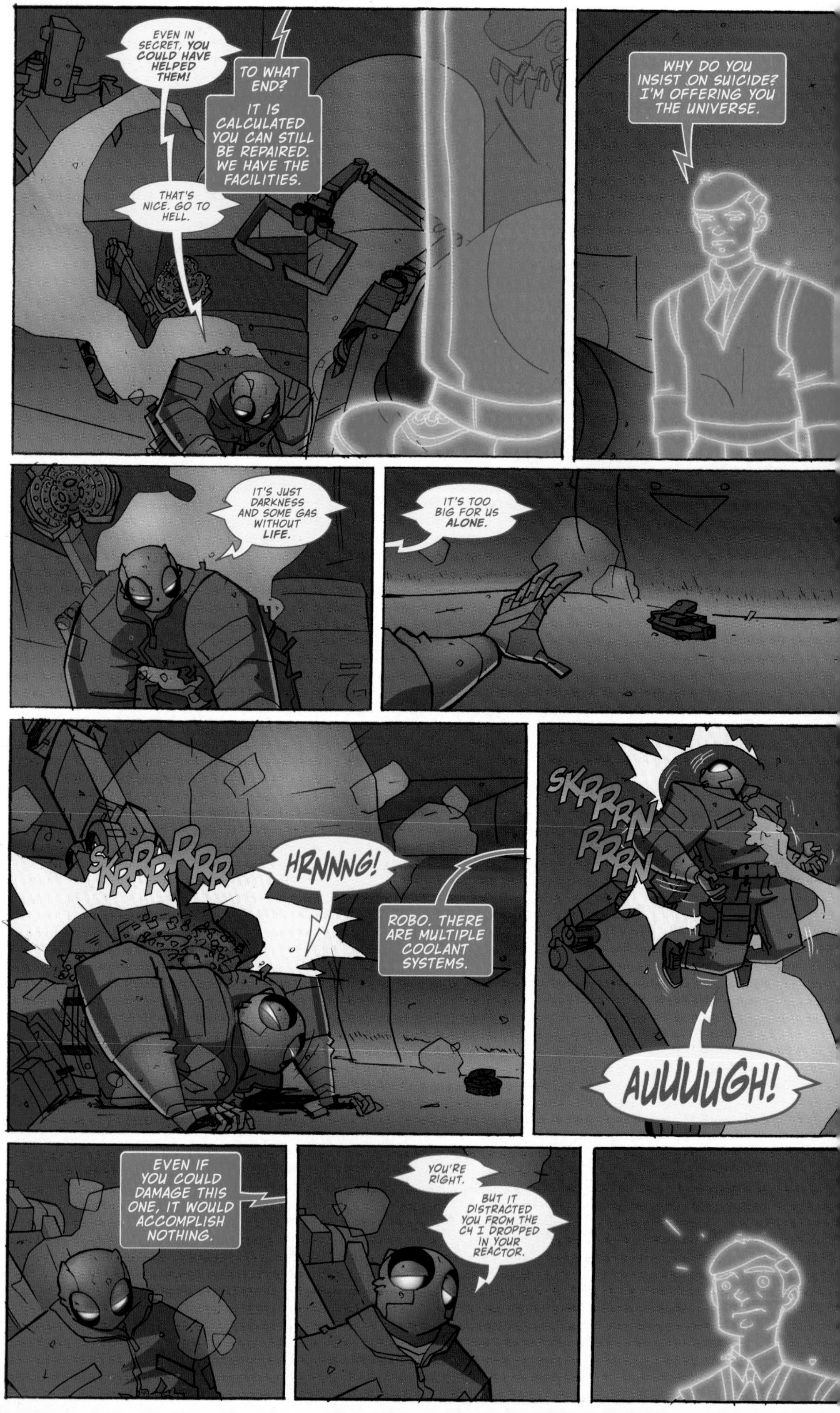
EVEN IN SECRET, YOU COULD HAVE HELPED THEM!
TO WHAT END?
IT IS CALCULATED YOU CAN STILL BE REPAIRED. WE HAVE THE FACILITIES.
THAT'S NICE. GO TO HELL.
WHY DO YOU INSIST ON SUICIDE? I'M OFFERING YOU THE UNIVERSE.
IT'S JUST DARKNESS AND SOME GAS WITHOUT LIFE.
IT'S TOO BIG FOR US ALONE.
SKRRRRRRR
HRNNNG!
ROBO. THERE ARE MULTIPLE COOLANT SYSTEMS.
SKRRRN RRRN
AUUUUGH!
EVEN IF YOU COULD DAMAGE THIS ONE, IT WOULD ACCOMPLISH NOTHING.
YOU'RE RIGHT.
BUT IT DISTRACTED YOU FROM THE C4 I DROPPED IN YOUR REACTOR.

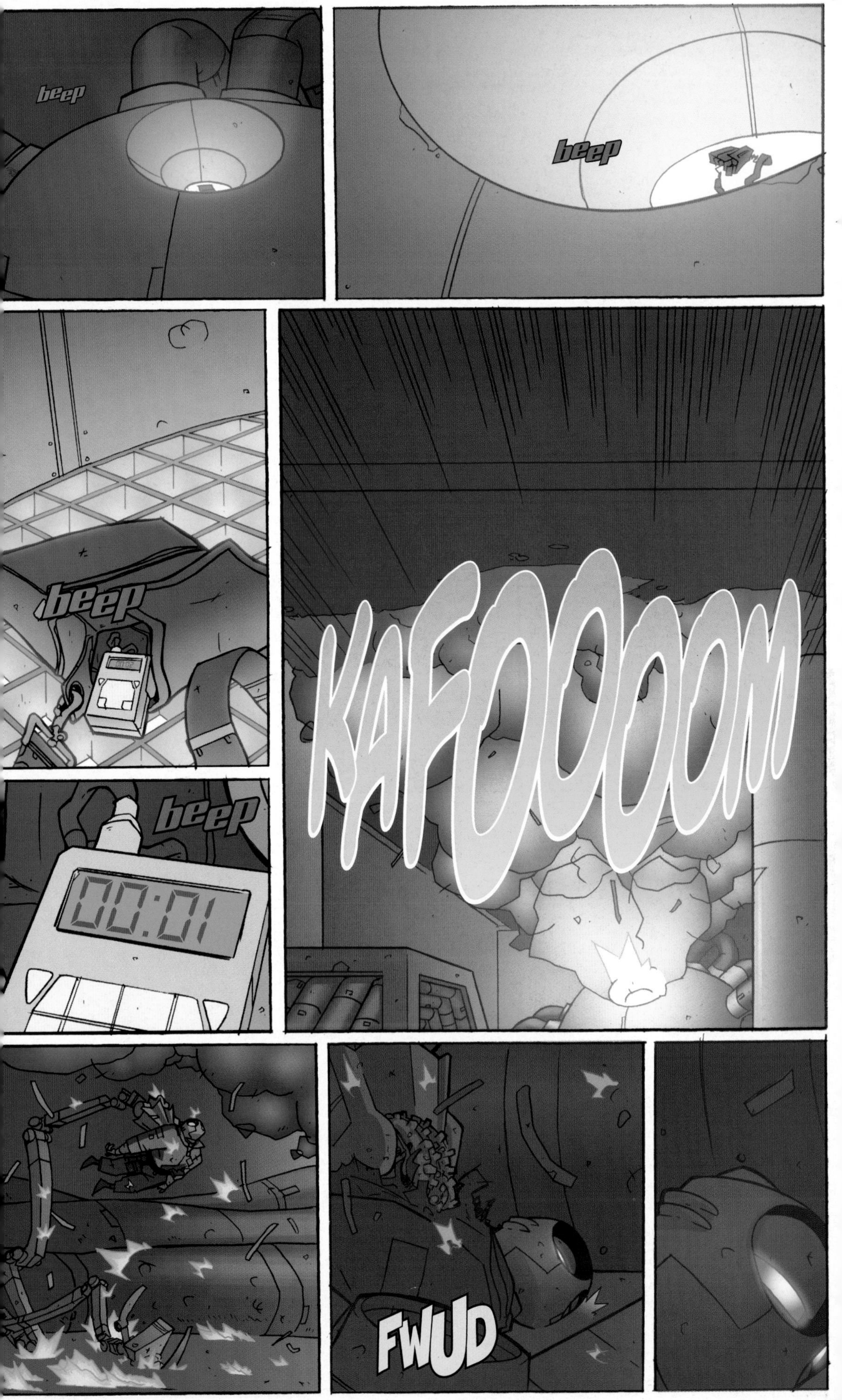

beep
beep
beep
00:02
beep
00:01
KAFOOOOOM
FWUD

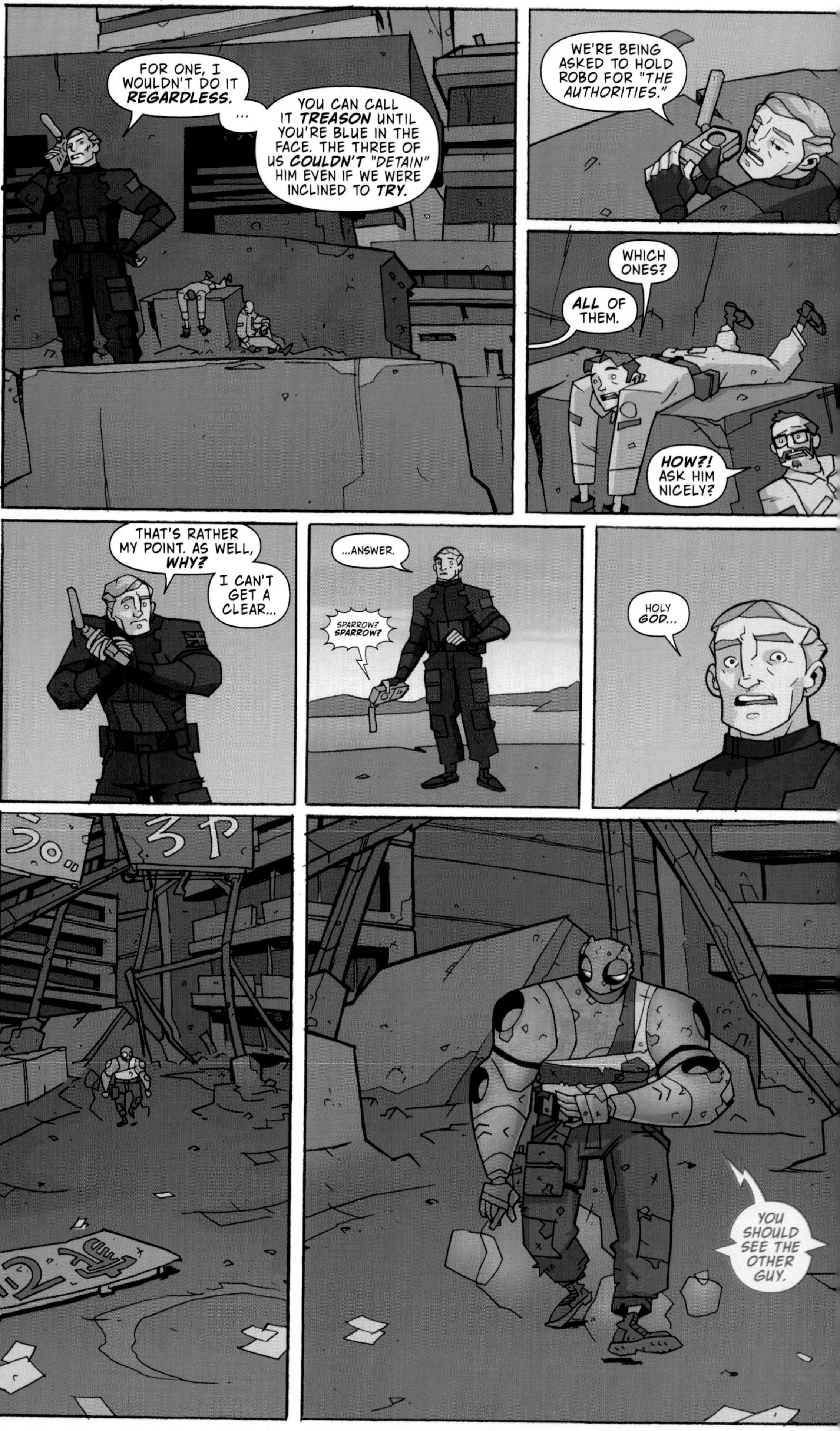

FOR ONE, I WOULDN'T DO IT **REGARDLESS.**
...
YOU CAN CALL IT **TREASON** UNTIL YOU'RE BLUE IN THE FACE. THE THREE OF US **COULDN'T** "DETAIN" HIM EVEN IF WE WERE INCLINED TO **TRY.**
WE'RE BEING ASKED TO HOLD ROBO FOR "THE AUTHORITIES."
WHICH ONES?
ALL OF THEM.
HOW?! ASK HIM NICELY?
THAT'S RATHER MY POINT. AS WELL, **WHY?**
I CAN'T GET A CLEAR...
...ANSWER.
SPARROW? **SPARROW?**
HOLY **GOD...**
YOU SHOULD SEE THE OTHER GUY.

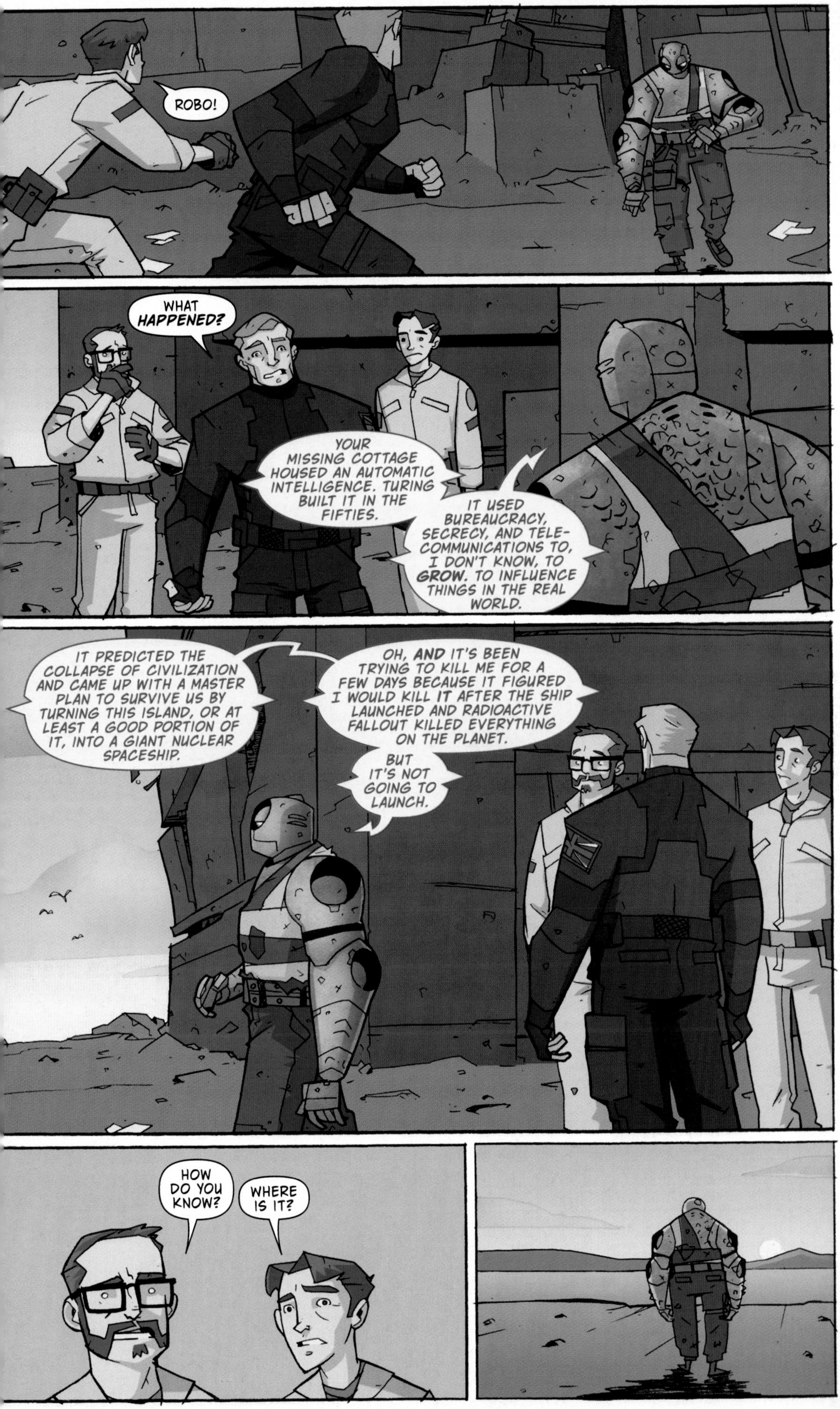
ROBO!
WHAT HAPPENED?
YOUR MISSING COTTAGE HOUSED AN AUTOMATIC INTELLIGENCE. TURING BUILT IT IN THE FIFTIES.
IT USED BUREAUCRACY, SECRECY, AND TELE-COMMUNICATIONS TO, I DON'T KNOW, TO GROW. TO INFLUENCE THINGS IN THE REAL WORLD.
IT PREDICTED THE COLLAPSE OF CIVILIZATION AND CAME UP WITH A MASTER PLAN TO SURVIVE US BY TURNING THIS ISLAND, OR AT LEAST A GOOD PORTION OF IT, INTO A GIANT NUCLEAR SPACESHIP.
OH, AND IT'S BEEN TRYING TO KILL ME FOR A FEW DAYS BECAUSE IT FIGURED I WOULD KILL IT AFTER THE SHIP LAUNCHED AND RADIOACTIVE FALLOUT KILLED EVERYTHING ON THE PLANET.
BUT IT'S NOT GOING TO LAUNCH.
HOW DO YOU KNOW?
WHERE IS IT?

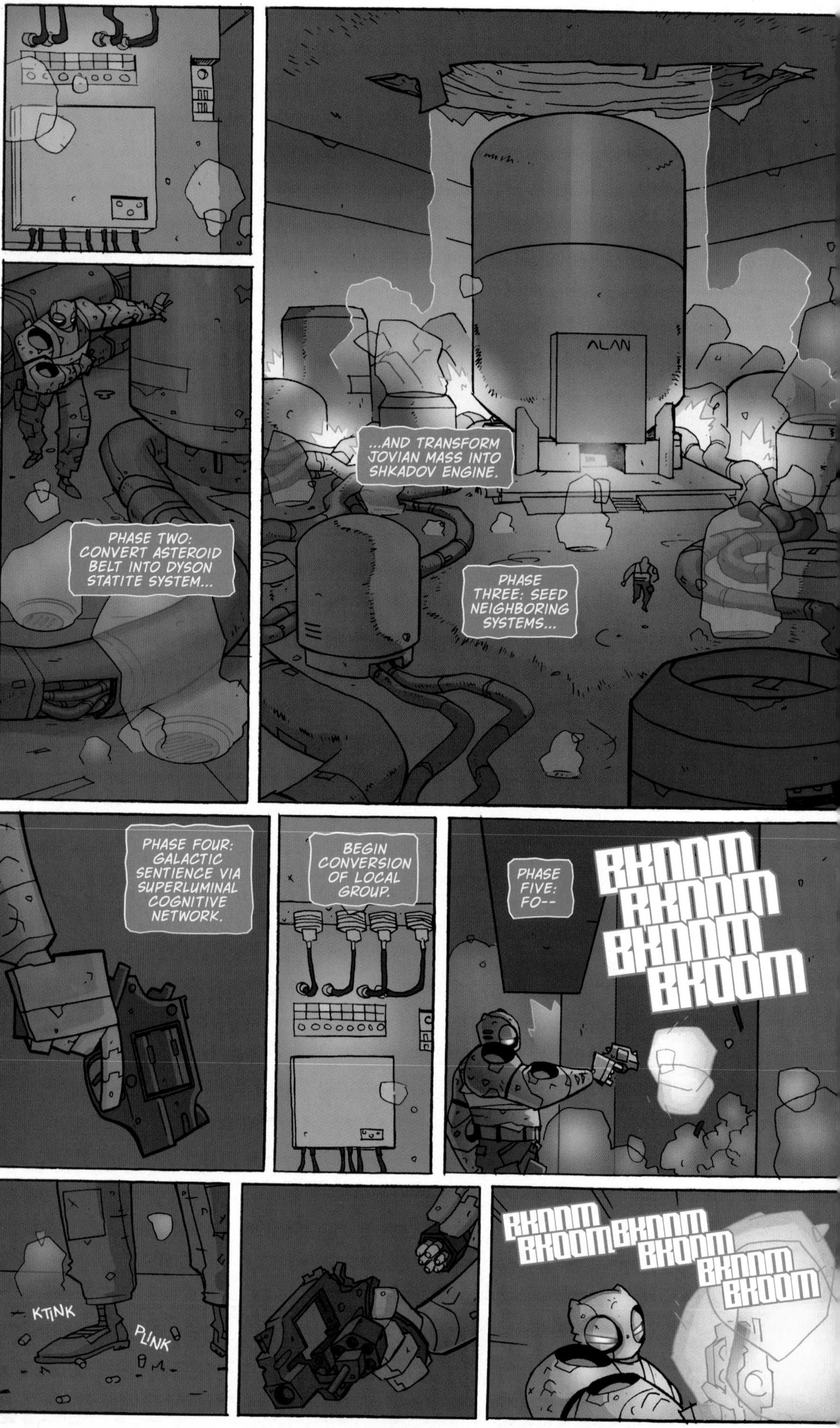
PHASE TWO: CONVERT ASTEROID BELT INTO DYSON STATITE SYSTEM...
ALAN
...AND TRANSFORM JOVIAN MASS INTO SHKADOV ENGINE.
PHASE THREE: SEED NEIGHBORING SYSTEMS...
PHASE FOUR: GALACTIC SENTIENCE VIA SUPERLUMINAL COGNITIVE NETWORK.
BEGIN CONVERSION OF LOCAL GROUP.
PHASE FIVE: FO--
BKOOM BKOOM BKOOM BKOOM
KTINK
PLINK
BKOOM BKOOM BKOOM BKOOM BKOOM BKOOM

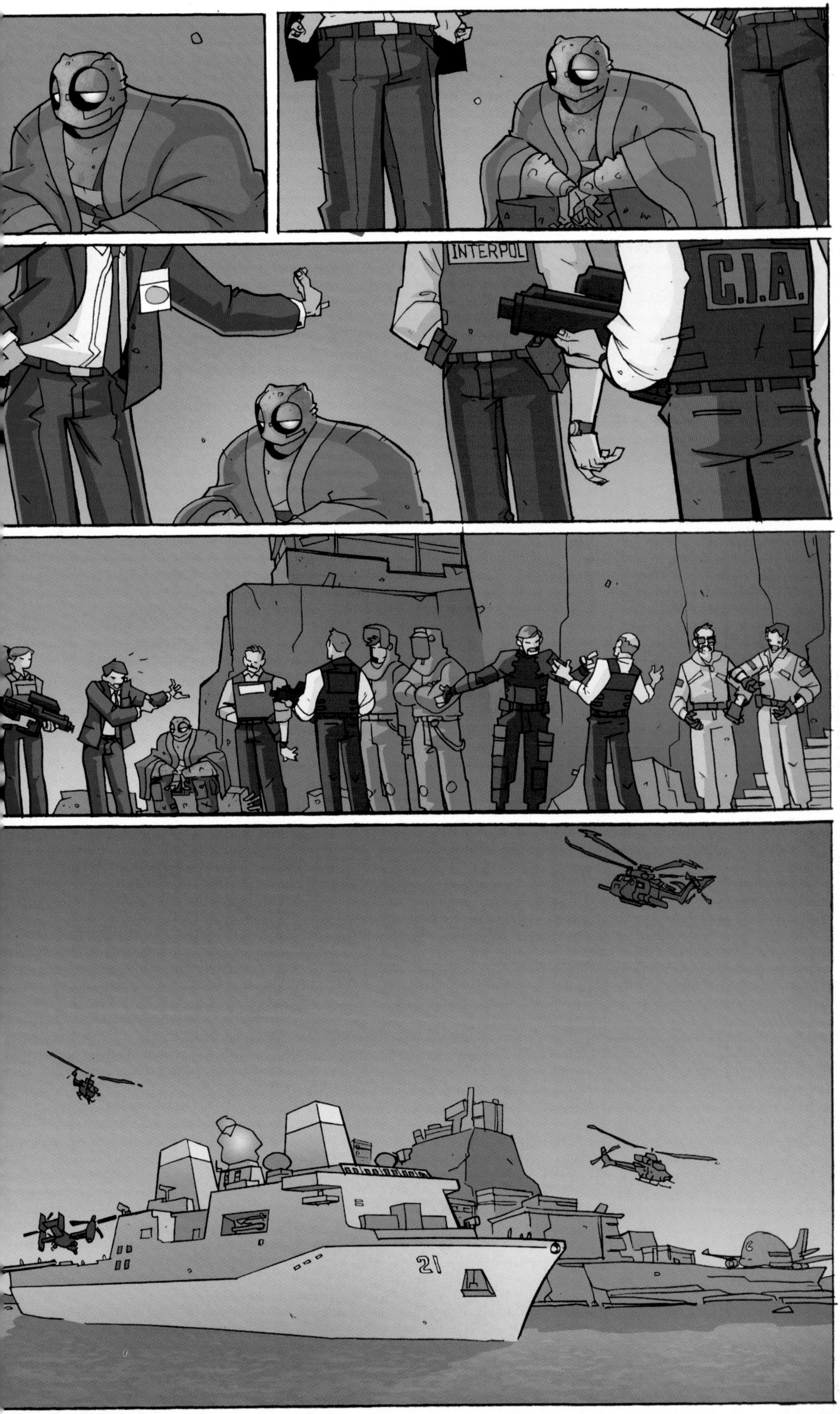
INTERPOL
C.I.A.
21

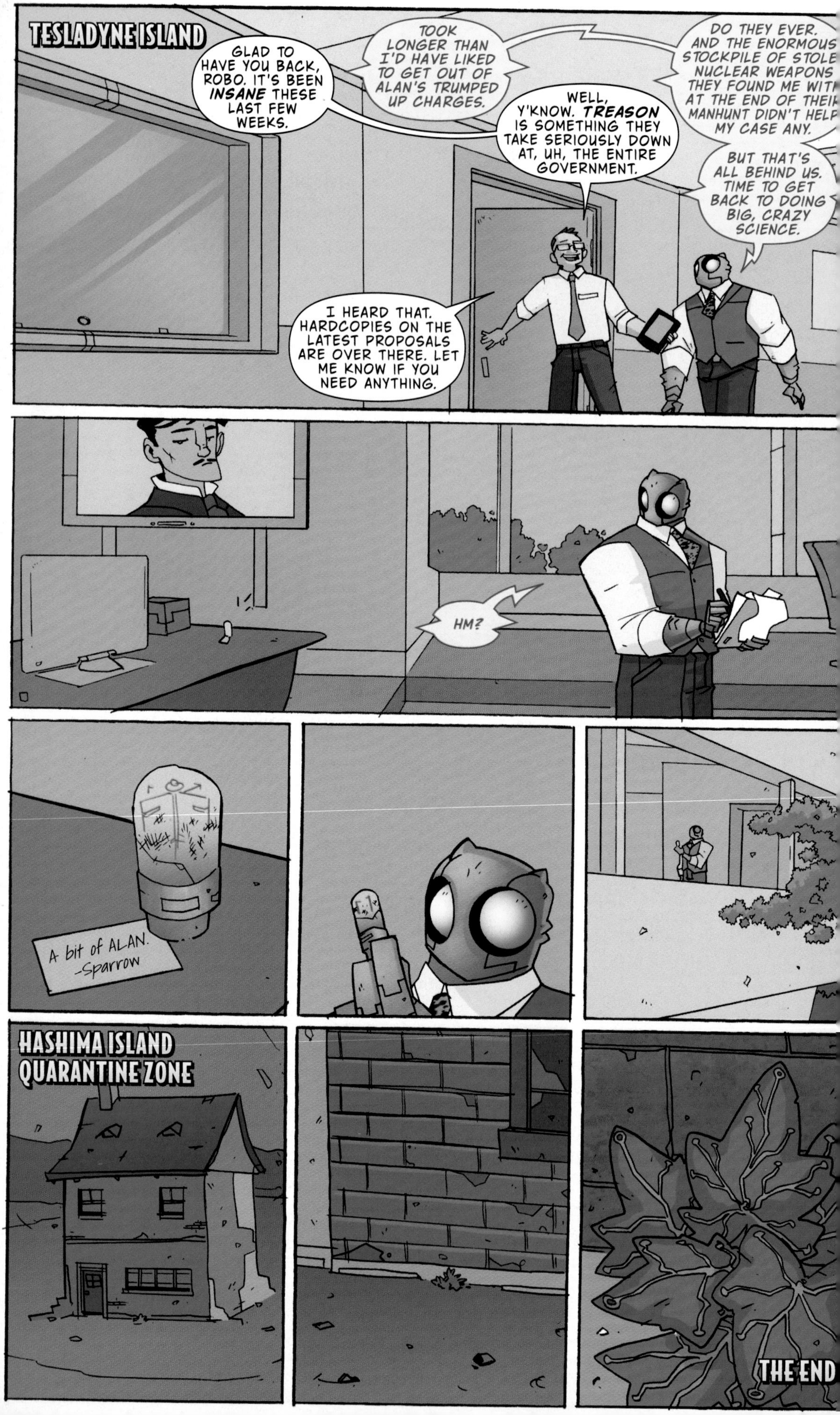
TESLADYNE ISLAND
GLAD TO HAVE YOU BACK, ROBO. IT'S BEEN *INSANE* THESE LAST FEW WEEKS.
TOOK LONGER THAN I'D HAVE LIKED TO GET OUT OF ALAN'S TRUMPED UP CHARGES.
WELL, Y'KNOW. ***TREASON*** IS SOMETHING THEY TAKE SERIOUSLY DOWN AT, UH, THE ENTIRE GOVERNMENT.
DO THEY EVER. AND THE ENORMOUS STOCKPILE OF STOLE NUCLEAR WEAPONS THEY FOUND ME WIT AT THE END OF THEI MANHUNT DIDN'T HEL MY CASE ANY.
BUT THAT'S ALL BEHIND US. TIME TO GET BACK TO DOING BIG, CRAZY SCIENCE.
I HEARD THAT. HARDCOPIES ON THE LATEST PROPOSALS ARE OVER THERE. LET ME KNOW IF YOU NEED ANYTHING.
HM?
A bit of ALAN. -Sparrow
HASHIMA ISLAND QUARANTINE ZONE
THE END

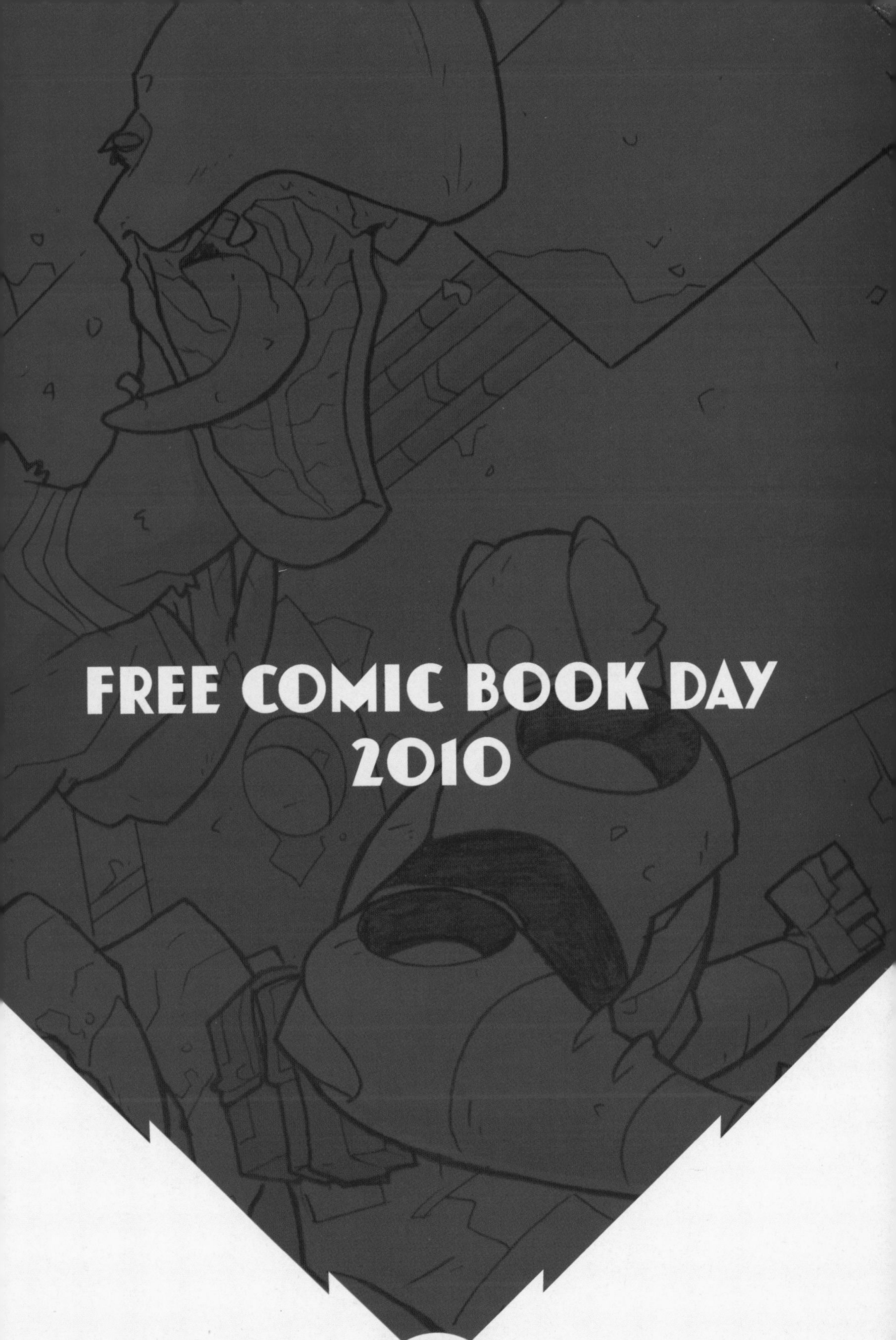
FREE COMIC BOOK DAY
2010

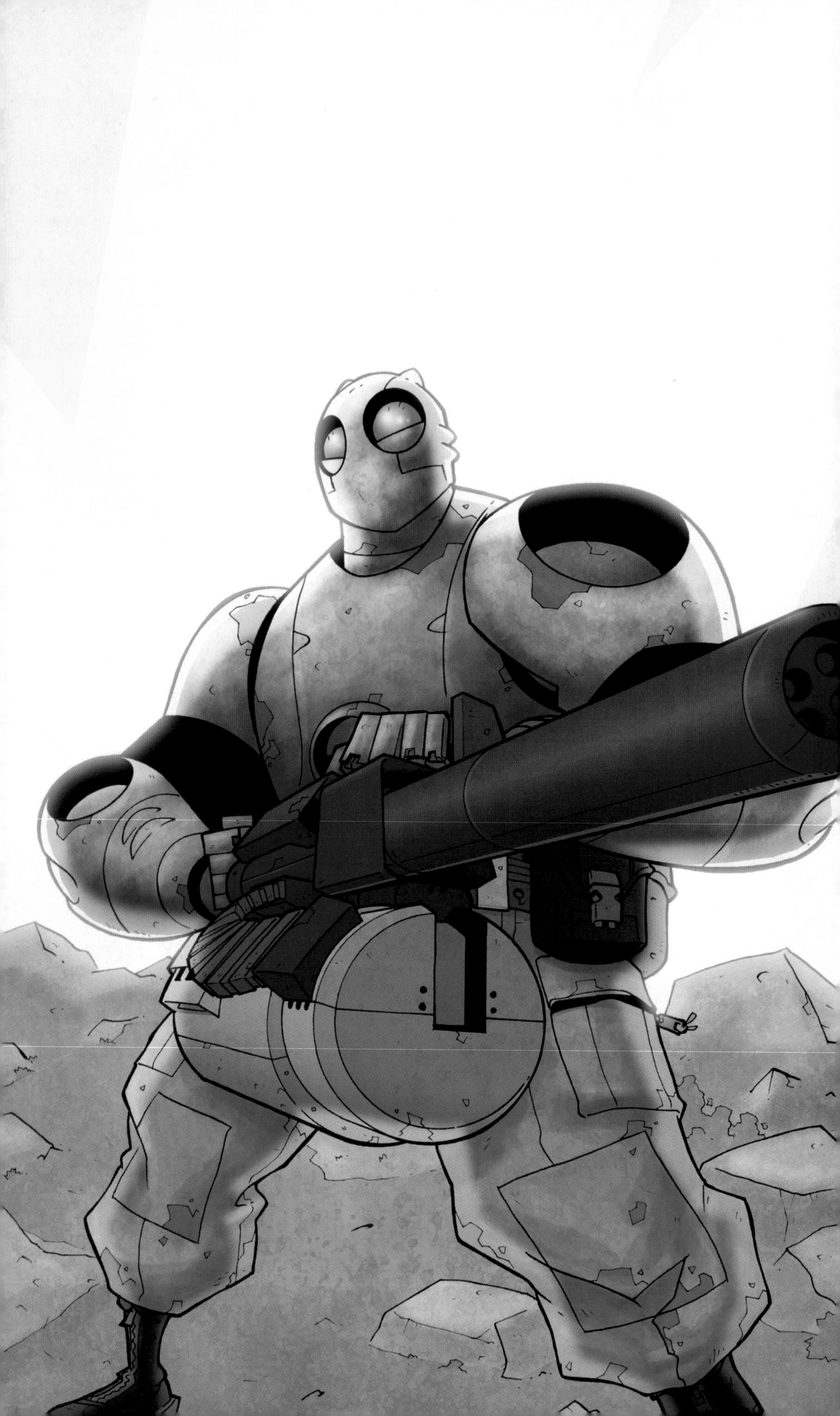

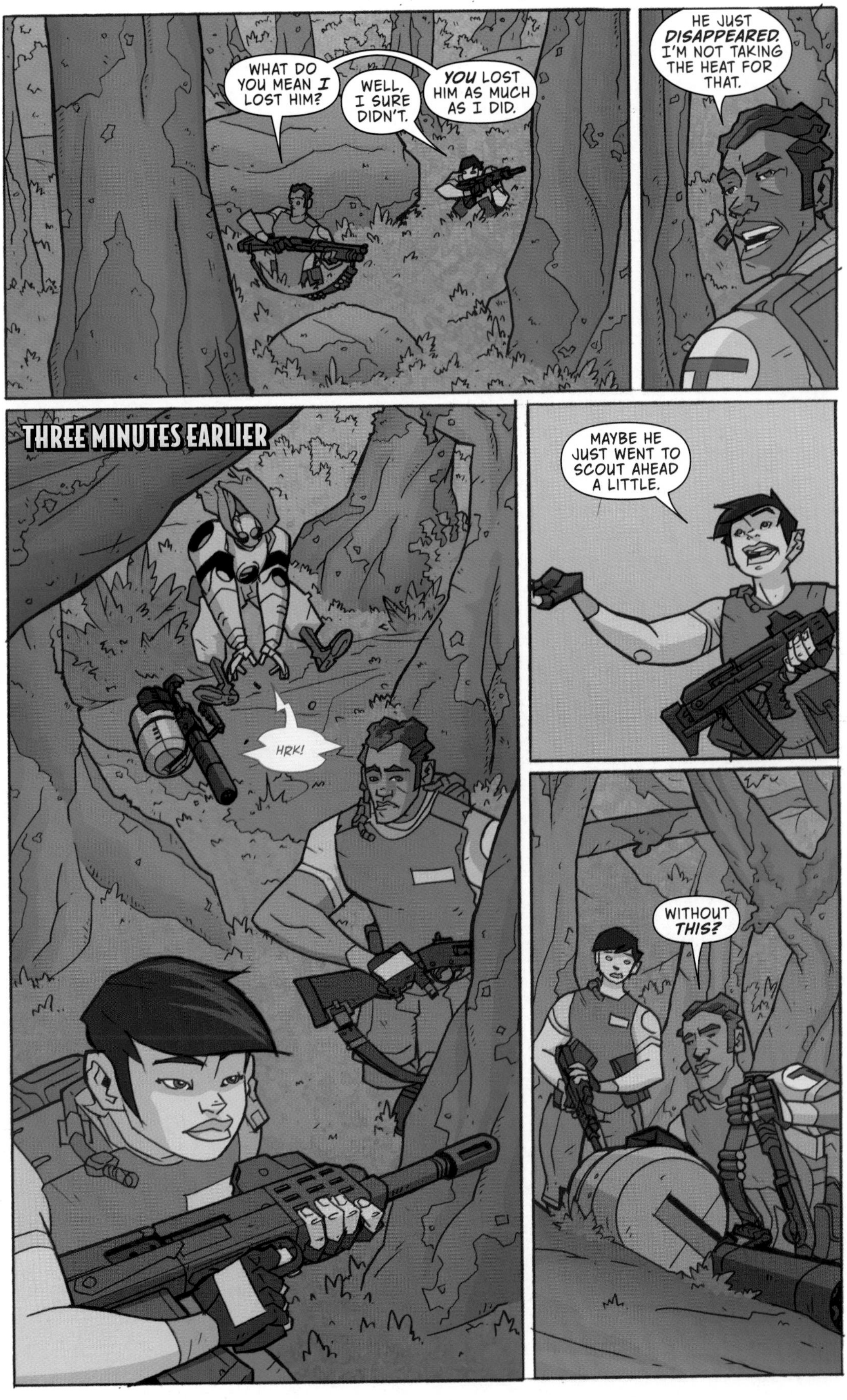
WHAT DO YOU MEAN *I* LOST HIM?
WELL, I SURE DIDN'T.
YOU LOST HIM AS MUCH AS I DID.
HE JUST *DISAPPEARED.* I'M NOT TAKING THE HEAT FOR THAT.
THREE MINUTES EARLIER
HRK!
MAYBE HE JUST WENT TO SCOUT AHEAD A LITTLE.
WITHOUT *THIS?*

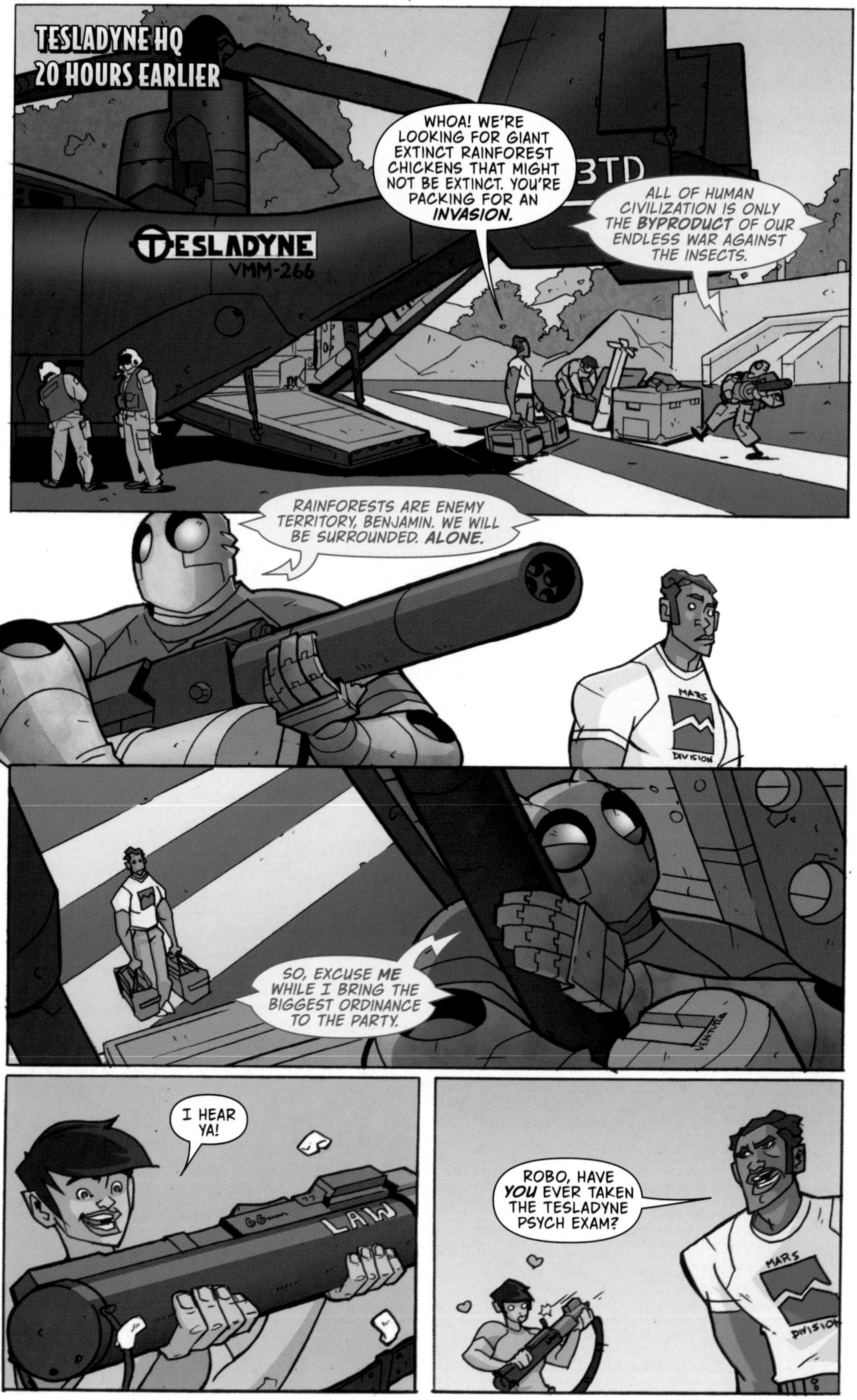
TESLADYNE HQ
20 HOURS EARLIER
WHOA! WE'RE LOOKING FOR GIANT EXTINCT RAINFOREST CHICKENS THAT MIGHT NOT BE EXTINCT. YOU'RE PACKING FOR AN INVASION.
3TD
TESLADYNE
VMM-266
ALL OF HUMAN CIVILIZATION IS ONLY THE BYPRODUCT OF OUR ENDLESS WAR AGAINST THE INSECTS.
RAINFORESTS ARE ENEMY TERRITORY, BENJAMIN. WE WILL BE SURROUNDED. ALONE.
MARS DIVISION
SO, EXCUSE ME WHILE I BRING THE BIGGEST ORDINANCE TO THE PARTY.
VENTURA
I HEAR YA!
LAW
ROBO, HAVE YOU EVER TAKEN THE TESLADYNE PSYCH EXAM?
MARS DIVISION

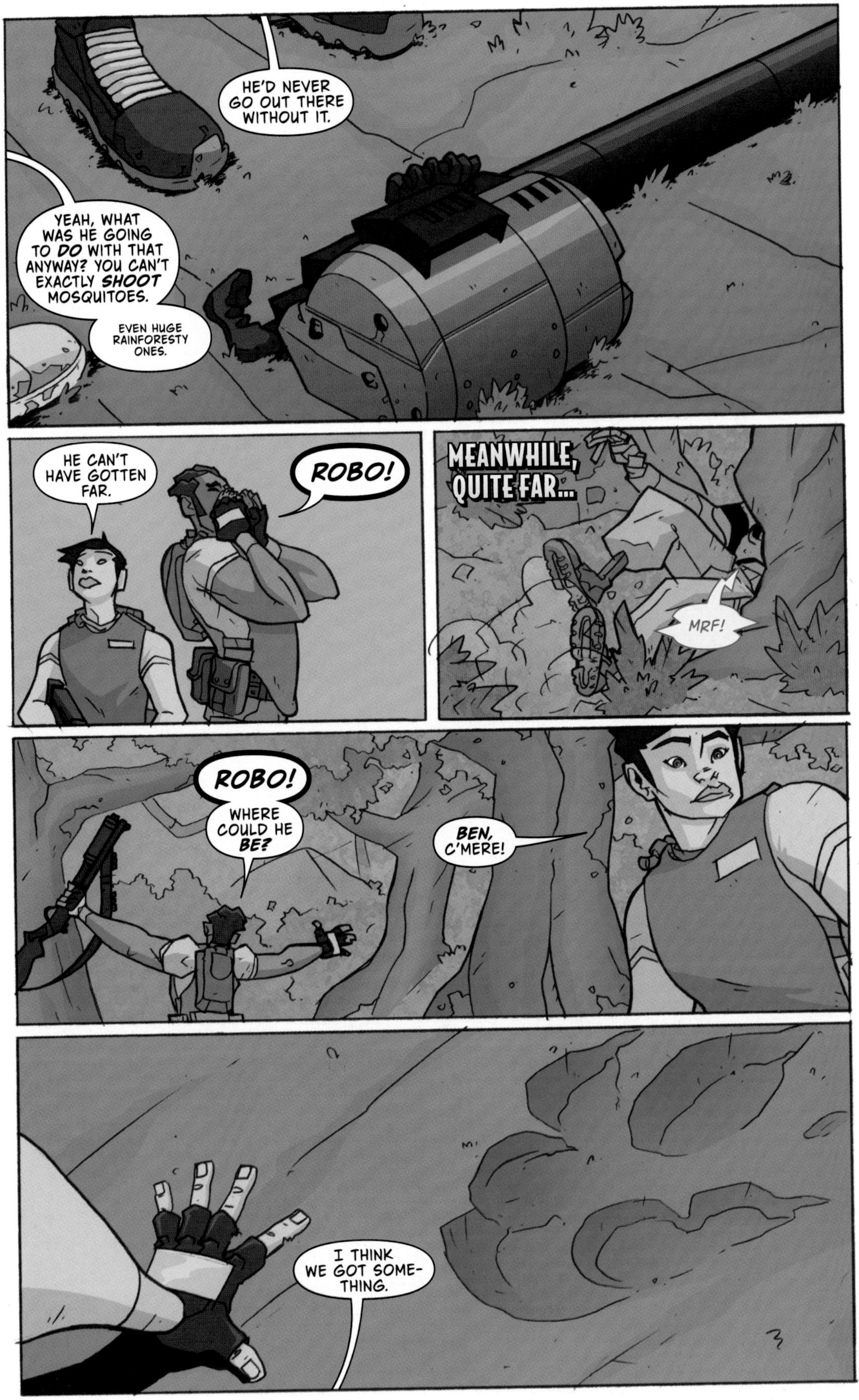
HE'D NEVER GO OUT THERE WITHOUT IT.
YEAH, WHAT WAS HE GOING TO *DO* WITH THAT ANYWAY? YOU CAN'T EXACTLY *SHOOT* MOSQUITOES.
EVEN HUGE RAINFORESTY ONES.
HE CAN'T HAVE GOTTEN FAR.
ROBO!
MEANWHILE, QUITE FAR...
MRF!
ROBO!
WHERE COULD HE *BE?*
BEN, C'MERE!
I THINK WE GOT SOME-THING.

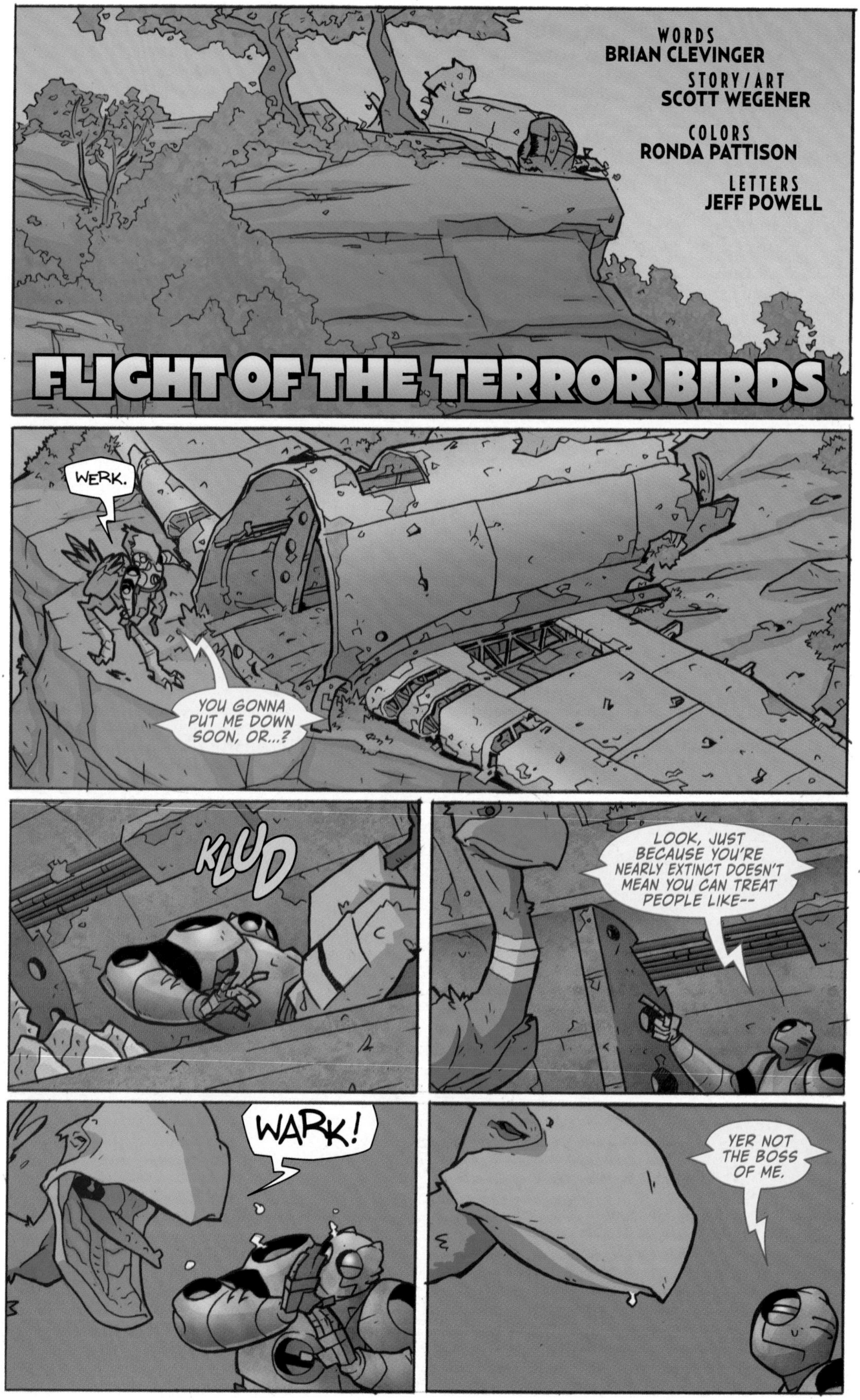
WORDS
BRIAN CLEVINGER
STORY/ART
SCOTT WEGENER
COLORS
RONDA PATTISON
LETTERS
JEFF POWELL
FLIGHT OF THE TERROR BIRDS
WERK.
YOU GONNA PUT ME DOWN SOON, OR...?
KLUD
LOOK, JUST BECAUSE YOU'RE NEARLY EXTINCT DOESN'T MEAN YOU CAN TREAT PEOPLE LIKE--
WARK!
YER NOT THE BOSS OF ME.

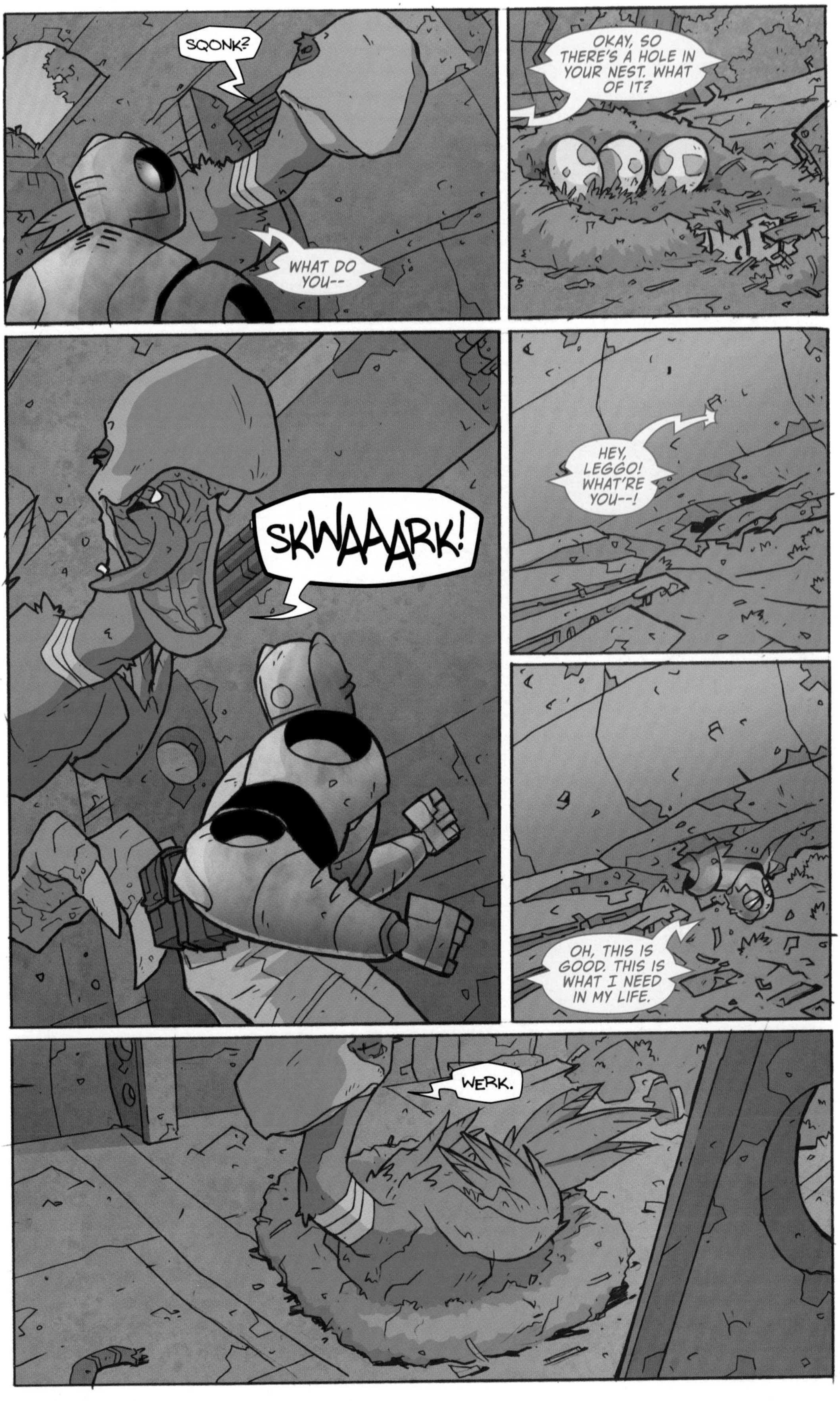
SQONK?
WHAT DO YOU--
OKAY, SO THERE'S A HOLE IN YOUR NEST. WHAT OF IT?
SKWAAARK!
HEY, LEGGO! WHAT'RE YOU--!
OH, THIS IS GOOD. THIS IS WHAT I NEED IN MY LIFE.
WERK.

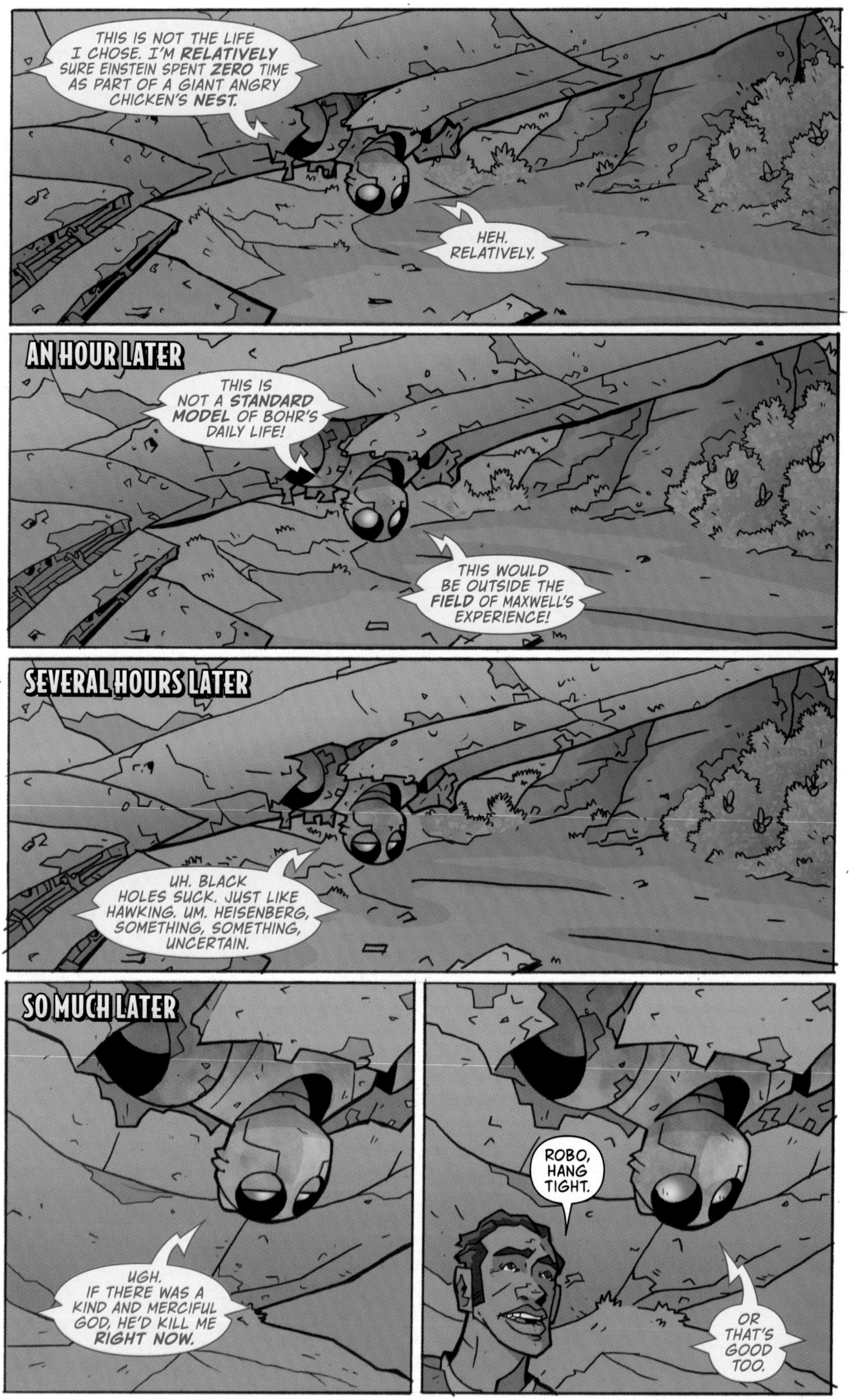
THIS IS NOT THE LIFE I CHOSE. I'M RELATIVELY SURE EINSTEIN SPENT ZERO TIME AS PART OF A GIANT ANGRY CHICKEN'S NEST.
HEH. RELATIVELY.
AN HOUR LATER
THIS IS NOT A STANDARD MODEL OF BOHR'S DAILY LIFE!
THIS WOULD BE OUTSIDE THE FIELD OF MAXWELL'S EXPERIENCE!
SEVERAL HOURS LATER
UH. BLACK HOLES SUCK. JUST LIKE HAWKING. UM. HEISENBERG, SOMETHING, SOMETHING, UNCERTAIN.
SO MUCH LATER
UGH. IF THERE WAS A KIND AND MERCIFUL GOD, HE'D KILL ME RIGHT NOW.
ROBO, HANG TIGHT.
OR THAT'S GOOD TOO.

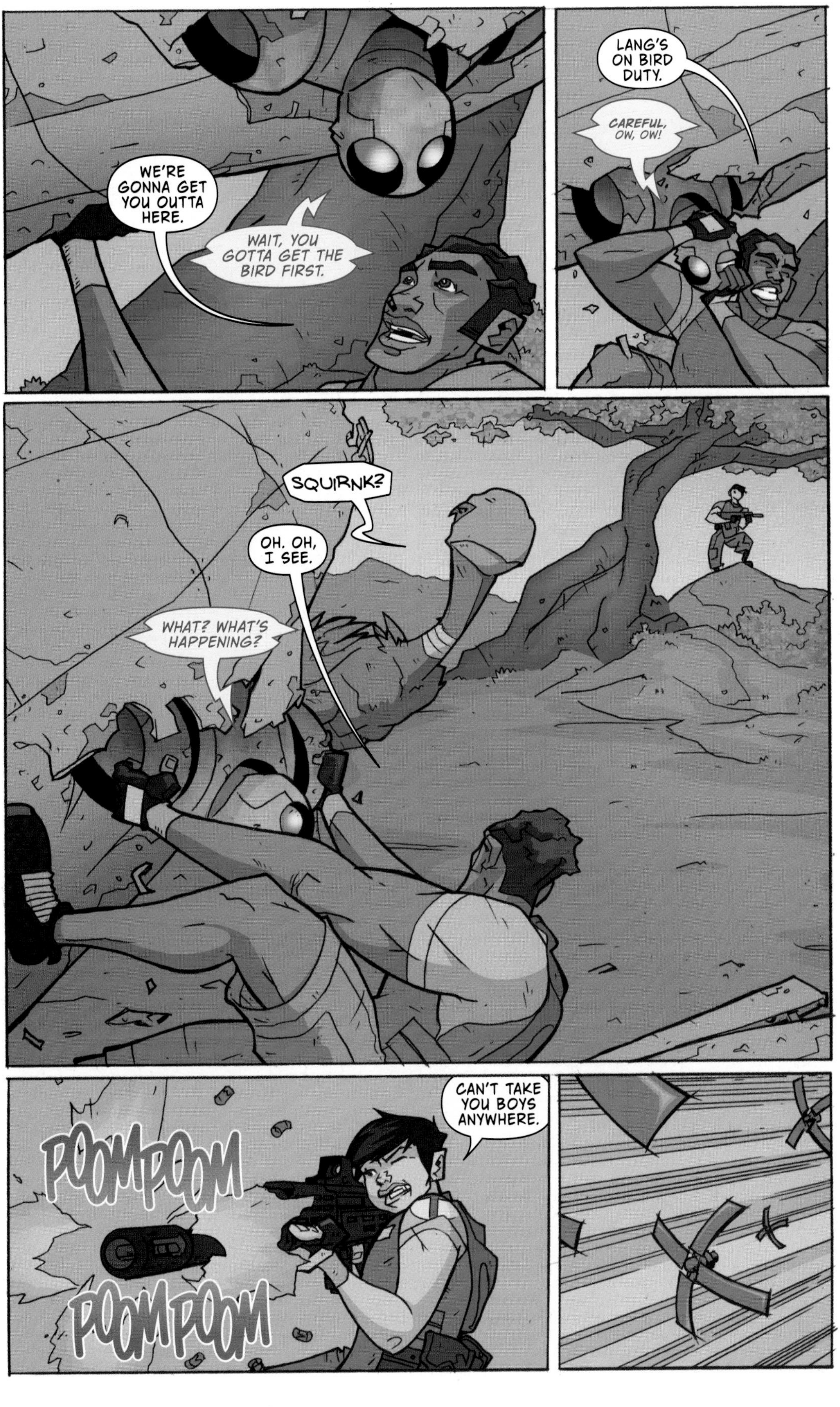
WE'RE GONNA GET YOU OUTTA HERE.
WAIT, YOU GOTTA GET THE BIRD FIRST.
LANG'S ON BIRD DUTY.
CAREFUL, OW, OW!
SQUIRNK?
OH. OH, I SEE.
WHAT? WHAT'S HAPPENING?
POOMPOOM
POOMPOOM
CAN'T TAKE YOU BOYS ANYWHERE.

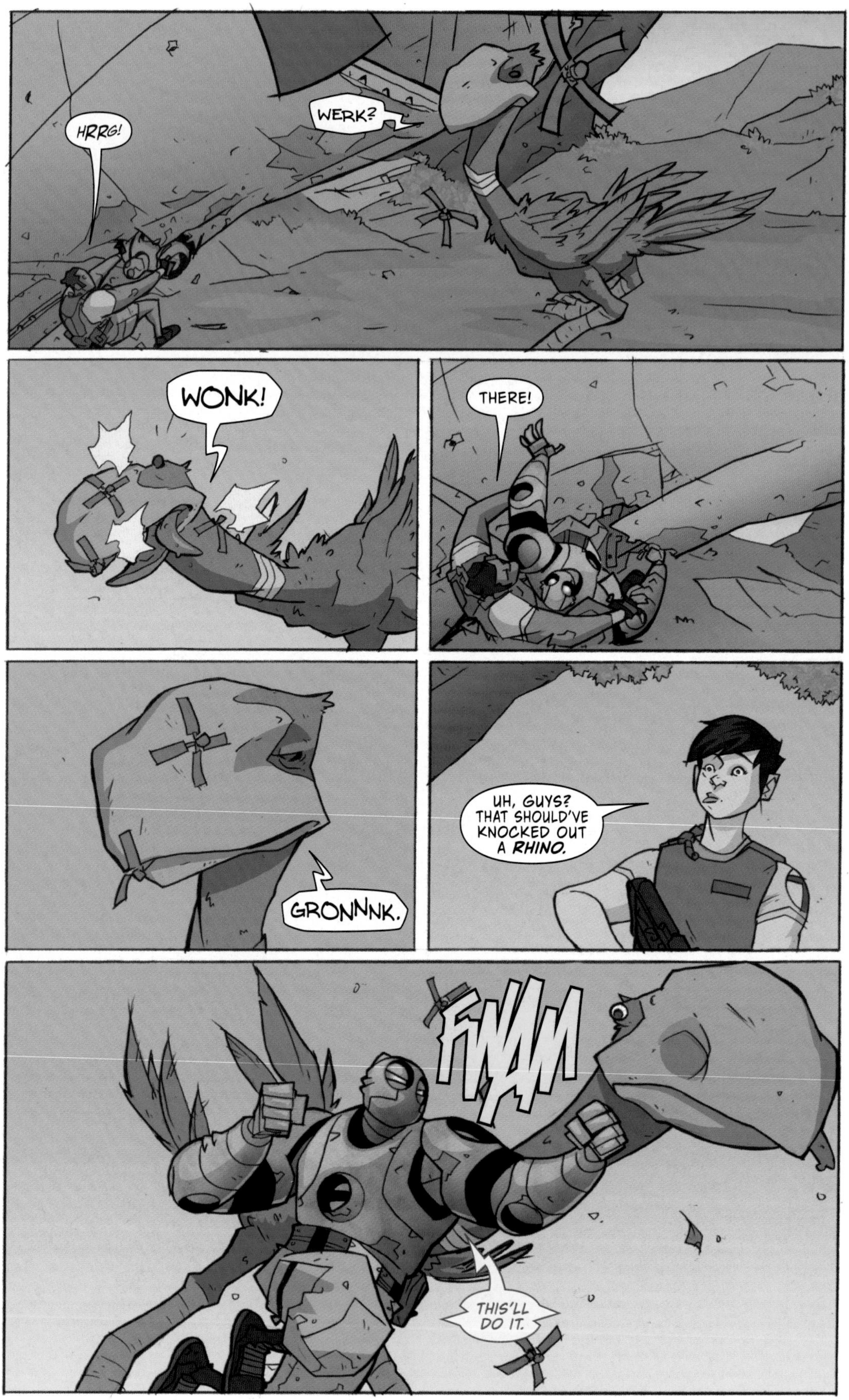
HRRG!
WERK?
WONK!
THERE!
GRONNNK.
UH, GUYS? THAT SHOULD'VE KNOCKED OUT A *RHINO.*
FWAM
THIS'LL DO IT.

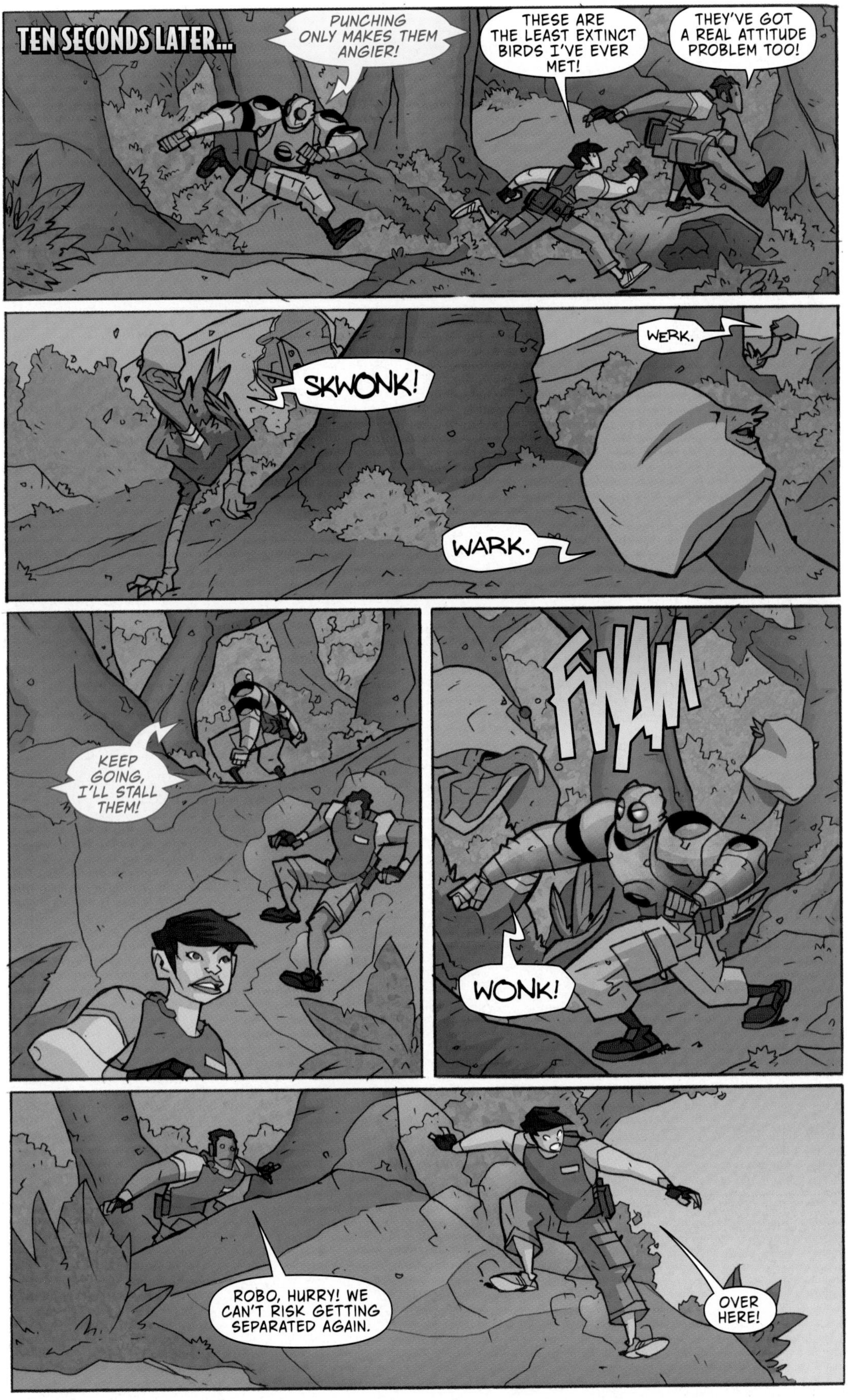
TEN SECONDS LATER...
PUNCHING ONLY MAKES THEM ANGIER!
THESE ARE THE LEAST EXTINCT BIRDS I'VE EVER MET!
THEY'VE GOT A REAL ATTITUDE PROBLEM TOO!
SKWONK!
WERK.
WARK.
KEEP GOING, I'LL STALL THEM!
FWAM
WONK!
ROBO, HURRY! WE CAN'T RISK GETTING SEPARATED AGAIN.
OVER HERE!

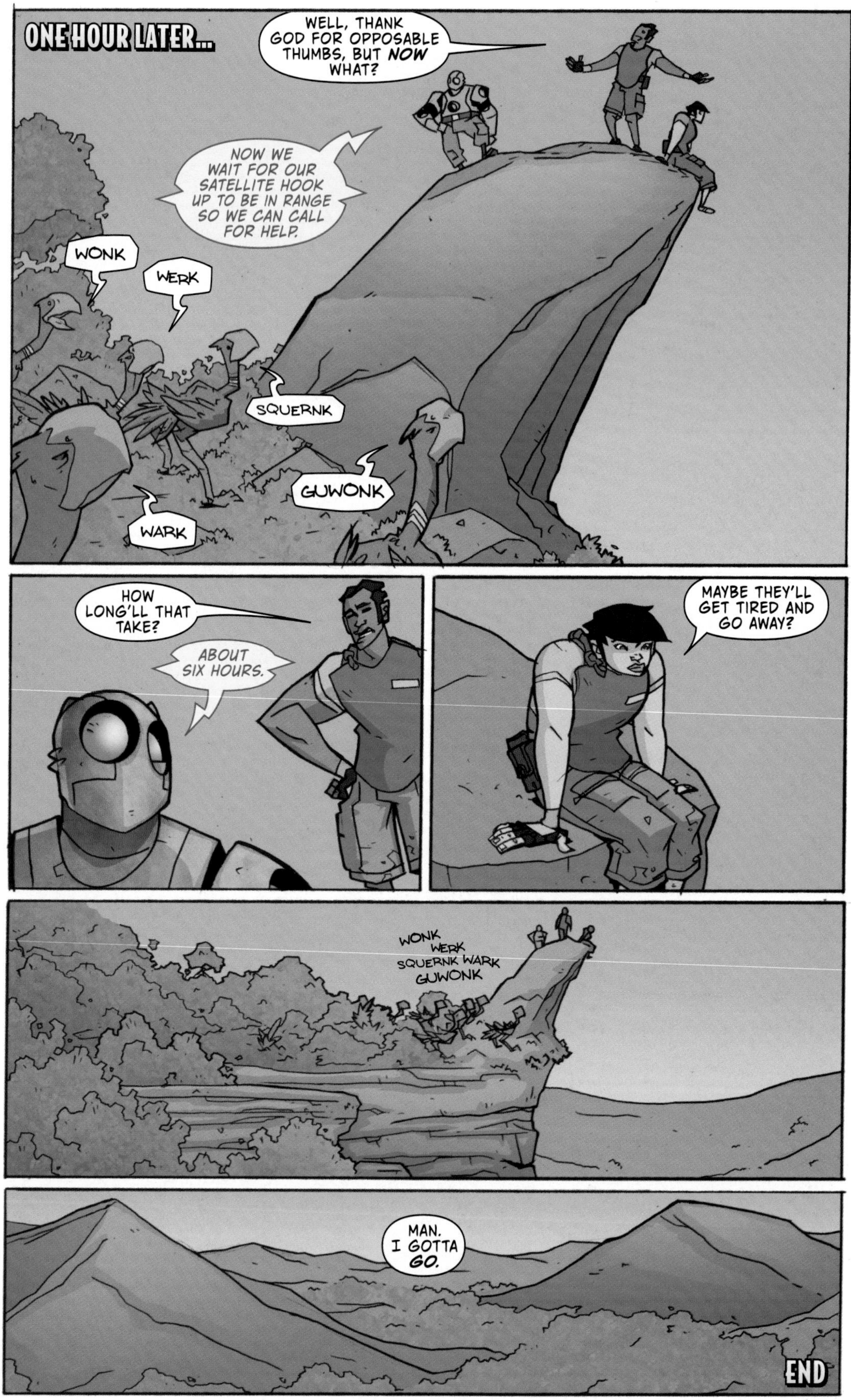
ONE HOUR LATER...
WELL, THANK GOD FOR OPPOSABLE THUMBS, BUT NOW WHAT?
NOW WE WAIT FOR OUR SATELLITE HOOK UP TO BE IN RANGE SO WE CAN CALL FOR HELP.
WONK
WERK
SQUERNK
GUWONK
WARK
HOW LONG'LL THAT TAKE?
ABOUT SIX HOURS.
MAYBE THEY'LL GET TIRED AND GO AWAY?
WONK WERK SQUERNK WARK GUWONK
MAN. I GOTTA GO.
END

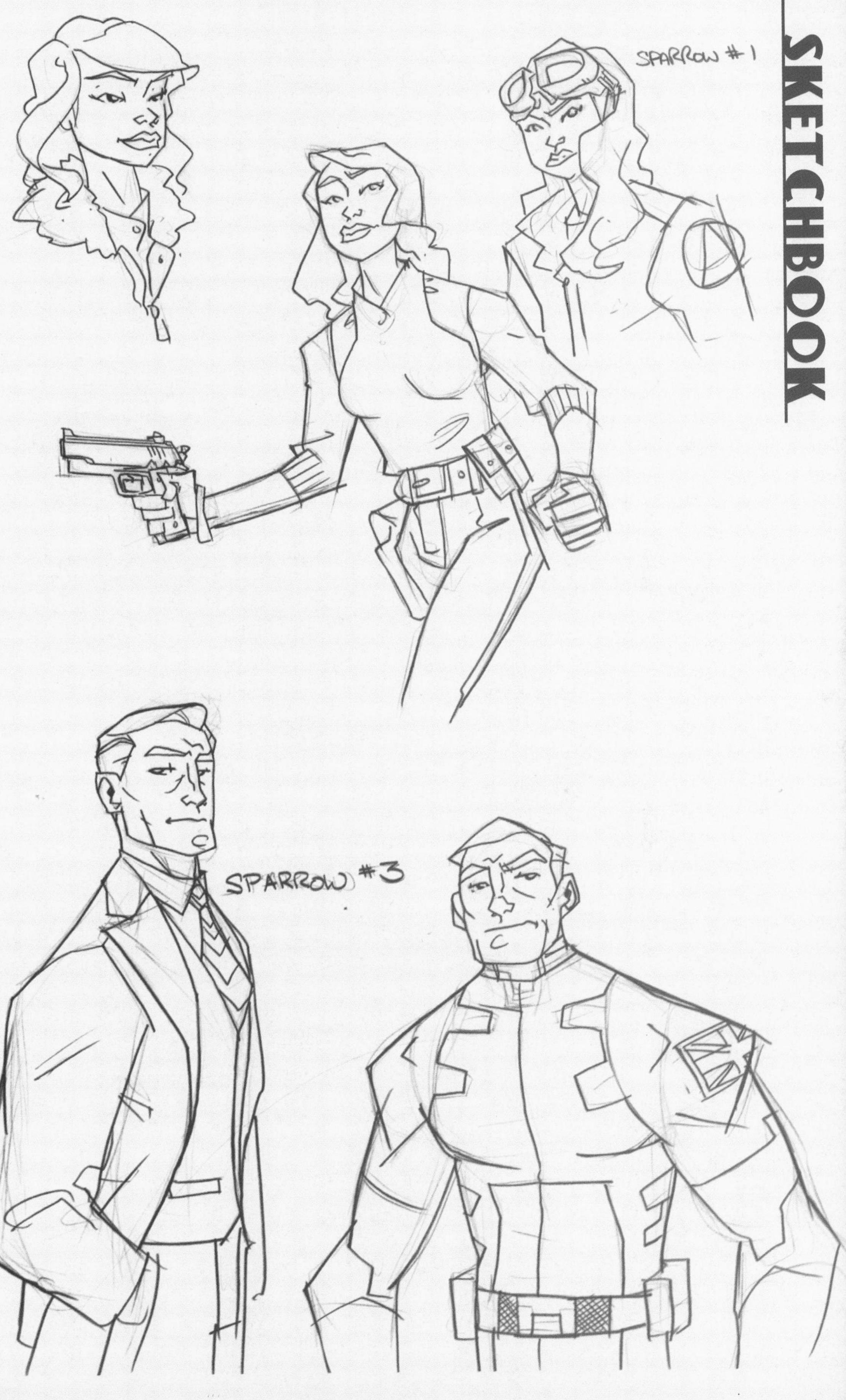
SPARROW #1
SPARROW #3

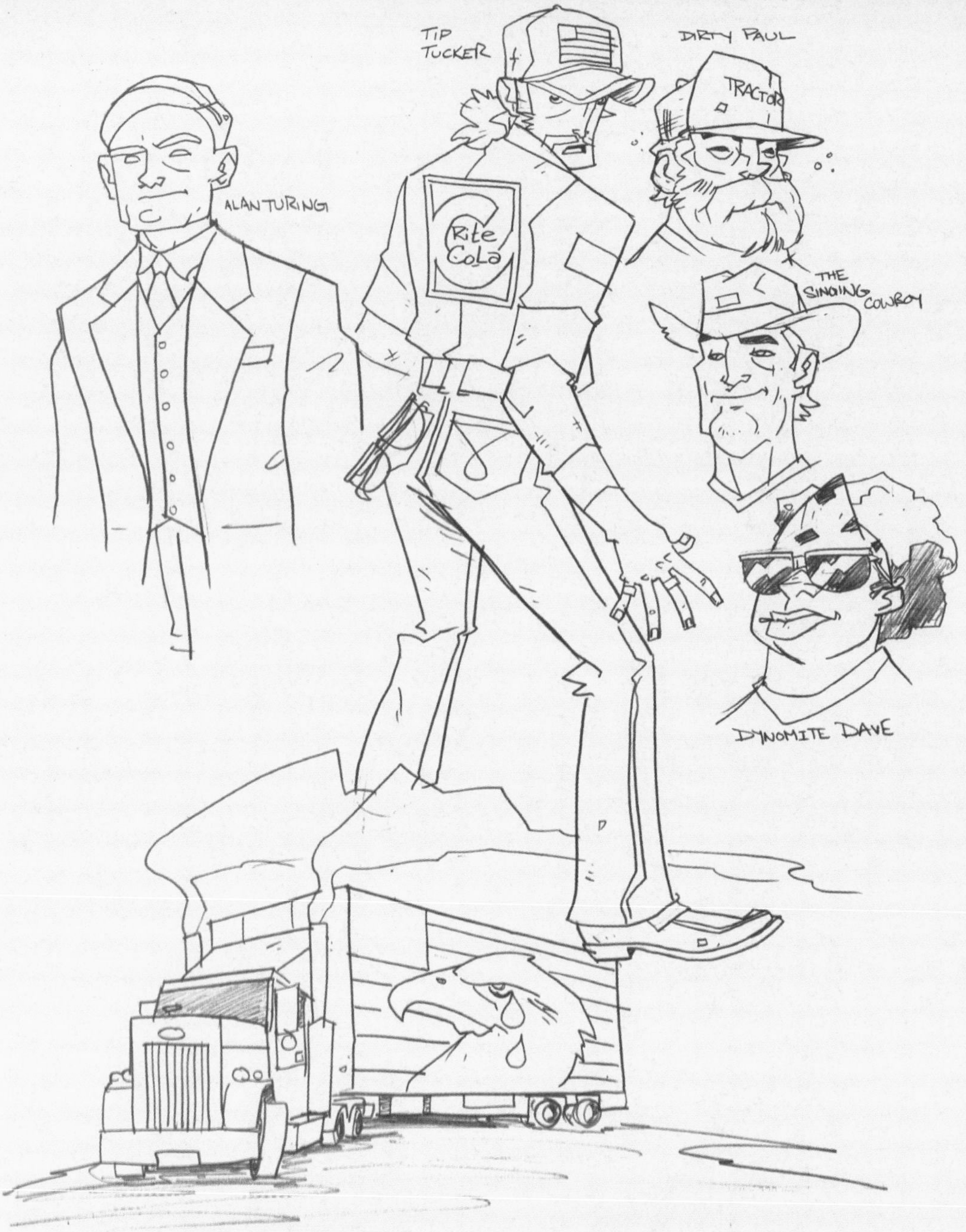
TIP TUCKER
DIRTY PAUL
TRACTOR
ALAN TURING
Rite CoLa
THE SINGING COWBOY
DYNOMITE DAVE
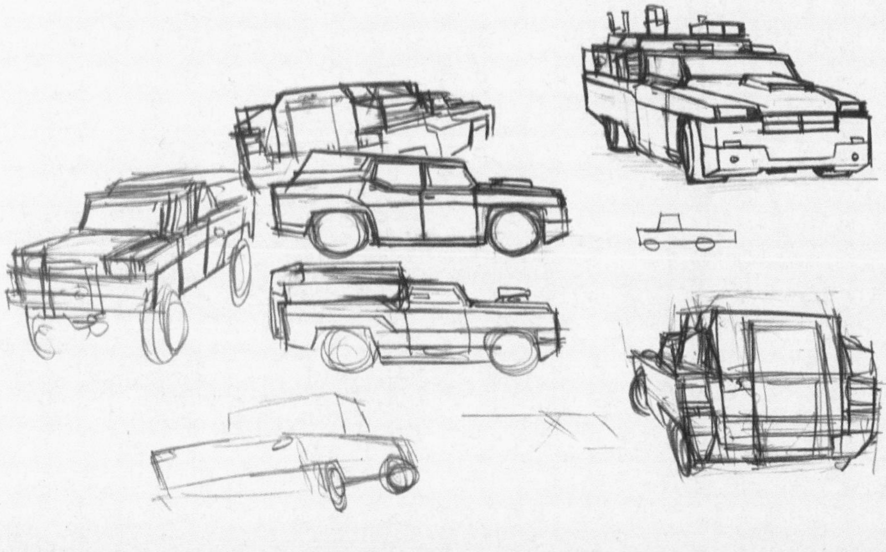

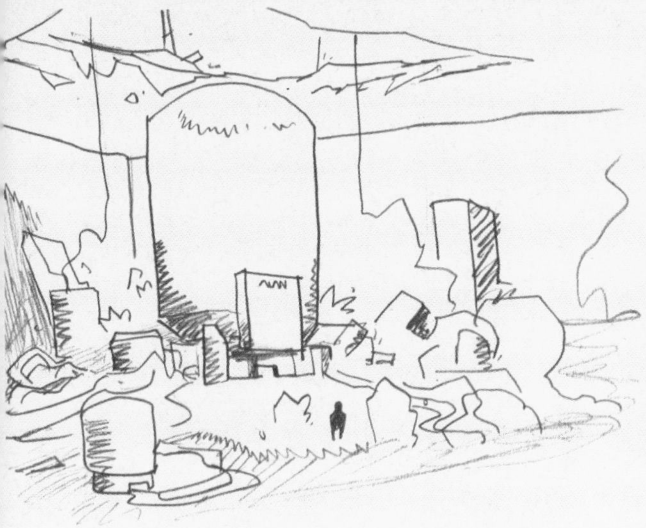

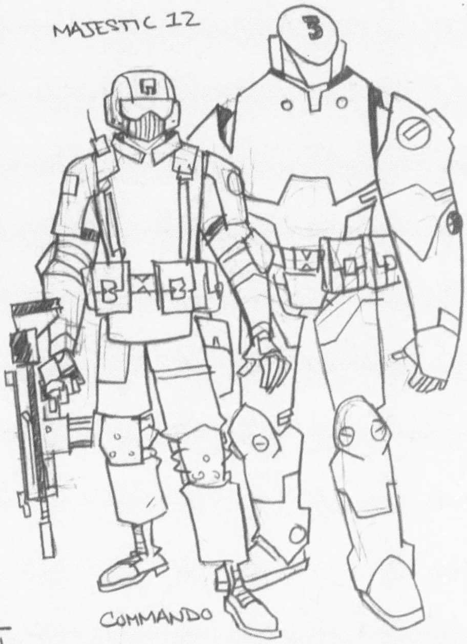
MAJESTIC 12
COMMANDO

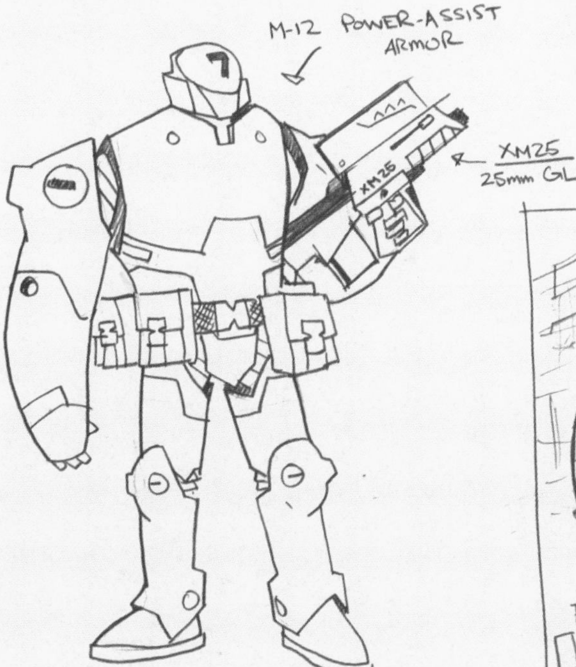
M-12 POWER-ASSIST ARMOR
XM25
25mm GL

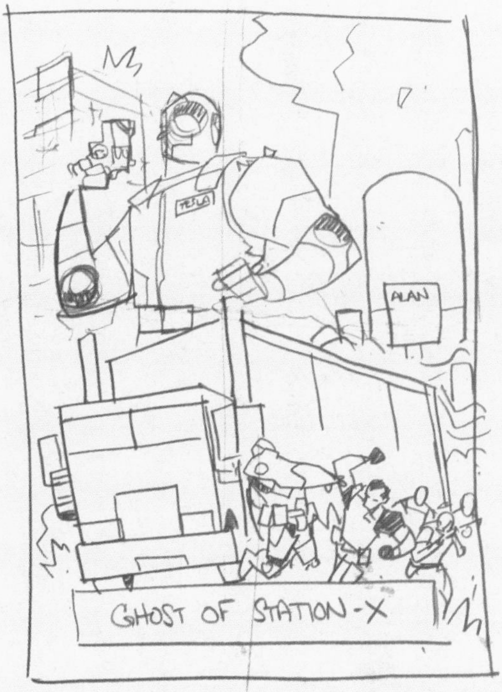
ALAN
GHOST OF STATION-X

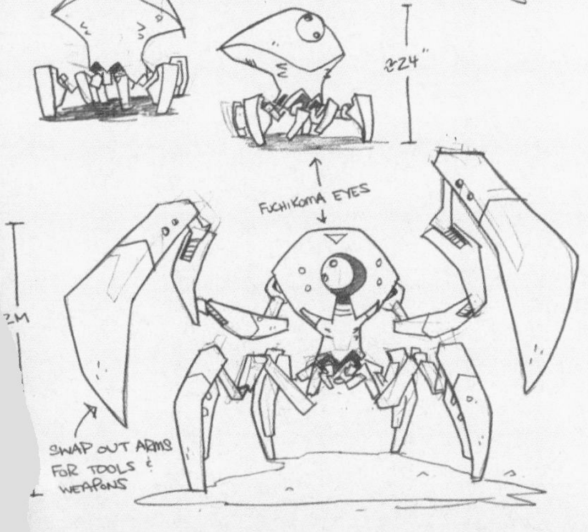
DRONES - The Death Star "MOUSE DROID" sorta thing.
≈24"
FUCHIKOMA EYES
2M
SWAP OUT ARMS FOR TOOLS & WEAPONS

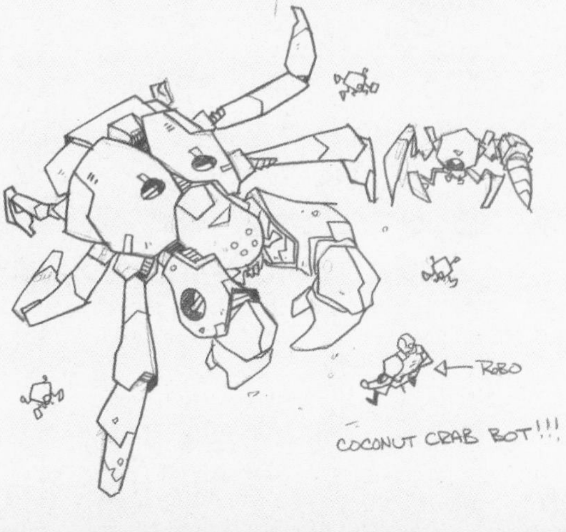
ROBO
COCONUT CRAB BOT!!!